Psychology Reviv⁻

Psychology

First published in 1927, the original blurb of *Psychology: Its Methods and Principles* reads: "In this book psychology is presented as the science of adaptive behavior. The writers are convinced that the study of such behaviour provides a more effective introduction to psychological science than the study of consciousness as such. They are not committed, however, to the tenets of any particular psychological 'school'. They have utilized both behaviouristic and introspective material without attempting to distinguish between 'introspection' and 'verbal report'. Throughout the text stress is placed upon the scientific methods by means of which adaptive behaviour is investigated in the psychological laboratory." Today it can be read in its historical context.

This book is a re-issue originally published in 1927. The language used and views portrayed are a reflection of its era and no offence is meant by the Publishers to any reader by this re-publication.

Psychology

Its Methods and Principles

**Fleming Allen Clay Perrin
and David Ballin Klein**

Routledge
Taylor & Francis Group

LONDON AND NEW YORK

First published in 1927
by Methuen & Co. Ltd

This edition first published in 2025 by Routledge
4 Park Square, Milton Park, Abingdon, Oxon, OX14 4RN

and by Routledge
605 Third Avenue, New York, NY 10017

Routledge is an imprint of the Taylor & Francis Group, an informa business

Publisher's Note
The publisher has gone to great lengths to ensure the quality of this reprint but points out that some imperfections in the original copies may be apparent.

Disclaimer
The publisher has made every effort to trace copyright holders and welcomes correspondence from those they have been unable to contact.

A Library of Congress record exists under LCCN: 26017502

ISBN: 978-1-032-94470-8 (hbk)
ISBN: 978-1-003-57092-9 (ebk)
ISBN: 978-1-032-94472-2 (pbk)

Book DOI 10.4324/9781003570929

PSYCHOLOGY
ITS METHODS AND PRINCIPLES

BY

FLEMING ALLEN CLAY PERRIN

AND

DAVID BALLIN KLEIN

METHUEN & CO. LTD.
36 ESSEX STREET W.C.
LONDON

First Published in Great Britain in 1927

PRINTED IN GREAT BRITAIN

PREFACE

In the present text psychology is presented as the science of adaptive behavior. The writers are convinced that the study of such behavior provides a more effective introduction to psychological science than the study of consciousness as such. However, they are not committed to the tenets of any particular psychological " school." They have utilized both behavioristic and introspective material, without attempting to distinguish between " introspection " and " verbal report." In fact, they are in entire accord with Hollingworth's position that the verification of psychological and other scientific phenomena finally is reduced to a question of statistical consistency. The writers use the term " stimulus-response " to designate the *program* of psychological investigation, but they employ this term in a strictly methodological sense. Throughout the text stress is placed upon the scientific methods by means of which adaptive behavior is investigated in the psychological laboratory.

In the writers' experience it has been found that the organization of the average text into chapters dealing with delimited topics — such as sensation, perception, intelligence, and imagination — induces the student to think of psychology in terms of " faculties." To minimize such suggestion of a faculty psychology they have articulated these topics with the larger problems of adjustment. The attainment of this objective necessitated a division of the text into relatively few but lengthy chapters containing numerous major and minor captions.

The writers are indebted to the following psychologists and publishers whose diagrams are reproduced in the text: W. F. Book, H. E. Jones, D. Starch, J. B. Watson, R. M. Yerkes, The Gregg Publishing Company and The Macmillan Company. They are also indebted to the editors of the *American Review* for the privilege of interpolating part of an article by one of the writers in Chapter II. They acknowledge their obligations to Professor Joseph Peterson, who read and criticized the original draft of Chapter V, and to Professor E. T. Mitchell and Mr. William Carr, who rendered generous service in reading the proof. They are particularly grateful to Professor Roger Thomas for his efforts in connection with the preparation of the entire manuscript.

F. A. C. P.
D. B. K.

THE UNIVERSITY OF TEXAS

CONTENTS

PSYCHOLOGY

ITS METHODS AND PRINCIPLES

PSYCHOLOGY—ITS METHODS
AND PRINCIPLES

CHAPTER I

THE PROBLEMS AND METHODS OF
PSYCHOLOGY

The fundamental aim of this book is to present psychology as a *science*. Careful consideration should be given to the implications of this statement. Essentially, a science comprises a group of organized facts along with such explanations or interpretations of these facts as the standards of logical thinking justify. In the majority of sciences, including psychology, the facts are ascertained primarily by controlled observation, or *experimentation*. Scientific interpretations are frequently tentative or *theoretical*, but in no science are purely speculative or " arm-chair " theories given precedence over those resting on a factual basis.

A genuine science is never finished or closed. The intelligent student cannot study history, government, economics, physics, chemistry, or biology without realizing that these sciences are progressing towards goals which recede as they come in sight. In the present text, therefore, the writers will not hesitate to introduce conflicting theories and to raise controversial points where occasion demands. Intellectual honesty renders such a proceeding necessary. It is better to leave the student unsettled than dogmatically to give him facts of dubious authenticity and interpretations of questionable validity.

3

Finally, a science is *critical* in its attitude. It questions beliefs which are supported solely by hearsay evidence, superficial observation, or prejudiced opinion. Even the evidence of " common sense " has often been criticized by the scientist. Common sense observation was once appealed to in support of the belief that the earth is flat and the center of the universe. Psychological science, in particular, frequently conflicts with popular or " common sense " opinions regarding mental phenomena. It will be profitable to consider a few phases of this conflict in some detail.

The Inadequacy of Popular Psychologizing. In the give and take of every-day life questions arise and decisions are made that are intimately related to the problems of the scientific psychologist. And just as the ancient and perennial necessity for taking care of the human body is responsible for many erroneous notions concerning health and disease, so the problems of mental and social adjustment are solved by dubious theories and formulae. In fact, a great many psychological half-truths and psychologically unwarranted assumptions control our conduct, direct our conventions, color our literature, and influence our choice of companions and friends. Plodding students to whom mastery of their lessons comes only at the cost of much time and weary effort, envious and mystified by the ease and rapidity with which their more intellectual fellow-students master the same lessons, comfort themselves with such assertions as " quick learning means quick forgetting," or " easy come, easy go." Or else they derive comfort from the belief that their abilities are essentially practical — by some implicitly assumed law of compensation, they will manifest superiority where the others will be conspicuous by their inferiority. Again, it is interesting to observe the definite attitudes that we unconsciously adopt when in the presence of the square-jawed individual, the shifty-eyed tradesman, and the frock-coated, bearded, and generally distinguished-looking gentle-man. To continue our examples, Miss Blank is given credit for a marvelous memory because of the ease with which she enumerates the details of the genealogical relationships of the town's leading family. Grandfather's eyesight is unim-paired as proved by the fact that he can read without eye-glasses. A pet dog is observed to overturn the milk bottle on the table and lap up the milk, and is said to have rea-soned out the way to get the milk. Sister does poorly in geometry because mathematics involves reasoning and " women can't reason." If an individual will only try hard enough, he is bound to succeed. All that is necessary to achieve perfection is constant and unremitting practice. Our friend at the club could not get the point of our uproar-iously funny story because he was English, and the British lack a sense of humor. The savage has keener eyesight and more acute hearing than the civilized man. Instances such as these are but examples of countless others whose implica-tions and manifest meanings we unquestioningly accept. As a rule we are prone to be irritated by a request for evidence upon which these alleged facts are based. They are so much a part of our social tradition and constitute so integral a portion of our common stock of ideas that we tend to regard them as almost self-evident or axiomatic.

In his endeavor to study human and animal nature sys-tematically and in accordance with the principles so success-fully employed in the field of the physical sciences the psy-chologist has not hesitated to question these generalizations. Vividly aware of the errors the human mind is heir to — due to bias, prejudice, random impressions, striking cases, intellectual inertia, and suggestion — he has become ex-tremely skeptical of a vast number of popular beliefs. Be-fore the psychologist can be induced to grant the truth of these beliefs he must be presented with evidence of a sort sufficiently cogent to meet an irritatingly large number of questions he is likely to ask the champion of the accepted current dogmas.

An Example of Psychological Method. By way of indicating the nature of the methods employed by the psychologist in attacking his problems, a concrete example may be considered. The previously mentioned instance of the common idea regarding the savage's superior vision and hearing may serve as a convenient case. In analyzing this matter we shall not be concerned with the establishment of any conclusions regarding the question. Our purpose is merely to show the differences between the popular and the psychological *methods* of handling a given problem.

According to popular belief the savage possesses keener vision, more acute hearing, and a more sensitive sense of smell than his civilized brother. He is presumed to hear and see things to which we are deaf and blind. As the matter is occasionally put, the price we pay for the development of our intellect is a progressive reduction in the efficiency of our sense organs. If the individual adhering to this view is asked how he knows this to be the case, he is likely to flare up and state that " common sense proves it," " it stands to reason that it must be so," " everybody knows it," or some equivalent form of rejoinder. Pressed for a more concrete line of argument he may allege that the literature of biography, travel, and fiction is replete with instances of the savage guide warning his party of explorers of impending danger when the members of the party were themselves unable to detect the slightest sign of danger. He may follow this up by pointing out that " in the very nature of the case " the savage must have better sense organs, for his very life depends upon their acuteness and accuracy. He has to see his game when it is still lurking in a thicket if he is to obtain his food supply. Menaced by hidden dangers on all sides, it is imperative that he learn to detect the first sign of such danger if he is to survive. In other words, the struggle with primeval forces renders it indispensable for him to be equipped with superior sense organs.

In some such fashion the discussion may proceed and the skeptic be convinced, for the *prima facie* case when so presented is superficially plausible. Let us assume, however, that the skeptic is a technically trained psychologist. He will not be so readily satisfied, not because of any bias in the matter for or against the effects of the civilizing process, but rather because of a disinterested love for the truth, whatever it may be and irrespective of whom it affects. We are altogether likely to hear him bring up a battery of questions he wants answered — questions that most of us never considered in connection with the problem. In general, he wants the following points cleared up:

(1) Does the statement that the savage possesses keener senses than civilized man mean that this alleged superiority is due to his training, or is it an inborn superiority? Has the year-old infant of the savage better eyesight and better hearing than the year-old infant of civilized man?

(2) Does the generalization mean that all savages are superior to all civilized men in sensory keenness? If not, what proportion is superior?

(3) How trustworthy is the evidence on which the generalization is based; that is, how competent are the civilized travelers to judge these things, since they did not actually measure the abilities of their savage friends? The evidence is more or less impressionistic.

However, the proponent of the accepted view may well state that the burden of proof rests upon the psychologist. Now how would the psychologist proceed to investigate the problem, assuming he were in a position to study it under ideal conditions? It will be well worth our time to study this matter in detail.

The psychologist would first formulate the problem in clear and unequivocal terms. When thus formulated the problem is seen to comprise several problems of a related sort, each calling for separate investigation. In this connection the psychologist must determine what is meant by the terms " savage," " civilized man," and " superior senses." He may decide to let the word " savage " refer to individuals living in a state of nature as opposed to people like ourselves who have been born into a relatively advanced environment. More specifically, he might cite the Australian bushman and the inhabitants of our large cities as examples of what he means. As has already been anticipated, the term " superior senses " may refer either to a superiority existing from birth, or to an acquired superiority. Of these two problems the one to be selected for prior solution is, of course, the one dealing with the existence of a difference in sensory capacity; for if the result should demonstrate the absence of such a difference, the problem of its origin would vanish.

Before doing anything of an experimental nature the psychologist consults earlier investigations bearing on the problem. By so doing he can profit by the work of others, avoiding their errors and availing himself of their successes. In the absence of any previous work he is compelled to plan his own method of procedure, involving such devices as his ingenuity may suggest. It is important to note that he does not endeavor to settle his problems by consulting authorities, whether travelers, explorers, or eye, ear, and nose specialists, in order to get their opinion. Such an anecdotal method is hopelessly inadequate as a means of ascertaining truth. For instance, it was used in old Salem days to prove the existence of witches. Although expert opinion may furnish the investigator valuable suggestions, it can never settle a question of fact. We may select a president by a majority vote, but the facts of nature refuse to be swayed or coerced by the opinions of men. In the time of Galileo the majority vote, both of the scholars and the laity, would have been to the effect that the earth was flat and stationary, but that did not make it so.

In devising an adequate plan for settling the question by an appeal to experimental investigation, a multitude of details have to be kept in mind and carefully controlled. The actual means to be employed in testing the keenness of vision are different from those to be used in testing hearing, smell, or touch. The fact that language cannot be employed to any marked extent in working with the savages presents additional difficulties in the way of settling upon a satisfactory technique. As far as practicable, tests to be chosen must call for a minimum use of language. Then there is the additional question of how many individuals of both groups must be subjected to a test before a reliable answer to the problem can be secured.

As soon as the psychologist endeavors to work out a scheme for testing the sense of vision, for example, he is beset with obstacles which must first be overcome before the tests can be administered. What is meant by a good sense of vision? Does it refer to the distance at which a given object can be seen and recognized? Does it refer to the distance at which colors can be seen and recognized? Has it to do with the width or extent of the field of vision? Possibly it means the fineness of discrimination, or the smallest distance that two points of light can be separated when the lights are at a given distance from the eye, and still be perceived as two lights and not as one. May it not really refer to the strength of the eyes, or the length of time they can be employed in a given kind of work without showing fatigue? Has it anything to do with the quickness of the eye, the speed with which objects can be perceived? Obviously, it has to do with all of these factors. But without experimentation we cannot say to what degree these different aspects of good vision occur in any single individual. In one aspect — say, color discrimination — the individual may be superior; while in another, say, fatigue of the eye, he may be inferior.

Furthermore, for testing each phase of the total complex of factors that constitute keen vision, a separate and distinct method of testing must be devised. It is laborious, time-consuming, requiring great skill, tact, and patience. The investigator must be careful to follow the same procedure each time he gives his series of tests to a different individual, since varying the procedure would render the results incommensurable. Not only that, but he must be sure to keep the conditions uniform. If he should test out the vision of ten savages in the morning and ten civilized men in the evening and find that on the average the savages are superior to the others, his results might be worthless for the simple reason that the time of day affects the integrity of our vision, especially when the eyes have been used all day.

Note further that with all these precautions observed and a practicable method of testing put into operation there still remains a vast amount of work to be accomplished. Let us assume for the sake of illustration that 100 Europeans and 100 savages have taken the tests. With 200 *subjects* (as persons who furnish data in psychological experiments are called) taking all the eye tests, there results an enormous number of measures. To handle such quantities of figures and mobilize them into meaningful relationships requires specialized statistical training. Not until the accumulated data are statistically elaborated, can any conclusion be drawn concerning the original problem. This process of drawing the correct conclusion from the figures requires alert discrimination and clear insight into all of the implications of the results. To get the figures is one thing; to interpret them is another.

Just as the problem of determining the differential status of eyesight in the two groups proves to be a complicated, exceedingly technical task, so the related problems involving the determination of other types of sensory efficiency (hearing, smell, and touch) are the jobs of specialists in each field. Only after all these results of detailed tests and separate investigations are secured, evaluated, and compared, and their reliability in turn worked out, is the psychologist in a position to answer the questions that prompted the research.

Since this problem has actually never been investigated in the manner outlined here, no certain answer can be given to it. What is of significance for present purposes is a full realization of the manner in which the psychologist's method of establishing the facts of human nature differs from our every-day methods of settling controversial points. His is a carefully planned, laboriously applied, and meticulously controlled method of attack. It is neither spectacular nor dramatic.

As is to be expected, it frequently happens that the upshot of the psychologist's investigation is merely to confirm a popular belief. This is one of the reasons why some of his work has been ironically characterized as an " elaboration of the obvious." It should be borne in mind, however, that the " obvious " in such cases is but a general and more or less vague, poorly defined relationship. What the psychologist's method of *quantitative* investigations serves to do is to transform such an " obvious fact " into a specific, delimited one. Everybody knows, for example, that the bright student possesses more intelligence than the dull student; but the amount by which he exceeds the stupid is not known. Frequently it is the *amount* of difference rather than the *fact* of difference that is significant in comparing individuals with reference to psychological traits.

Fact and Interpretation in Psychological Research. Some of the difficulties involved in the establishment of psychological facts have just been described. In connection with this description, a distinction was made between the establishment of a fact and its interpretation. Too much stress cannot be placed upon this distinction. It is well illustrated by a little incident reported to one of the writers by a young mother whose training in psychology was responsible for her interest in the matter. According to her report, each time her two-weeks-old infant cried its grandfather insisted on approaching the crib and playing with the baby, because, as he alleged, " it was lonely and wanted somebody to come and talk to it." She, on the other hand, objected to his reasoning on the ground that the youngster was crying either because of organic discomfort or " just for exercise." In fact she was able to discount the former possibility by a careful examination of the child. The friendly disputants were agreed on the fact of the baby's crying. This was manifest and observable. Their dispute centered on the *interpretation* of this observed fact. Why did the baby cry? Now no one can deny that when the grandfather maintained the baby was crying for companionship he was furnishing a possible explanation. In the same way the mother's explanation must also be considered as a possible one. The question is which is the better or truer explanation? From the scientific point of view which of the rival interpretations is to be preferred? Of course what the mother meant by saying that the child was crying " just for exercise " was that it was " letting off steam." That is, the energy obtained from food and air has to be expended in some way. In such a young baby the greater part of it is used to regulate growth, but any excess that an older child would dissipate in play activity is here discharged by such random, circumscribed activity as kicking the legs, waving the arms, and crying. The mechanisms underlying such crying responses are rather well established; they are known to be present in young infants; and they are present in the new-born child and function without special training.

So far as we know the desire for companionship and " to be talked to " is one that is acquired, not inborn. This is very obvious. In her explanation the mother proceeded upon the already established fact that very young infants possess the tendency to " cry for exercise," as she puts it. The grandfather, on the contrary, invoked an explanatory principle which while applicable to older, experienced children has never been demonstrated to exist in two-weeks-old infants. It is thus clear that the mother's view explains the unknown in terms of the known or demonstrated, while the grandfather's view proceeds from the unknown to the unknown. In accepting the latter explanation we make *two* assumptions: that the baby cries for companionship and that this is the reason for its crying. In accepting the mother's explanation we make but *one* assumption: that the mechanism of " crying for exercise " covers the particular case. Because of the fewer assumptions involved in it, the mother's explanation is the more scientific one.

The Law of Parsimony. This principle of selecting an explanation or theory that makes the fewest necessary assumptions to cover the facts is usually referred to as the *Law of Parsimony.* Scientists always prefer to limit their assumptions to the fewest number necessary to explain the phenomena being studied. They like to stick to facts; and assumptions are not facts until so proved. The psychologist is governed by this law in interpreting the phenomena of mental life. He does so because it enables him to keep closer to the facts.

The Stimulus-Response Program in Psychology. Modern psychological investigation is conducted largely on the principle that all psychological phenomena exhibit two aspects, the stimulus and the response. In fact, the term *stimulus-response* is of such fundamental importance that the psychologist Woodworth has suggested it as a suitable motto for the psychological laboratory. Since, as the ensuing discussion shows, it expresses the general system or method by which psychological facts are ascertained, it is known as a psychological *program*.

The stimulus-response principle refers to the relationships between the activity of the organism and the factors causing this activity or behavior. The causative factor is the stimulus and the behavior is the response. Such behavior is shown by the simplest forms of animal life. As animals become more complex structurally they react proportionately to groups of stimuli rather than to stimuli in isolation, such groups being known as *situations*. Thus, while lower organisms, the amoeba for example, respond to light, heat, gravity, contact, and chemical substances, man reacts to automobiles, thunderstorms, symphony concerts, books, sermons, dinners, animals, his fellow-creatures. A situation is not merely an aggregate of stimuli, for these stimuli inaugurate sensory nerve impulses that are correlated in sensory areas of the brain before they cause action. The chief factor in their correlating process is past experience, represented by neural " traces." Hence, in examining a locomotive, an individual reacts not only to visual, auditory, olfactory, and thermal stimuli, but to the object itself. These stimuli function by arousing nerve mechanisms in his brain, mechanisms that represent his previous experience with locomotives. Higher animals react to situations rather than stimuli because their reactions also are modified by their past experiences.

All higher organisms are stimulated *through* specialized bodily structures known as sense-organs or receptors; and they respond by means of other specialized structures, called the effectors. Certain receptors, such as the eye, the ear, and the organs of touch, pain and temperature, are on the body surface, while others are internally located. The effectors are the muscles and glands. All acts are executed by the effectors.

The behavior of higher animals and of man consists chiefly of complex and interrelated acts. As we have just intimated, stimuli come from *within* the body as well as from without, requiring systems of internal sense organs or internal receptors. Such stimuli are variously known as organic states, drives, emotions, and motives. Moreover, many of these states are both stimuli and responses. Anger is a response, aroused, say, on the occasion of an insulting remark; but it is also a stimulus in that it prompts the individual in whom it has been aroused to action. Since many internal stimuli are more or less permanent or recurring, as is true of hunger and a grudge, the resulting behavior is likewise permanent or recurring. Frequently a response made to a stimulus furnishes the stimulus for an ensuing response. This occurs when the pouncing reaction made by the cat to the running mouse results in the capture of the prey; for the mouse, when held in the cat's mouth, becomes a combined touch and taste stimulus for further and different conduct. In many other respects stimulus-response behavior is complicated, particularly in the social life of man. It is even true, as the psychologist Thurstone asserts, that the organism seeks certain stimuli and avoids others.[1] It does not follow, however, as Thurstone argues, that the stimulus-response principle is inadequate in explaining complex behavior. This fact and the considerations just advanced merely show that a narrow interpretation of stimulus and response is grossly inadequate.

The Control and Prediction of Behavior. As the psychologist Watson explains, the stimulus-response principle is basically involved in psychological *prediction*.[2] Knowing the response we infer the stimulus; and knowing the stimulus we predict the response. The two possibilities become significant when we realize that science aims at and is judged by its predictive achievements. Our popular respect for astronomy is caused by the fact that astronomy is a highly predictive science; eclipses, for instance, occur on scheduled time. Many chemical phenomena are just as predictable. A greater margin of error is found in biological science, particularly in the applied phases of biology. In medicine, for instance, prediction is not always safe.

Since psychology is a biological and social science prediction in that field has reached the same degree of accuracy attained by these sciences, but human nature is not the uncertain, intangible thing it is sometimes assumed to be, for otherwise social organization would be impossible. To " know " an individual is to predict with a reasonable degree of accuracy how he will behave in a given situation. Furthermore, even insane behavior can be predicted: the psychiatrist knows his patients just as the teacher knows her pupils. In other words, human responses are adjustments to the physical and social environment, and they tend towards uniformity because human organisms are structurally similar, while the environment, both physical and social,

[1] Thurstone, L. L. " The Stimulus-Response Fallacy in Psychology." *Psychological Review*, 1923, 30, 354-369.

[2] Watson, John B. *Psychology from the Standpoint of a Behaviorist.*

shows relatively little change. Human nature is much the same, in all ages and the world over.

We should observe that an "adjustment to the environment" is not a pedantic phrase to be memorized by a student. Rather, it expresses an attempted solution for a very real problem. Taking an examination, applying for a position, selecting a rooming-house, crossing a crowded street, running to catch a train, inquiring one's way in a new city, striving to appear at ease in an embarrassing social situation, are adjustments to environment. In the typical psychological experiment the essential stimuli elements in an environment, with the irrelevant factors eliminated, are presented to the subject. The adjusting process takes place whenever an organism reacts in any way to any environment.

Now, in many instances of adjustment in social and economic life, the stimulus-response conditions are relatively well controlled. For instance, this is true in advertising, where it is economically necessary to predict responses from the stimuli. It would seem, then, that the professional advertiser must be a psychologist, even though he lacks training in the science. In speaking to a professional psychologist a business man is likely to say, "I don't know a thing about psychology, yet I use it every day in the world"; and in many cases he is correct. It is possible to employ psychological methods and to determine many laws of human behavior without training in scientific psychology.

But even the professional advertiser, to all intents and purposes working in a field far removed from scientific pursuits, finds that many of his problems can be solved most expeditiously by the use of scientific methods. By regarding advertising media (newspapers and magazines, posters, etc.) as stimuli, and by regarding the effects of these upon human beings as responses, he approaches his problems from the psychological standpoint. Likewise all individuals interested in studying or controlling human nature — police officers, scout-masters, parents, teachers, lecturers, physicians, lawyers — can profitably employ the psychological methodology that we have described. However, introductory psychology is not a vocational subject — unless the art of living with and understanding one's fellow and one's self is considered a vocation. On the contrary, introductory psychology aims at the fundamentals of the science. And as our ensuing chapter shows, the underlying principles of psychology are biological in character.

The preceding discussions have emphasized certain fundamental characteristics of psychology, particularly its problems, methods, and governing principles. It should thus be evident that the business of the psychologist is to apply scientific method to a study of human and animal nature. There are many ways of accomplishing this business. From the standpoint of this text the most efficient way is to study human and animal nature as it is revealed in concrete behavior.

CHAPTER II

THE BIOLOGICAL FOUNDATIONS OF BEHAVIOR

Psychology is intimately related to the biological sciences, particularly to zoölogy, anatomy, and physiology. This relationship is due to the fact that the behavior of an organism is determined primarily by its anatomical and physiological organization. To illustrate, birds fly because they have wings; dogs bark because their vocal apparatus renders it possible for them to do so; human beings are enabled to laugh, cry, talk, and gesticulate by virtue of their anatomical equipment. The expression " animal nature " refers to the characteristic behavior tendencies of animals made possible by their bodily structure. In this sense it is " natural " for the squirrel to eat nuts, and for the carnivorous beast to capture and devour its prey. Likewise human nature is basically a product of the human bodily constitution. The behavior of all organisms from amoeba to man is thus innate in so far as it is determined by structural and physiological factors. Since the psychologist undertakes to explain behavior, his first concern is with its innate basis.

But psychology must not be identified with biology. It differs from the various biological sciences in being concerned with the behavior of the organism as a whole. The psychologist studies such phenomena as emotion, learning, skill, talent, intelligence, and personality. All of these are forms and aspects of behavior manifested by intact organisms, and conversely, none of them are exhibited by separate organs or systems of the body. Structurally the amoeba is far more simple than the human heart, but unlike the heart it is a complete living organism, maintaining an independent existence and showing the rudiments, at least, of intelligent behavior. In a way psychology begins where biology ends.

As its title suggests, this chapter is devoted to the biological facts and principles which underlie behavior. We have already noted that corresponding to the two aspects of psychological phenomena described in the previous chapter we find in the higher organisms both special organs of stimulation and special organs of response. Connections between these two systems of organs are brought about by the nervous system. Following the logical sequence we shall discuss in order (1) the organs of stimulation, (2) the connecting neural mechanisms, and (3) the organs of response. In a given act of behavior, however, the three systems function as one mechanism, hence the three-fold distinction should be regarded as purely arbitrary and convenient.

Organs of Stimulation: the Receptors

The specialized organs of stimulation are commonly known as sense organs, but since their function is to receive forms of stimuli they are more properly called receptors. Notwithstanding the fact that human beings and the higher animals respond to situations rather than to isolated stimuli, the latter are the actual, physical agencies which affect the receptors. The best approach to the study of stimuli is through the receptors upon which they act.

As a preliminary consideration, attention should be called to an erroneous belief concerning the number of receptors. The notion that there are five senses has prevailed for centuries, whereas, as a matter of fact, there are at least twenty. The cutaneous or skin senses alone number four; namely, touch, pain, warmth, and cold. Each is mediated undoubt-edly by a specialized structure or sensitive cell. Inciden-tally, it should be noted that the skin itself is not a receptor. The cutaneous receptors are located in and beneath the skin, just as the visual receptor is located behind a movable skin and muscle covering, the eyelid. The skin is no more the organ of touch than the eyelid is the organ of vision. Fur-thermore, many of the receptors described below are located within the body and stimulated by forces from within. These are completely overlooked in the five-fold classifica-tion of the senses, one made before psychology became a science.

The Function of Receptors. As the name indicates, a receptor is a receiving device. It receives some form of physical stimulus for which it is structurally adapted. The eye receives light waves; the ear receives sound waves; the organ of smell receives gaseous particles; the organ of taste receives food particles in solution; the cutaneous receptors receive thermal and mechanical stimuli; and the internal receptors receive thermal, mechanical, and chemical stimuli. Still other forms of stimuli are described subsequently in this chapter.

The fact that a receptor receives stimuli is the first con-sideration involved in ascertaining its function. Having acted upon the sensitive cells in the receptor, the stimulus has completed its task. It then disappears, or moves be-yond the range of sensitivity of the organism; or the organ-ism moves away from the stimulus; or perhaps the stimulus if continuous is regulated or shut out by the receptor itself. An example of a receptor regulating a continuous stimula-tion is found in the contraction and dilatation of the pupil of the eye. If the stimulus is excessively intense, the organ-ism makes convulsive responses designed to eliminate it or scatter its physiological effects. No receptor can withstand an intense stimulus indefinitely, for it eventually becomes fatigued, and it may suffer permanently from the overstimulation.

The Classification of Receptors. The receptors can be classified in terms of their functions. Both the physiologist Sherrington (10) and the neurologist Herrick (4) have grouped receptors in this way. The following table represents a combination of their respective systems:

A. THE SOMATIC RECEPTORS: (I) EXTEROCEPTORS AND (II) PROPRIOCEPTORS

(I. Exteroceptors)

1. Distance receptors
    (a) Organ of vision — the eye
    (b) Organ of audition — the outer ear, middle ear, vestibule and cochlea of inner ear
    (c) Organ of smell (also an interoceptor) — olfactory epithelium of nose
2. Contact receptors — the cutaneous sense organs
    (a) Organs of touch and pressure
    (b) Organs of heat
    (c) Organs of cold
    (d) Organs of pain (in addition to interoceptors for visceral pain)

(II. Proprioceptors)

1. Organs of position and equilibrium — semicircular canals, saccule and utricle of the internal ear
2. Organs of kinaesthetic functions
    (a) Organs in muscles
    (b) Organs in tendons
    (c) Organs in joints, or on articular surfaces

B. The Visceral Receptors:

(III. Interoceptors)

1. Receptors of the digestive system
   - (a) Organs of smell (listed above)
   - (b) Organs of taste — taste-buds on tongue and pharynx
   - (c) Organs or sensory cells of hunger — in stomach
   - (d) Organs or sensory cells of thirst — in mucous membrane of pharynx
   - (e) Organs or sensory cells of nausea — in stomach
2. Receptors of circulatory system
3. Receptors of respiratory system
4. Receptors of reproductive system

We shall now study this table in some detail. According to Sherrington, a given receptor is attuned to a particular force or stimulus, so that the organism can react adequately to small amounts of this stimulus. However, in developing structures that are particularly sensitive to specific forms of stimuli the organism loses the power to respond to these forms in the absence of such structures. Although the human eye is more sensitive to light than is the entire body of the amoeba, the remaining structures of the human being are much less sensitive to light. In this general respect, highly developed receptors are comparable with the specialists of modern economic society, who are much better qualified to do one thing and much less qualified to do other things than the jack-of-all-trades of primitive society.

In order to understand the specific functions of the various classes of receptors it is necessary to distinguish between the *somatic* and the *visceral* parts of the body. The viscera consist of the digestive, circulatory, excretory, respiratory, and reproductive systems of the body. Most of the visceral organs of a fowl are removed when it is cleaned for cooking. The viscera are directly controlled by a division of the nervous system called the autonomic nervous system. Visceral organs such as the stomach, kidneys, heart, and lungs must not be confused with the visceral receptors or sense organs belonging to this system. The latter are sensory nerve structures, microscopic in size, located on or near the visceral organs. The somatic part of the body includes primarily the skeleton, the skeletal muscles, the outside skin, the cerebrospinal nervous system, and the receptors directly connected with this system. Somatic receptors are sensory nerve structures found on the body surface, on the joint surfaces, in the muscles and tendons, and in one case, in a bony cavity within the head. The responses elicited by stimulation of visceral receptors are glandular secretions and movements of visceral organs. Responses elicited by somatic receptors adjust the organism to its environment. In other words, visceral functions are apparently involved in motives, emotions, and feelings, while somatic functions are associated with intelligent behavior. The implications of this statement will be developed later.

(I) **The Exteroceptors.** As the term signifies, the exteroceptors are external receptors, located on the body surface. It follows that they receive stimuli from without the body. Since certain external stimuli come from a distance, while other forms affect the body through contact, these organs are further divided into distance receptors and contact receptors.

As we have just stated, the exteroceptors guide the organism in its overt adjustments to the environment. They inaugurate and control gross movements, such as locomotion, manipulating objects, and assuming bodily postures and attitudes with reference to the environment. The stimuli from the exteroceptors prompt such responses as dodging an approaching automobile, discovering and picking up a purse, locating a gas leak, reading, listening to music, and recognizing friends by hearing their voices, seeing them or perhaps touching them. Exteroceptors are thus seen to be involved in important life-adjustments. Helen Keller and Laura Bridgman are two well-known cases of individuals practically deprived of distance receptors; but we have no cases of individuals surviving in the absence of contact receptors. To use a very crude analogy, the exteroceptors correspond to those parts of an automobile, such as the steering gear and its connections, that place it in efficient contact with the environment.

(1) Of the three distance receptors, one, the organ of smell, is in part an interoceptor. To the extent that an organism, say a dog, seeks food or follows a scent the olfactory organ is an exteroceptor; but when the organism sniffs at an odorous substance, thereby getting a favorable or unfavorable verdict from its stomach regarding the food properties of the substance, this same organ is an interoceptor. In many instances both functions are manifested simultaneously. The eye and the organ of hearing are *bona fide* extero- and distance receptors, sensitive to stimulations from a distance that travel from stimulating objects to them as vibratory energy.

The different forms of stimuli acting on the distance receptors should be noted. Light consists of vibrations projected from luminous or reflecting bodies; its exact nature is hypothetical, but it is related to electrical phenomena. Sound waves are periodic or non-periodic molecular vibrations in solids, liquids, and gases. The olfactory stimulus consists of gaseous particles thrown off by the olfactory substance. Thus it is possible for objects removed some distance from the organism to affect sensitive cells on the surface of that organism in two ways: its stimulating energy is conducted to the organism as vibrations in some medium, or it discharges particles of itself into the surrounding environment. Recent research in physics suggests that the two forms are ultimately identical.

(a) The eye is usually described as similar in operation to a camera. The counterparts of a camera found in the eye (Fig. 1) are as follows: the eyelid is the external shut-

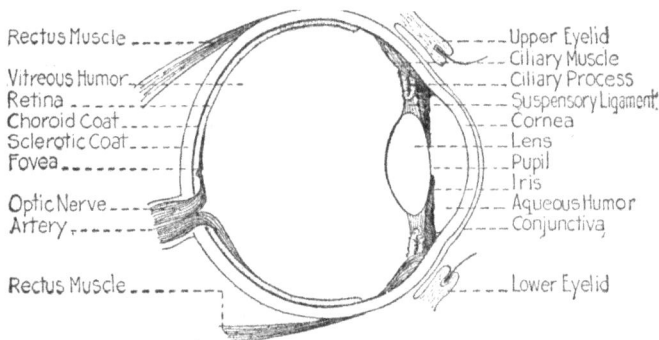

Rectus Muscle
Vitreous Humor
Retina
Choroid Coat
Sclerotic Coat
Fovea
Optic Nerve
Artery
Rectus Muscle

Upper Eyelid
Ciliary Muscle
Ciliary Process
Suspensory Ligament
Cornea
Lens
Pupil
Iris
Aqueous Humor
Conjunctiva
Lower Eyelid

A. STRUCTURE OF THE EYE

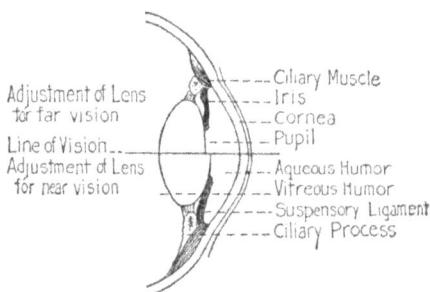

Adjustment of Lens for far vision
Line of Vision
Adjustment of Lens for near vision

Ciliary Muscle
Iris
Cornea
Pupil
Aqueous Humor
Vitreous Humor
Suspensory Ligament
Ciliary Process

B. MECHANISM OF ACCOMMODATION

FIG. 1. — Cross-section of the eye. *A* shows the parts of the eye and some of the structures adjacent to the eye-ball. *B* shows the difference in the curvature of the lens for far and for near vision.

ter; the pupil is the aperture that admits the light; the iris is the diaphragm; the lens resembles the camera lens; the dark, choroid coat of the eye, like the black inner surface of a camera, absorbs excessive light; and the retina corresponds to the sensitive plate or film. In the camera focusing is accomplished by getting the proper distance between (1) lens and plate, and (2) lens and object to be photographed; in the eye focus is obtained by (1) varying the curvature of the lens, and (2) adjusting the distance between eye and object. Changes in the curvature of the lens are effected by the ciliary muscles to which is attached the suspensory capsule in which the lens is enclosed; the process is called *accommodation*. While the space within a camera is filled with air, the eyeball spaces are filled with two transparent substances, the aqueous humor and the vitreous humor. The retina is similar to the sensitive plate in that it contains a photochemical substance; but in the eye this photochemical substance, being organic protoplasm, is being constantly renewed by metabolic processes. Moreover, retinal processes in the higher animals, particularly in man, are differentiated to react to " colors," or vibration rates of different frequencies. In brief, both eye and camera are mechanically constructed to receive the same physical stimulus and to direct this stimulus upon a chemically sensitive, plate-like structure.

In adjusting the eye to the stimulus accommodation is not the only process involved. Just as the photographer moves his camera in position before regulating the focus of the lens, so the eyes are also moved into " position." Such movement is accomplished by muscles attached to the outer or sclerotic coat of the eye (Fig. 2). By means of these muscles the eyes may be moved horizontally, vertically, and obliquely. These are called *conjugate* eye movements. In addition, in fixating upon near objects, as in reading a book, the eyes move *convergently* or toward each other. In fixating upon distant objects, as in witnessing a football game, the eyes assume a less convergent position. We thus have two principal kinds of eye movement, conjugate and convergent.

The eye should be thought of as a distance receptor that enables the organism to *act* with reference to certain features of its environment. Even though we are poetically justified in regarding the eye as preëminently " the window of the soul," and in thinking of it as the organ through which we see and enjoy color, form, and distance, such a

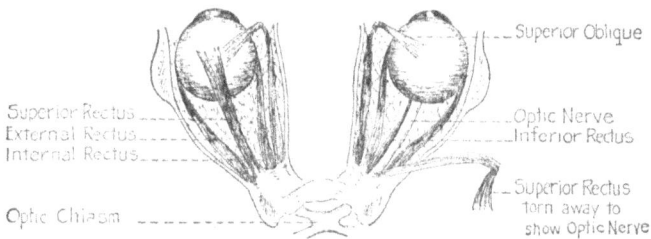

FIG. 2. — Muscles regulating eye movements.

concept does scant justice to the function of vision. In spite of such romancing the fact remains that a blind person is handicapped primarily because he avoids threatening objects with difficulty, and in general fails to respond adequately to objects in his environment.

Experimental as well as observational evidence justifies this emphasis upon the function of vision. The psychologist Stratton (12) once devised an instrument that, when fastened over one eye, the other eye being blindfolded, completely reversed the field of vision. Everything was seen upside down and all right-left relationships were reversed. When Stratton first put on this instrument he experienced pronounced difficulty in executing the daily tasks that are normally quite habitual and mechanical. For example, his attempts to eat dinner were almost disastrous. When, however, his everyday habits became adjusted to the inverted visual field, his visual experience ceased to appear unnatural. Stratton became habituated to the reversed visual cues in much the same manner that the student gets accustomed to the reversed and inverted movement of a microscopic slide.

Contrary to popular belief, the fact that the retinal image is normally inverted has no special psychological significance. We " see things right side up when the image is upside down " because our habits are adjusted to this situation. As a matter of fact, we do not see the retinal image at all, for we react to visual stimuli. Through vibration rates that it directs into the eye an object causes certain chemical changes in the retina of the eye; these in turn inaugurate nerve impulses that traverse the optic nerve; and finally, these impulses result in a discharge of nerve impulses to the muscles. The end result is an act of behavior, for the function of vision is to facilitate our response to objects in space.

Certain of these responses to spatial situations are demonstrably modified by the fact that we have two eyes. A diagram (Fig. 3) representing the pathways of stimuli to the two eyes shows the mechanism of binocular vision. The retinal images (i.e., the loci of stimuli on the retinas) of the two eyes are slightly dissimilar, the image on the right retina representing relatively more of the right side of a three-dimensional object, the image on the left side representing more of the left face of the object. This is the natural or habitual situation that obtains when one views a solid object; hence, when this condition is reproduced artificially, we have the illusion of depth. This illusion can readily be demonstrated by means of the *stereoscope*. The depth values of binocular vision are also demonstrated by the diminished accuracy with which an individual habituated to the use of his two eyes judges distances in the third dimension with one eye closed. He is considerably less accurate in such performances as picking up an object or threading a needle.

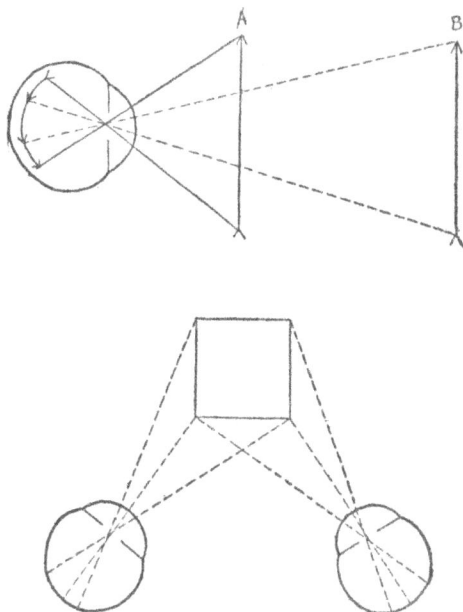

FIG. 3. — The mechanism of monocular and binocular vision (schematic). The upper figure shows (a) the inversion of the retinal image and (b) the relationship between the size of the image and the distance between the object and the eye. The lower figure shows the difference in the retinal images of the two eyes when the stimulating object is solid.

(b) The organ of hearing (Fig. 4) is a complicated structure encased in the temporal bone of the head. The external ear is a crude trumpet for directing sound waves into the tube leading from it, the external auditory meatus.

Deaf people frequently reinforce this function by holding their hands back of their ears while listening. Sound vibrations are transmitted through the middle ear by various structures, including a membrane and a lever-like arrangement of three small bones, that decrease the amplitude and increase the intensity of these vibrations. The actual organ

FIG. 4. — Cross-section of the ear.

of hearing is an exceedingly complicated device in the cochlea of the inner ear, immersed in liquid. Just how this organ operates is not definitely known save that it selects various vibration rates and transforms them into nerve impulses.

It is difficult to describe a specialized function of audition. The fact that auditory stimuli do not elicit definite spatial responses is well known. In a familiar laboratory experiment the inadequacy of auditory localization is demonstrated by the marked inability of a blindfolded subject to point to the source of clicking sounds, produced at various places around him. Since the two ears receive the same sound with different degrees of intensity, he is accurate only in locating the sound to the right or to the left of his head.

The vocalizations of animals and the articulate speech of

man perhaps represent the chief way in which sound is utilized. That the two are closely related is obvious. If forced to choose either deafness or blindness as the lesser of two evils most people, possibly with good logic, would elect deafness; nevertheless deafness seems a greater social handicap than blindness. Were it not for the device of lip-reading deaf people would be almost completely deprived of ordinary normal social relationships. Thus audition ranks high as a factor in social behavior.

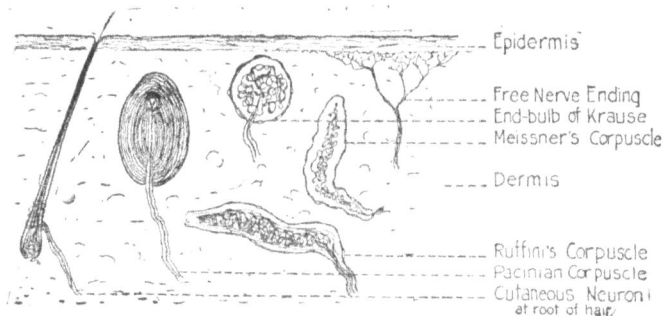

FIG. 5. — Cutaneous receptors.

Although the olfactory receptor does not possess the complicated accessory structures found in the eye and the ear, mechanisms for placing it in contact with its stimuli are not lacking. These are expressed in the act of scenting and sniffing, involving body and head adjustments, movements of the nose itself, and respiratory changes. This adaptive act literally brings the olfactory stimulus to its receptor; a counter-adaptation is the act of holding the breath and sometimes the nose.

(2) The contact receptors are small organs found for the most part in and just beneath the skin. Some idea of their appearance can be formed by studying Figure 5. According to some authorities they include, in addition, numerous

organs deeply embedded in bodily tissues, called the Pacinian corpuscles. These corpuscles may mediate deep sensitivity. Several organs seemingly are responsible for touch, including nerve endings in the hair bulbs at the roots of the hairs. It is usually assumed that Merkel's corpuscles and Meissner's corpuscles are touch receptors. Two other structures, Ruffini's cylinder and the end-bulb of Krause, are supposed to mediate warmth and cold respectively. The structure ordinarily regarded as the organ of pain is merely a free nerve ending, or a nerve with no receptor attached.

Sensitivity to the four kinds of cutaneous stimuli is not found uniformly over the skin, but is distributed irregularly over the body surface, touch spots, in particular, being found on areas of the skin (end of the tongue and finger tips) used for exploratory purposes. By employing a rather simple experimental technique, involving the application of various stimulating instruments to the skin, it is possible to locate the four classes of sensitive spots on a given skin area.

Since the membranes found within the body as well as the skin are composed of epithelial tissue the possibility of internal touch, warmth, cold, and pain is suggested. But evidence points to the absence of tactile and temperature sensitivity in the viscera, and to an irregular distribution of pain sensitivity. In general, while visceral organs are relatively insensitive to pain, portions of their surrounding membranes, such as the peritoneum, the pleura, the pericardium, and the meninges, are partly or entirely sensitive to certain forms of pain stimuli. Some forms of visceral pain are accurately localized by subjects or patients; other forms, known as referred pains, are projected to parts of the body quite removed from the source of stimulation. Thus a pain caused by an ulcerated condition in the colon or large intestine may be experienced in the shoulder. The explanation of this phenomenon involves the principles of the nervous system, described below. It is found in the fact that when the sensory neurons or nerve cells from the viscera reach the ganglia just outside the spinal cord they connect with sensory neurons coming from the body surface. The neuron from the body surface carries the visceral as well as its own nerve impulses with the result that the visceral pain is referred to the exteroceptive source.

Such acts of behavior as are made in response to stimulation of contact receptors show certain characteristics that explain their function. In studying human and animal behavior we observe that certain responses are easily aroused by cutaneous stimuli, examples being scratching parts of the skin, preening feathers, moving the tail, quivering, trembling, starting and withdrawing movements, licking parts of the body surface. Evidently skin sensitivity serves to bring beneficial stimuli in closer contact with the body, and to remove obnoxious stimuli from the body. In general, cutaneous reflexes are definite and well developed, for they are elicited by stimuli touching the organism itself. Responses made to distance receptor stimulation are characteristically anticipatory or preparatory in that they lead up to a final and culminating response. As opposed to these, responses to contact are necessarily final, for whether the stimulus is amicable or inimical, it is at hand and it must be disposed of. The cringing, withdrawing response caused by touching a repulsive object is, on the whole, even more violent than the same response aroused by seeing the object. A corresponding greater intensity of the cutaneous response can be observed when the stimulus evokes a forward-going reaction. In describing their own reactions people testify to the compelling nature of cutaneous stimuli. For instance, if " the skin you love to touch " produces an intense favorable response, a skin that is repulsive, by virtue of its color or perhaps its hygienic condition, produces an unfavorable response no less marked. In terms of behavior, repulsive and attractive as applied to stimulating objects are no mere figures of speech. They express the demonstrable behavior tendencies of the organism confronted with certain stimulating objects; and these tendencies originated as contact responses.

(II) **The Proprioceptors.** The receptive organs of the body, such as the semicircular canals of the ear, as well as those found in the muscles and tendons and on the joint surfaces, are called proprioceptors because their adequate stimuli are furnished by (or are the " property " of) the organism itself. The canals contain a liquid, variations in the pressure of which presumably stimulate adjacent sensitive nerves. The proprioceptors embedded in the muscles and tendons are stimulated by the surrounding tissue. The stimulations become strong when the muscles are active or tense. The proprioceptors on the joint surfaces are stimulated by movements of the joints.

The proprioceptive system can be compared with the differential of an automobile, a device that automatically regulates the fine movements of a car by distributing the power in correct proportions to the rear wheels. Although gross motor responses are effected by exteroceptors, the muscular coördination that normally characterizes these responses is effected by proprioceptors. The latter are divided into two classes, the organs of static sense, and the kinaesthetic organs. Each has a special function in effecting coördination.

(1) The organs of static sense and bodily equilibrium are the semicircular canals, including the saccule and utricle of the inner ear. They regulate automatically the responses of the organism whereby its equilibrium is maintained, illustrated by the balancing reflexes of the trained (or untrained) tight-rope walker; and they regulate in general all efforts of the organism to maintain and alter its bodily pos-

tures and attitudes. As stated above, it is commonly assumed that the stimulus for the organ of the static sense is its own liquid, pressing with varying and changing degrees of intensity at different places on the confining walls of the organ as the head moves. By setting the appropriate neuromuscular mechanisms in action the organ coördinates adjustments that otherwise would be jerky and awkward. It is usually held that the receptors of the semicircular canals are activated in turning or rotary movements, while the saccule and utricle are activated in straight line or rectilinear movements.

In connection with semicircular canal functions, Titchener (13) mentions the danger attending deaf mutes who indulge in rides on merry-go-rounds, or in deep water diving. In the one case they tend to sit upright, irrespective of the speed at which they travel, whereas the normal person unconsciously " banks " in toward the center; and consequently they are in danger of being thrown off. In the case of deep water diving the deaf mute is in danger of losing his spatial orientation and consequently of drowning.[1] In both cases, of course, the deafness is purely incidental, for the injury to the canals, located near the organ of hearing, is the cause of the difficulty.

(2) The kinaesthetic organs are located in the muscles and tendons (Fig. 6), and on the joint surfaces. The term kinaesthetic literally means feeling of motion, but since we are seldom conscious of the sensations caused by these organs our chief interest is in their functioning. The endings, or functionally the beginnings, of afferent neurons (that is, nerve cells which carry impulses from the receptors to the brain or spinal cord) are found in the muscles, wound spirally around individual muscle cells. On tendon surfaces are found branch-like beginnings of afferent nerves, and the

[1] *Op cit.*, pp. 178-179.

synovial membrane lining the joints is supplied with receptors. We have already noted that kinaesthetic receptors are stimulated by the contraction of muscle cells, the tension of

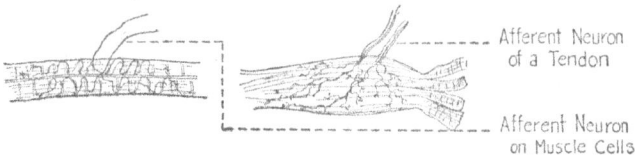

FIG. 6. — Kinaesthetic receptors in muscles and tendons.

the tendons, and the rubbing of one joint surface on another when some muscular act is taking place. Kinaesthetic stimuli are thus forms of contact stimuli.

Kinaesthetic receptors function by generating nerve impulses that regulate muscular activity. Their importance is demonstrated in the familiar mirror-tracing experiment, in which a subject traces some simple design, usually a star, with a pencil, on the design reflected from the mirror. Under the conditions of the experiment the visual cues are reversed, thus breaking up the established visual-kinaesthetic cues, and making the execution of the act quite difficult. These cues are combined through habit, for in the everyday acts of dressing and shaving before a mirror the same conditions obtain that characterize the mirror-tracing experiment.

In the disease *tabes dorsalis*, also called *locomotor ataxia*, a degeneration in the spinal cord primarily affects nerve tracts from the cutaneous receptors and proprioceptors. The resulting symptom is an extreme clumsiness of gait and of manipulatory habits. When the normal individual with both legs or feet " asleep " tries to walk he practically duplicates the tabetic gait. In the absence of kinaesthetic cues from his feet and legs he relies on visual cues that are inadequate for smooth or coördinated muscular activity.

D

(III) The Interoceptors. Notwithstanding the fact that the proprioceptors are located internally, they belong to and are adjuncts of the exteroceptors. The true internal receptors are located in the viscera. Aside from the organs of taste and smell they have not been definitely identified or described. Since many visceral activities, such as the secreting functions of the gastric glands, may take place independently of nerve control, we cannot assume that interoceptive stimulation is the sole condition for visceral functioning, either muscular or glandular. There are, however, afferent (leading from the receptors) connections between the viscera and the cerebrospinal nervous system, as well as connections in the autonomic system that are both afferent and efferent (leading to the muscles and glands), so that the existence of interoceptive impulses cannot be questioned.

According to Herrick, taste in man is wholly interoceptive, in the sense that nerve impulses from the taste organs affect internal and visceral functions, and not the orientation of the body. Nevertheless, taste stimuli come from without so that logically taste could be exteroceptive; and in fact it is partly exteroceptive in certain fishes.

Human gustatory receptors or taste buds are located on the tongue and in various places on the pharynx. The adequate stimuli for taste are chemical substances in solution, producing the four taste responses, sour, salt, sweet, and bitter. The obvious function of taste is to provide for the intake of proper and the rejection of improper food. However, this function should not be described in the language of poetry — taste buds do not send " messages " to either the brain or the stomach, but together with the thermal and touch exteroceptors located on the tongue they send nerve impulses that discharge into certain neuromuscular and glandular mechanisms. If the stimulus is customary, and chemically suitable, these impulses result in mastication, swallowing, peristalsis, and glandular activity; if unusual or chemically noxious, they inhibit these activities and occasionally produce antiperistalsis.

CONNECTIONS BETWEEN RECEPTORS AND EFFECTORS: THE NERVOUS SYSTEM

It would be grossly misleading to think of the receptors as functionally distinct from the response organs or effectors, and from the neural mechanisms which connect the two. They have been discussed in a separate section of this chapter solely in the interests of convenience. The receptors function by converting the energy of the stimulus into nervous energy — that is, by generating or inaugurating nerve impulses as the result of being stimulated. These impulses go to nerve centers over the nerves connecting the receptors with the centers where they are " re-directed " — to use a convenient expression — back to the effectors or response organs, consisting of the muscles and glands. The nerves leading from the receptors to the nerve centers are ingoing or *afferent*. The nerves going from the centers to the muscles and glands are outgoing or *efferent*. In the older terminology afferent and efferent are called sensory and motor respectively. Thus receptors, nerve connections, and effectors together constitute a system of neural circuits, known as reflex circuits or arcs. The brain, popularly referred to as the organ of thought, is a part of this reflex system: it is that part of the nervous system in which the most elaborate connections between afferent and efferent impulses are found. The brain and spinal cord together contain all the connecting centers of the body save those in the viscera, which belong to a special division of the nervous system, the autonomic division. Both brain and spinal cord (Fig. 7) are compact masses of nervous tissue, lodged in bony cavities. The nerves of the body consist entirely of afferent and efferent elements whose sole function is the conduction of nerve impulses from receptor to brain and spinal cord, and from these centers out to the muscles and glands. Since these nerves are located outside of the brain and cord rela-

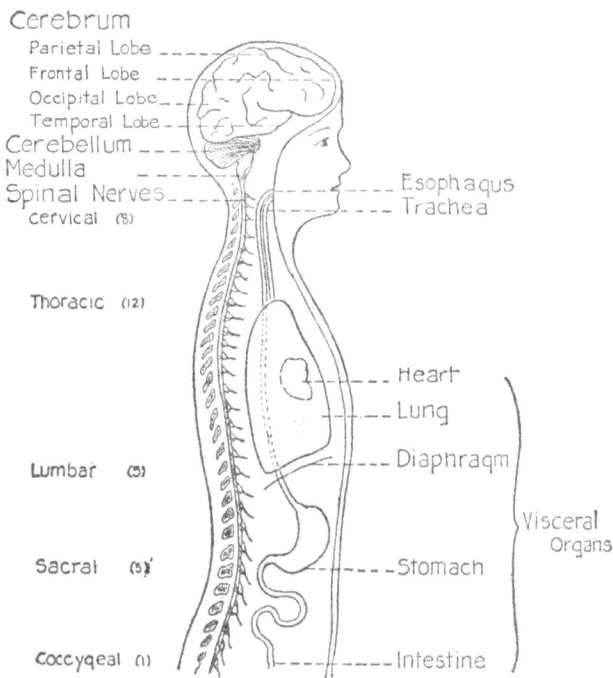

Cerebrum
Parietal Lobe
Frontal Lobe
Occipital Lobe
Temporal Lobe
Cerebellum
Medulla
Spinal Nerves
cervical (8)

Thoracic (12)

Lumbar (5)

Sacral (5)

Coccygeal (1)

Esophagus
Trachea

Heart
Lung
Diaphragm

Visceral
Organs

Stomach

Intestine

FIG. 7. — Schematic diagram of the central nervous system. Note that the 31 spinal nerves are grouped into five divisions.

tively nearer the surface of the body they are sometimes designated as the peripheral nervous system. The peripheral nervous system and the central nervous system (brain and spinal cord) together constitute the cerebrospinal nervous system.

Perhaps this preliminary sketch of the nervous system would be rendered more intelligible by the use of an analogy. The nervous system is frequently compared with a telephone exchange. The central nervous system or the brain and the spinal cord corresponds to the telephone switchboard, housed in a building, while the peripheral system is represented by the cables and individual wires that follow the streets of the city. The receptors and effectors are analogous respectively to the transmitters and receivers of the telephone instruments. It should be noted that the general comparison is inadequate in one essential respect: nerve cells of the cerebrospinal nervous system are polarized — that is, they carry impulses in one direction only — whereas telephone wires transmit impulses originating at either end. But in another respect the comparison is illuminating: stated negatively, electrical impulses of the telephone system are not human voices, and nerve impulses are not " messages " or sensations. Both kinds of impulses are forms of energy sent from a beginning to a terminal structure by means of a connecting medium.

From the standpoint of psychology the distinction between the cerebrospinal and the autonomic nervous systems is important. The former consists of exteroceptive and proprioceptive reflex circuits and their inter-connections, while the autonomic system comprises connections with the interoceptors. The former is involved in such psychological phenomena as thinking and intelligence and the acquisition of motor habits. It represents the neural mechanisms by which the organism reacts to its social and physical environment. The latter is primarily responsible for the drives, emotions, feelings, and other organic states, that motivate the organism in its contact with the environment. It must not be forgotten that both systems function together, for they are both parts of one nervous system. As a matter of fact, the two kinds of psychological phenomena just distinguished likewise are so closely associated that they can be separated only for purposes of verbal description.

Neurons, Nerve Impulses, Synapses, and Reflexes. From the standpoint of morphology or structure the unit of the nervous system is the microscopic nerve cell or *neuron* (Fig. 8). In appearance the neuron differs from other cells

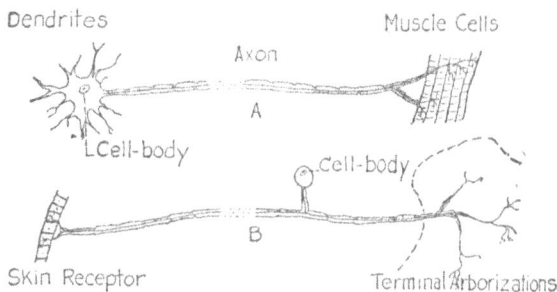

Fig. 8. — Efferent and afferent neurons. A, efferent neuron; B, afferent neuron. The axons are broken to indicate that they are disproportionately short in the diagram.

of the body (muscle, epithelial, connective tissue, bone, and fat cells) by virtue of its branching processes. One of these processes, the axon, is frequently so long that it makes the neuron a wire-like structure. The remaining processes are called *dendrites*. Both axon and dendrites are branches from the third part of the neuron, the *cell-body*. In traversing the neuron nerve impulses travel in one direction only — from dendrites through cell-body and out over the axon. The axon often has collateral branches extending from it at right angles that connect with the dendrites of other neurons. The minute plate-like endings of axons and collateral branches are called *terminal arborizations*. Axons and collaterals correspond to the outside wires of the telephone system, and like (many) such wires they are covered by an insulating substance. The insulation, called the *medullary sheath*, is found uniformly in the mature cerebrospinal nervous system; the final covering, the *neurilemma*, is found in the peripheral but not in the central division of the cerebrospinal system.

The *nerve impulse* is a form of physiological energy that travels, as we have said, from dendrites out over the axon. Normally it is generated or liberated in the receptor, and it becomes transformed into behavior energy at its final destination, the effector (muscle or gland). Its rate of transmission in higher mammals has been estimated at about 125 meters per second. The nerve impulse is undoubtedly both electrical and chemical in nature, for it liberates CO_2.

The student must not confuse nerve impulses with sensations, or conscious states resulting from stimulation of the receptors. When the eye is normally stimulated, the former and not the latter travel from the retina of the eye to the brain, and the resulting conscious reaction is the sensation of red, blue, etc. The nerve impulses are not correspondingly colored. Neither are the auditory impulses from the ear to the brain sounds or musical notes. And when the hand is painfully burned the "pain" does not follow the course of the nerve from the hand, up the arm, into the spinal cord, and up to the brain. In fact, the pain normally is localized at the anatomical seat of the injury. The nerve impulse is a purely physiological phenomenon that interests the psychologist because of its rôle in behavior.

Nerve impulses go from one neuron to another, more specifically from the terminal arborizations of one neuron to the dendrites of another, at places of contact called *synapses*. It is commonly believed that the synapse offers a resistance to the nerve impulse, and that habit formation involves the breaking down of synaptic resistances; but this view has been questioned, notably by Lashley (7). The important point is that synapses are selective or differential, in that they direct impulses over certain specific neurons instead of sending them out indiscriminately over all possible neurons. Theoretically axons of several neurons may discharge their nerve impulses into one common neuron, or one neuron may connect with several other neurons. Neurons also show a serial arrangement. There are at least three sensory neurons from somatic receptor to the brain (cerebral) surface, and two motor neurons from the brain surface to the muscle. A group of synapses having a common function is called a *center*, if the group is located within the central nervous system. When located outside of this system such a group is termed a *ganglion*. For example, the cell-bodies of the sensory neurons entering the spinal cord are located outside of the cord near its dorso-lateral surfaces. However, the true centers or synapses of the cerebrospinal nervous system are located in the spinal cord or brain — that is, in the central nervous system. None are found in the arms, legs, or in the body. Synaptic connections of the visceral system are scattered in various parts of the body. In terms of our analogy, the synapses constitute the switchboards of the telephone system. A complete neural circuit without central synapses is theoretically possible, just as direct telephone connections between houses is possible. But neither arrangement provides for varieties of connections, hence neither is ever actually found.

The act of behavior that results when a relatively simple group of nerve impulses go from receptor to effector is called a *reflex*, or a *reflex act*. Examples are hand-withdrawal as the result of painful stimulation, the pupillary reflex to light in the eye, respiratory reflexes such as sneezing and coughing, circulatory reflexes such as blushing, paling, and heart acceleration, reflexes of the skeletal musculature such as balancing, grasping, waving the arms, extending the fingers.

The flow of saliva and tears are glandular reflexes. Corresponding to the two kinds of effectors, reflexes are motor or glandular. Reflexes vary greatly in complexity. The importance of the principle underlying reflex behavior will be brought out repeatedly in this text.

The Spinal Cord and Spinal Reflexes. The spinal cord is approximately eighteen inches long and two-thirds of an inch in diameter. It is surrounded by three membranes or sheaths separated by a liquid, and the membranes in turn are surrounded by the spinal column. When these membranes or meninges become inflamed the disease is called *spinal meningitis*. The nerves of the body enter and leave the cord in thirty-one pairs, called the spinal nerves. They are really double pairs, since each member of the pair, either the right or the left, divides into two branches close to the cord within the spinal column, one branch entering dorsally and one ventrally. Small spaces between the vertebrae permit the spinal nerves to extend from the body of the cord.

The spinal cord has two main functions. The first function is that of conduction. Afferent neural impulses from the sensory nerves entering the cord are conducted upward to higher levels of the cord or to the brain. Efferent impulses from the brain and higher centers are conducted downward in the cord until they are carried out over the neurons in the spinal nerves to their ultimate destination, the muscles and glands. The outer portion of the cord, or the " white " matter, consisting of a cable of neurons, performs the function of conduction. Bundles or cables of axons appear white because the relatively thick medullary sheath surrounding the individual axons is whiter than the axis cylinder; centers or groups of synapses are grey because they consist of cell-bodies and dendrites not covered by the medullary substance. The ascending afferent neurons occupy the dorsal half of the cord while the descending efferent neurons lie ventrally.

The second function of the cord is to establish connections between afferent and efferent neurons. These connections or synapses, the spinal reflex centers, are found in the central part or the " grey " matter in the cord. In a cross-section of the cord this grey matter is seen as a capital H. It is sometimes assumed that the afferent neuron makes a direct connection with the efferent, but according to most authorities at least one neuron is found interpolated between them. Interpolated neurons of this kind in the spinal cord are called *connecting* neurons; in the brain they are known as *associational* neurons. By means of collateral branches

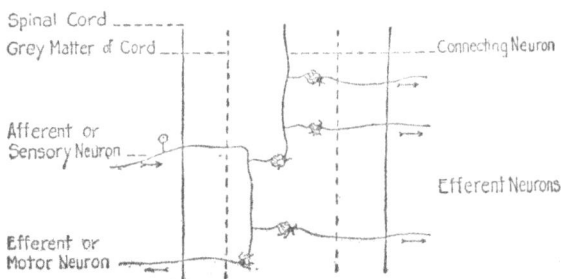

FIG. 9. — Schematic diagram representing some of the synaptic connections in the spinal cord.

afferent impulses entering the cord are distributed in three ways: they go to efferent neurons at the same level of the cord at which they entered, they go to efferent neurons at other levels, and they are conducted up to the brain and higher centers. Efferent impulses descending from the brain are similarly distributed to the spinal nerves at different levels of the cord. Thus the mechanisms for every complex coördinated movement are provided for in the central grey matter of the cord (Fig. 9).

We may now note some of the essential features of spinal reflex behavior. An animal whose brain has been removed or destroyed is called a *spinal animal*, since its behavior must be explained largely in terms of spinal cord mechanisms. For example, the spinal frog will show coördinated as well as simple reflexes: stimulation of the foot will elicit the leg withdrawal responses. According to the physiologist Howell (6), " If the animal is suspended and various spots on its skin are stimulated by the application of bits of paper moistened with dilute acetic acid the animal will make a neat and skillful movement of the corresponding leg to remove the stimulating body." [2] In a familiar physiological experiment the tissues of a decapitated cat are kept alive by artificial respiration so that the spinal reflexes of the animal can be studied. Upon proper stimulation the tail will twitch and the legs will be flexed or extended. Since this animal is more highly organized than the frog its spinal reflexes are more mechanical and less fully coördinated. The available evidence indicates that human spinal reflexes are even more dependent upon the brain centers and upon the nervous system functioning as a whole.

The Medulla, Pons, and Cerebellum. The upper extremity of the spinal cord is enlarged to form the *medulla oblongata*. This structure contains special nerve centers that partly control respiration and circulation, known respectively as the *respiratory* and *vasomotor* centers. Several other special centers are also located in this region. The medulla is also the region where most efferent neurons coming from one half of the brain cross to the opposite half of the spinal cord — the remaining efferent neurons cross below at different levels in the cord.

Since the cerebellum is housed in the skull cavity it is, in a way, part of the brain. Actually it is relatively inde-

[2] Seventh Edition, Chapter VII, p. 143.

pendent, showing the same type of organization found in the major part of the brain, the cerebrum. Its outside surface uniformly shows fine convolutions separated by fissures, so that this surface area is more extensive than the size of the cerebellum would seem to indicate. This area is the surface of a thin layer of centers or synapses called the *cerebellar cortex;* the inner portion of the cerebellum consists primarily of bundles of axons crowded together in a mass of tissue. The axons belong to two sorts of neurons: (1) afferent and efferent, both communicating with the spinal cord and brain, and (2) *commissural,* connecting the two halves or lobes of the cerebellum. The commissural axons form a horse-shoe structure with its concavity dorsalwards, called the *pons* (or bridge).

The functions of the cerebellum are imperfectly understood. In general, physiologists regard it as a coördinating center for the muscular reflexes involved in locomotion and equilibrium. For example, when an individual undertakes to walk a tight rope his tendencies to fall towards either the right or the left are counteracted more or less successfully by reflex jerks in the opposite direction; and it is assumed that these reflexes are due to motor impulses sent from the cerebellum when the proprioceptive impulses caused by the falling motions are received by the cerebellum. According to this theory of its function, the cerebellum is physiologically related to the proprioceptors, that is, to the organ of static sense in the ear and to the kinaesthetic organs of the muscles, tendons, and joints.

The Cerebrum. The greater part of the skull cavity is occupied by the *cerebrum.* Both cerebrum and cerebellum are separated from the inner surface of the skull by the meninges. The cerebrum is divided into two hemispheres by the great longitudinal fissure. Its surface shows many convolutions separated by fissures that are fairly constant in normal animals of the highest type, as well as human beings. Two of these fissures, the Fissure of Sylvius and the Fissure of Rolando, are especially noteworthy. As in the case of the cerebellum, the convolutions increase the surface area.

Cerebral Cortical Areas. The cerebral cortex occupies the surface of the cerebrum to a depth of 2-4 millimeters. It is a layer of synapses which presumably are organized into centers. It consists of three recognizable kinds of areas, as follows: (1) sensory areas, where the axons of neurons in the afferent path from the receptors terminate; (2) motor areas, containing cell-bodies which send axons down into the cerebrum and spinal cord to connect with other axons leading to the effectors; and (3) associational areas, containing the cell-bodies and other parts of neurons which connect the various regions of the cortex, including the sensory and motor areas. The various areas are indicated in Figure 10.

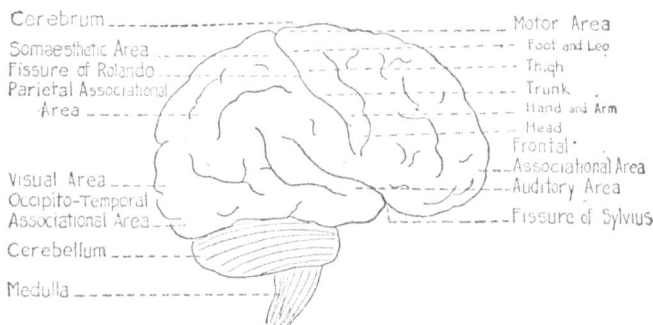

FIG. 10. — Right half of the brain, showing some of the chief cortical areas. The function and location of these areas are hypothetical.

The connections between the cerebral cortex and the receptors and effectors may be sketched briefly (Fig. 11). In noting them we should not overlook the fact that many afferent connections are made between the proprioceptors and the cerebellum. Receptors of the exteroceptive and proprioceptive systems located in the trunk and extremities are connected with the spinal cord by afferent bipolar neurons. Axons of the bipolar neurons constitute in part the spinal nerves. We have seen that they make synaptic connections

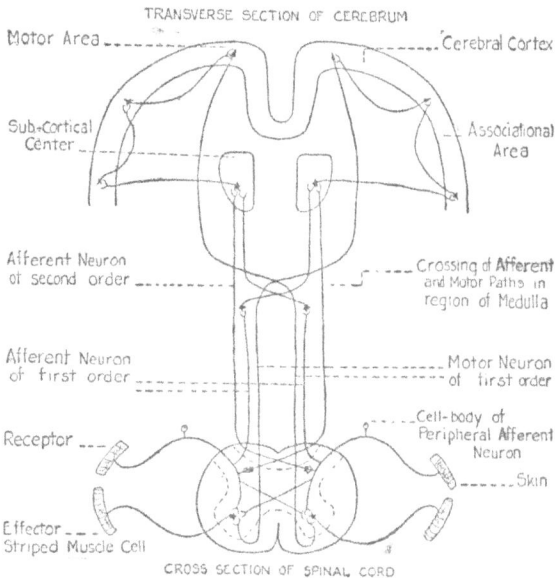

FIG. 11.—Some of the connections in the central nervous system between the cutaneous receptors and the somatic effectors.

with efferent neurons in the spinal cord. In addition to making these connections, the bipolar neurons send axons upward in the cord which terminate in the region of the medulla. Either in this region or at lower levels in the cord they form synapses with neurons which cross to the opposite side of the cord, and then continue upward into a collection of centers located in the middle of the cerebrum. Because of their location, these centers are known as *subcortical* centers.

From the subcortical centers a third series of neurons goes to a particular area of the cortex known as the *somesthetic* area. This is, therefore, the sensory area of the cortex which receives exteroceptive and proprioceptive impulses from the body. The term, " somesthetic," means " bodily feeling."

Receptors located in the head connect with the brain stem, or that part of the brain between the spinal cord and cerebrum, through the cranial nerves. They also make synaptic connections in the subcortical centers, and with the exception of the receptors for vision, audition, taste, and smell, they finally connect with the somesthetic area. Afferent impulses from these four receptors eventually reach special sensory areas on the cortex known respectively as the visual, auditory, gustatory, and olfactory areas. Many neurons in the afferent path from receptors located in the head cross to the opposite side of the cerebrum, but not in the definite way which characterizes the spinal afferent paths. In general, at least three afferent neurons constitute the path from receptor to cerebral cortex.

As we said above, the motor areas of the cortex constitute a discharging, efferent station and not a receiving, afferent station. They contain the cell-bodies of efferent neurons. Many axons from these neurons extend down into the brain and cord without entering the subcortical centers and terminate in the central grey of the cord. Here they form synaptic connections with neurons that leave the cord and go to the muscles. Thus there are at least two efferent neurons in the path from the motor areas to the muscles.

The synaptic connections made in the associational areas of the cortex are exceedingly complicated. It is important to know that neurons extend from the different sensory areas to the associational areas, and that other neurons extend from the associational areas to the motor areas. These two series of neurons complete the links in cerebral reflex circuits, thereby forming cortical connections between receptors and effectors. Numerous other connections are made in the cerebral cortex.

The Doctrine of Phrenology. It is obviously impossible to reconcile the known facts of cerebral anatomy and physiology with the belief, once generally accepted but now fortunately dying out, that different circumscribed areas on the cerebral surface are the locations of specific human traits. In the first place, even the simplest of psychological processes involves cerebral activity that is widely scattered over the cortex. The perception of a locomotive, for instance, involves activity in (1) the visual area of the cortex at the back of the brain, (2) the auditory area on the sides, and (3) the somesthetic area, where cutaneous and kinaesthetic impulses are received, above and in front of the auditory area; moreover, it involves associational areas as well. The various " faculties " of the phrenologist, such as sublimity, ideality, time, veneration, comparison, secretiveness, destructiveness, parental love, or amativeness, are exceedingly complex as compared with acts of perception. Incidentally, the notion that specific, over-developed brain areas are represented by bumps on the skull or even thinned spots in the skull bones is physiologically highly improbable. In the second place, as is fully explalned in our chapter on *Intelligent Behavior*, the " faculties " of phrenology are not actual human traits at all, but artificial abstractions. There is no " faculty " of *good judgment*, for an individual could be a good judge of clothes and at the same time a poor judge of horses. The doctrine of phrenology would merit no consideration at all were it not for its frequent popular acceptance. It was originally formulated by Gall and Spurzheim a century ago in a sincere attempt to explain cerebral functions.

Cephalization. Our chief interest is in cerebral functions rather than cerebral structures, so as to obtain a better understanding of the mechanisms of behavior. Possibly the best approach to an understanding of cerebral functioning can be made by noting the developmental history of the central nervous system. The annelid or segmented worm, of which the common earthworm is an example, possesses a central nervous system extending the length of its body and consisting of a double chain of ganglia, or reflex centers. In moving around in its environment the head of the worm obviously bears the brunt of the environmental attack: it is the head of the animal rather than the other segments of its body that first encounters food or harmful substances. The result of this situation is that the receptors, notably the receptors used in locating, selecting and ingesting food, tend to develop in the head of the organism. Moreover, as the course of development in animals higher than the worm shows, the specialized receptors or higher senses, vision and hearing, develop in the head. As the receptors appear at one extremity of the organism there also appears at this extremity a corresponding growth of the central nervous system. An increase in the number of afferent-efferent connections necessarily accompanies the increase of sense organs. This general process of head development is called *cephalization.* Our interest is in the fact that the group of ganglia developing in the head is the forerunner of the brain.

Special attention is called to the conclusion that logically follows from the developmental facts just stated: with respect to origin and function the brain is essentially a system of connections between afferent and efferent neurons. As our subsequent discussion of correlation, association, and co-ordination shows, these connections are tremendously complicated and involved; but they are neural connections nev-

E

ertheless. Another way of stating the matter is to say that the entire nervous system, including the brain, is organized on the reflex basis. The brain is the " organ of thought " only in the sense that cerebral activity constitutes part of the more widely distributed physiological activity with which thinking is related or identified. Since neuron systems in the brain function fundamentally in connection with receptorial and effectorial systems, the physiological counterpart of the thinking process includes all the bodily organs and structures involved and not merely those composed of nervous tissue.

Correlation and Coördination. The principle of cephalization corroborates the view that the central nervous system functions by receiving afferent impulses and organizing them into efferent impulses which are sent out to the muscles and glands. The terms *correlation* and *coördination* are used to designate respectively the afferent and efferent aspects of this organizing process. Sometimes the term *association* is used to describe the process as a whole.

Correlation refers to the process by which afferent impulses from the various receptors are brought together, fused, and modified before they reach motor centers. According to Herrick, much of the central portion of the spinal cord and the greater part of the subcortical regions of the cortex consist of correlation centers. One of these regions, the *thalamus*, is a particularly important correlation center. All afferent impulses reaching the cerebral cortex, with the exception of those coming from the olfactory receptor, pass through the thalamus. The sensory areas of the cortex likewise perform this same function. The correlation centers are thus arranged in different levels of complexity. In fact, all afferent impulses which finally reach the cerebral cortex are first subjected to a preliminary correlating process.

The principle of correlation explains the fact that organisms react to situations rather than to isolated stimuli. To use a former illustration, the individual who inspects a locomotive regards it as a unitary object and not as an assortment of unrelated visual, auditory, thermal, and olfactory sensory elements. The afferent impulses corresponding to these forms of stimulation in a way lose their identity before they are permitted to discharge into motor areas and effect a response. We may regard such correlated impulses as patterns or configurations. Sometimes the German word *Gestalt* is used to describe such configurations. In reading a familiar phrase like " very truly yours " we do not react to the isolated letters separately, but to the phrase as a whole. Its *Gestalt* or general form evokes the reading response.

Coördination is the companion term for correlation. It describes the way in which nerve impulses are discharged from the central nervous system to the effectors. In terms of behavior, well coördinated acts are skillful and graceful, whereas poorly coördinated acts are inefficient and awkward. Theoretically, complete absence of coördination is the condition in which responses to stimuli are so spasmodic and erratic that they are in no sense adjustments to the stimuli, but such an extreme condition is found only in pathological cases, such as strychnine poisoning.

Various parts of the central nervous system have coördinating functions. That part of the cerebral cortex known as the motor area is a coördination center; other such centers are the corpus striatum, one of the subcortical centers, and the (vertebrate) cerebellum. For practical purposes we may say that impulses coming from the receptors are redirected toward the effectors in the central nervous system, and that impulses cease to be afferent and become efferent when they " turn the corner." Herrick states that the neurons in front of the corners differ structurally from those behind the corners. Functionally, the distinction between correlation and coördination will be more clear after an examination of muscular action.

Perhaps the best way to appreciate coördination is to picture its opposite state. If all motor pathways were open indiscriminately to all sensory impulses the resulting behavior would be a medley of reflexes. The normal coördinated response to a painful stimulus applied to the hand is a hand or arm withdrawal, but with a nervous system bereft of all coördinating centers it might be a convulsive movement toward the stimulating object. Due to the fact that they are largely acquired, coördinated responses are on the whole adaptive.

The elements of coördination include the direction, force, duration, and timing of responses. The example just given illustrates the element of direction. The respective amounts of force behind a blow in playful boxing and a blow similarly directed in a desperate prizefight differ considerably. Duration and timing likewise are characteristic of all coördinated acts, but they are particularly valuable in those responses, such as swimming and dancing, that represent forms of locomotion. All the elements of coördination are involved in the simplest response.

It is evident that coördination implies a highly organized distribution of motor impulses. In picking up an object, for instance, hundreds of impulses are distributed to the proper muscle fibers of the arm, hands, and fingers involved. The coördinations required in playing a symphony on the piano are, of course, infinitely more complex. As described by Howell, the act of mastication involves about six different muscles, while deglutition or swallowing consists of many specific movements all timed to appear in their proper sequence. Many acts practically involve the musculature of the entire body.

Facilitation and Inhibition. The processes of correlation and coördination involve certain principles of neural activity that are not fully understood. Thus *facilitation* refers to the fact that an act of behavior is frequently intensified or accelerated by introducing stimuli over and above those directly responsible for the act itself. When an individual is apparently exerting all his strength upon a hand dynamometer (an instrument that measures the strength of hand-grip) an auditory stimulus may result in a perceptible increase in his grip. Conversely, *inhibition* is found when extraneous stimuli retard or weaken a response. It is illustrated by the act of pressing on the upper lip to ward off a sneeze. Presumably facilitation involves the reinforcement of certain neural impulses by others, whereas inhibition involves interference among impulses.

Inasmuch as the principles of facilitation and inhibition apply to cerebral as well as spinal cord activity, they help explain many phases of behavior for which the cerebrum is primarily responsible. What is ordinarily called will-power or *volition* is largely a demonstration of restraint or inhibition. The student who forgoes the pleasure of a dance or theater party in order to prepare for final examinations exerts a commendable will or restraint that is represented neurologically by the inhibitory effects of certain neural impulses upon coördination centers. The so-called influence of mind over matter again illustrates inhibition. Thus, the belief that states of fear or worry exert a depressing effect upon the digestive process is well-founded. It has been demonstrated experimentally in the case of a cat suddenly confronted with an angry dog. When the cat sees, hears, or smells the dog the afferent impulses originating in its corresponding receptors in some way affect the efferent impulses involved in digestion. It will be noted that both the cat and the student presumably illustrate cortical inhibition, since the restraining neural impulses come from the cortex. This conception has led many psychologists and physiologists to emphasize the inhibitory functions of the cerebral cortex. They argue with some logic that education itself is largely a process of establishing inhibitions. In other words, its effect is the substitution of training and discipline for primitive impulsiveness. However, facilitation as well as inhibition characterizes cortical activity, in the sense that education and training result in better adaptation to the environment. Broadly speaking, the trained individual as compared with the untrained is one who can order a meal, write a letter, solve a geometrical problem, select a new suit, control his subordinates, or converse with his associates more efficiently and more effectively. Thus both facilitation and inhibition are cerebral activities that are closely related to intelligence.

Vicarious Functioning in the Central Nervous System. In order to explain many phenomena connected with injuries to the central nervous system it is necessary to assume that functions can be transferred from parts of this system to adjacent parts. The principle involved is known as *vicarious functioning.* Under certain conditions, including a period of relearning, a function lost as the result of injury to or disease in the brain or spinal cord can be regained. One might suppose that the nerve tissues heal or regenerate, but this process takes place only in the peripheral nervous system. The neurilemma, or the membrane surrounding the medullary sheath, apparently acts as the regenerating agent, and the neurilemma is not found in the brain and spinal cord. The bilateral structure of the central nervous system suggests that the function of a part is taken over by its symmetrical part, on the opposite side of the body; but vicarious functioning seems to operate homolaterally as well as bilaterally. Like facilitation and inhibition it is an explanatory principle inferred from observed facts.

Cerebral Localization of Function. We have noted the salient facts of cerebral structure, and we have explained the basic principles of cerebral functioning, but as yet, except in a general way, we have not discussed the possible localization of functions in different parts of the cerebrum. The available evidence regarding such localization is by no means conclusive. The anatomical facts seem to justify the general view of the cerebrum and the central nervous system sketched above: afferent paths go from receptors to spinal cord and subcortical centers, and from these centers to the cerebral cortex; efferent pathways lead from the motor areas of the cortex to the musculature of the body; and associational tracts lead from sensory to associational areas, and from these areas to the motor cortex. Moreover, the subcortical centers seem to be complete reflex mechanisms, since efferent paths go from these centers to the effectors. In general the clinical and physiological evidence supports this view. For instance, when the motor areas of the cortex are exposed in the living animal and explored by a pair of electrodes, contractions of various muscles of the body are plainly observable. The location of the motor areas of the cortex given in Figure 10 is based primarily on experiments of this kind. In studying the functions of the sensory and associational areas the method of electrical stimulation cannot be used. It is necessary to remove the specific areas in question and note the effect of the operations upon the behavior of the animals.

The results of such physiological experiments warn us against generalizing too freely upon anatomical evidence. Franz (2) has published the results of several investigations tending to show that destruction of cortical areas does not in all cases result in the loss or the impairment of the functions ordinarily attributed to these areas. In one series of experiments performed by Franz and Lashley (3) it was found that contrary to a prevailing view, the destruction of the frontal lobes of the cerebrum of the white rat does not greatly interfere with learned reactions. In another paper (8) these psychologists report that the maze [3] may be learned by a white rat after a good part of its cortex has been removed. This result is somewhat startling in view of the fact that removal of the cortex is supposed to destroy the intelligence of the animal so treated.

Lashley (9) has also advanced some new views concerning the motor areas of the cortex. It is generally assumed that the motor areas function in so-called voluntary acts, as in deliberately lifting the arms. According to the traditional view the neural process involved comes from the motor area down the cord to the level of the arms and then out on the efferent nerves at that level to the arm muscles. But Lashley found that extirpation or removal of the motor areas in white rats resulted primarily in a difficulty in maintaining bodily posture and not in an inability to initiate movements. In other words, he obtained results similar to those ordinarily associated with cerebellar disturbances. Upon destroying the motor areas in monkeys he found that their habits of manipulating objects were retained along with their habits of visual discrimination. Lashley suggests the possibility that the motor areas in some way prime or instigate other centers more directly responsible for coördinated acts. Both Lashley and Franz found that *specific* motor functions are not located in any absolute and fixed way within the motor area.

The pathological condition known as *aphasia* sheds some light on the nature of cerebral functions. Taken literally aphasia means " loss of speech," but in actual usage it is restricted to loss or imperfections of speech due to lesions or hemorrhages in the cerebral cortex. Occasionally there may be a case of aphasia for which no structural cause can be

[3] See Chapters IV and V for descriptions of the maze experiment.

found. It is then referred to as a *functional* disturbance. There are two kinds of aphasia, sensory and motor. *Sensory aphasia* is the inability to understand language. It is further differentiated into word-blindness and word-deafness, depending upon whether the patient's difficulty is with language seen, or with language heard. Since his receptors are unimpaired he sees the word in the one case and hears it in the other, but in both cases it is unfamiliar. The two defects are ordinarily ascribed to different cortical areas, both however located in a strip back of the Fissure of Rolando that extends into the parietal lobe. In *motor aphasia* the speaking vocabulary of the patient is lost or impaired. There is no actual paralysis of the muscles of articulation. Motor aphasia takes various forms: the patient has a vocabulary of only a few words, or he uses words and syllables in wrong combinations, or perhaps he can articulate words only when he sings. A defect closely related to motor aphasia is *agraphia*, or the inability to write.

A neurological explanation of aphasia should be advanced with extreme caution. We cannot conclude that language is seen by one part of the cortex, heard by another, and articulated by a third. Such an interpretation goes back to the phrenology of Gall and Spurzheim. We may surmise that the language functions impaired in word-blindness and word-deafness respectively are provided for by relatively separate correlation systems; but we do not know that these systems are located in circumscribed cortical areas. Possibly the areas in question contain only the higher units of the correlation systems, the remaining units being scattered over various parts of the cerebral cortex, or even the sub-cortical areas. It is also possible, following Lashley's suggestion regarding the functions of the so-called motor areas, that these areas send out impulses which in some way "prime" the real centers of the correlation systems, located elsewhere; but an adequate explanation of aphasia presupposes a more complete knowledge of the nervous system than we now possess.

Summary of Views of Cerebral Functions. From the foregoing discussion it can be inferred that there are two opposed views of cerebral functioning. According to one of them, specific functions are localized in definite, circumscribed regions of the cerebrum, particularly on the cerebral cortex. Phrenology represents the oldest view of this kind. This doctrine was superseded by the theory which assigns three functions, namely, sensory, associational, and motor, to the three corresponding areas on the cortex. Moreover, this theory regards each area as a collection of centers for special functions. According to the opposed view, the cerebrum functions as a whole: it is one organ and not a system of organs. The conclusions of Herrick, Lashley, and the other investigators mentioned stand somewhere between these extreme views.

Although conclusive evidence regarding the nature of cerebral functions is lacking, we can clarify the issues involved by asking what is meant by the term, *function*. The answer to this question is found in the stimulus-response principle, explained in our introductory chapter. From a psychological standpoint a function is a *complete* stimulus-response phenomenon. Not the mere act of withdrawing the hand, but withdrawing the hand in response to a pain stimulus is a function. And not merely a fear response, but a fear response to a stimulating object, say a burglar, is a psychological function. It is misleading to speak of sensory functions, associational functions, and motor functions, for the reason that the simplest act performed by an organism involves all three. We might as well say that a man " purchased," without implying that he purchased something.

Psychological science is interested in the physiological

mechanisms underlying concrete stimulus-response events. The simplest of these mechanisms includes the receptor, the afferent path, the correlating and coördinating centers in the central nervous system, the efferent path, and the effector. But the majority of functions analyzed in subsequent chapters of this book are far more complex than the simple reflexes. Any single emotional response, any learning process, or any intelligent act in all probability involves the entire physiological and neurological equipment of the organism concerned. The problem of describing cerebral cortical functions is therefore the problem of ascertaining how various parts of the cortex coöperate on a given occasion with all parts of the body concerned.

The Autonomic Nervous System. Visceral effectors receive their nerve impulses from a special nervous system, the autonomic, that is an extension of the efferent cerebrospinal nervous system. Stiles (11) negatively but adequately defines the autonomic system as that part of the efferent system that does not control the skeletal muscles.[4] The afferent fibers found in the autonomic system properly belong to the cerebrospinal system.

The autonomic system consists of a chain of ganglia on either side and in front of the spinal column, several plexuses or ganglia in the viscera of the body cavity, and three small ganglia in the head, together with the nerves connecting these ganglia with each other.

It should be noted that efferent fibers do not leave the central nervous system and proceed to the visceral effectors as they do to the somatic effectors. Instead, there is always an additional motor neuron in the path from the central nervous system to the visceral effector. Corresponding to this structural arrangement is the fact that visceral functions are not directly subject to cortical control. We " vol-

[4] *Op. cit.*, p. 115.

untarily" wink, cough, gesticulate, register facial expressions, and produce vocal sounds; but we do not "voluntarily" control heart beat or intestinal peristalsis. The term "voluntary" is exceedingly misleading, but it expresses in a crude way the direct control of higher brain centers over the somatic as opposed to their indirect control over the visceral effectors. A more detailed analysis of this fact and of autonomic functions is made subsequently in our discussion of emotion.

ORGANS OF RESPONSE: THE EFFECTORS

It is theoretically and to a large extent practically possible to analyze all human responses in terms of their component elements. A smile differs from a frown as regards the play of the specific muscles involved in the two acts. Emotions are patterns or characteristic groupings of more circumscribed responses, and the patterns as well as the units are yielding to experimental analysis. Habits involving gross muscular coördinations are analyzed with relative ease. In fact, certain habitual adjustments made in bricklaying and other vocational activities have been analyzed with reference to their relative effectiveness. Human responses are concrete *acts*, representing coördinations executed by specialized structures of the body.

A very elementary knowledge of physiology suffices to reveal the organs of response. It is evident that such movements as are involved in adjustments to the environment are effected by muscle or muscle-bone mechanisms. A smile is primarily a muscular coördination; the act of turning a door-knob involves bones as well as muscles. In addition to the support it gives to the body as a whole, the skeleton provides the arms for the numerous muscle-bone levers of the body. Muscles that are directly or indirectly attached to bones are known as skeletal muscles. Hence one group of response organs consists of the skeletal muscles with all of their bone attachments and neural connections. Since these organs are located in and constitute largely the soma, they are known as the somatic effectors. They are directly stimulated by the exteroceptors and proprioceptors.

The viscera consist largely of response mechanisms, the smooth muscles and the glands of the body. Smooth muscle and glandular responses correspond to the lubrication and feed systems of the automobile.

Thus we may describe two chief classes of response organs, the somatic and visceral. The first consists of skeletal muscles and their connections; the second includes two sub-classes, the smooth muscles and the glands.

(A) The Somatic Effectors

The Somatic Response Organs. As we have said, the somatic effectors are the muscle or the muscle-bone units exclusive of the visceral musculature of the body. There are approximately 200 bones and 500 skeletal or striped muscles in the human body. In one kind of response mechanism the striped muscle connects with itself or with movable parts of the body. The muscle surrounding the mouth cavity, the muscle of the eyelid, the exterior muscles of the eyeball, and the muscles of the scalp are examples of this kind. In the second and more typical kind of response mechanism the two ends of the muscles are attached respectively to two articulating bones. This mechanism is therefore a lever. Muscles are attached to bones by tendons. Both kinds of response are due directly to contractions of the muscle itself, caused by nerve impulses discharged upon the individual muscle cells or fibers.

The muscle cell or fiber is the structural unit of the muscle, just as the neuron is the structural unit of the nervous system. It is a hair-like structure one or two inches in length and 1/5000 inch in diameter. Each muscle fiber is surrounded by a membrane or sac, the *sarcolemma;* while the muscle fiber itself is the muscle *plasma.* It shows numerous minute crossbands which give it the name *striped* muscle. Living muscle plasma is assumed to be a semi-liquid. Obviously, thousands of muscle fibers are necessary to constitute even a small muscle. Connective tissue surrounds the individual muscle fibers and the muscle as a whole.

Upon reaching a muscle an efferent nerve subdivides into small branches, the smallest branch being a division or collateral branch of the nerve fiber or axon. It will be remembered that the axon is the filament of the neuron that conducts the nerve impulse away from the cell body. The collateral branch terminates on the muscle fiber in a structure called an *end-plate.* Thus the number of axons supplying a given muscle is usually smaller than the number of muscle fibers in that muscle. The greatest number of axons per number of muscle fibers is regarded by Stiles as the neuromuscular unit.

The salient characteristics of muscular activity should be noted. *Muscle tonus* or tonic contraction refers to the fact that the muscles are never completely relaxed, even in sleep. They are in a state of constant incipient tension and they are consequently ready for overt action. Closely related to this phenomenon is the fact that motor neurons show definite *rhythms* of nervous discharge, ranging, according to Herrick (5), from forty to several hundred vibrations per second.[5] A continuous stream of nervous discharges results in prolonged or *tetanic* contraction, as distinguished from single muscular contractions. All so-called voluntary mus-

[5] *Op. cit.,* p. 116.

cular activity is probably tetanic. Another important principle is the law of *reciprocal innervation*. It has been found that when muscles responsible for a given act are stimulated, the muscles responsible for the opposed act are automatically inhibited. Thus in bending or flexing the arm, the flexor muscles are stimulated and the extensor muscles are inhibited. The phenomenon of *fatigue* is in part a function of the end-plate connecting the motor axon with the muscle fibers. Stiles compares this end-plate with a safety-fuse, designed to blow out when destruction of its contiguous structures is threatened. The end-plate, of course, does not have to be replaced by a new one in the living organism. There are other phenomena of neuromuscular activity too complex for elementary discussion.

(B) The Visceral Effectors

(1) **The Smooth Muscles.** The typical visceral muscle is smooth in the sense that its fiber does not have the striated or striped appearance of the skeletal muscle. The smooth muscle fiber is shaped like a spindle and it contains, as distinguished from the striated muscle, only one nucleus. Smooth muscle tissue is found in the alimentary canal and other visceral organs, the blood vessels and lymphatics, the bronchial tubes, the internal muscles of the eyeball, and the muscles attached to the hair follicles. Contrary to what would be expected, however, the heart muscle is striated. The smooth muscles are the non-skeletal muscles of the body. Very frequently skeletal and non-skeletal muscles respectively are called voluntary and involuntary, but these terms are confusing and should be avoided.

The two distinguishing characteristics of smooth muscle contraction are sluggishness of movement and the tendency to maintain muscular tone. Whereas sudden movements are more useful in the skeletal muscles, because they are re-sponses to the external environment, slower reactions are better adapted for such organic processes as digestion. When sudden contractions of the smooth muscles occur they indicate an unusual visceral condition. In a subsequent dis-cussion of the psychological aspects of smooth muscle func-tioning these characteristics again will be noted.[6]

(2) **The Glands.** The glands are secreting organs of the body. They are true response organs because they are ac-tivated by stimuli. Certain glands as well as some of the smooth muscles react directly to the stimuli, while most of them react normally to efferent nerve impulses, but in either case they effect the response. Some of the glands discharge their secretions through ducts into body cavities or on the body surface while others manufacture secretions that are taken directly into the blood stream. The former are the duct glands and the latter are the ductless glands or the *endocrines*.

Among the chief glandular effectors possessing ducts are the salivary glands, the glands of the stomach and intestine, the pancreas, the liver, the kidneys, the sweat glands, and the sebaceous glands of the skin. Some of the digestive glands also have endocrine functions. While the duct glands are primarily concerned with vital physiological processes, they are, as Watson points out, indirectly of great psycho-logical interest in that their reflex activities are in part modi-fied by external stimuli. For example, evidence shows that the flow of gastric juice can be accelerated by the sight of objects that have been associated with pleasant meals. In other words, their responses become associated with extrane-ous stimuli and thus contribute to the general tone of the organism.

The endocrines are attracting much scientific and popu-

6 Chapter IV.

lar attention on account of their somewhat spectacular contributions to the physiological balance among life processes.
Their active chemical principles are sometimes called hormones (from the word meaning " I excite ") but since these
principles sometimes inhibit physiological processes, they
are better known as autacoid substances (from " acos," a
remedy), so that hormones and chalones (" to relax ") respectively refer to stimulating and inhibiting autacoids.   It
should be understood that endocrinology is a new and somewhat hypothetical branch of physiological science.

Since autacoid substances are in effect drugs that circulate in the blood stream their psychological effects are secondary.   It is known that they influence physical growth,
energy, and the digestive and reproductive functions ; and
it is assumed by certain physiologists that in so doing they
influence emotions and temperament.   But psychologists
should be conservative in their assumptions regarding the
latter effects.

The endocrines vary in size and appearance, and in function (Fig. 12).   The *pineal body* is a small structure situated on the posterior surface of the brain stem between the
cerebral hemispheres.   It attains its greatest glandular development during childhood, and seems to inhibit excessive
growth of the skeleton and reproductive organs.   The *pituitary* body is lodged in a bony cavity at the base of the
brain.   It is divided into two lobes, an anterior and a posterior.   Hyperfunctioning (excessive functioning), of the anterior lobe is supposed to produce gigantism by stimulating
the growth of the skeleton ; functioning of the posterior lobe
exercises a tonic effect upon the smooth muscles, promotes
secretory functions of several other glands, and facilitates
the changing of glycogen into sugar.   Little is known about
the *thymus* gland, situated in the chest below the neck near
the upper part of the breast bone.   Since it atrophies after

F

puberty it is assumed to have an important function during early life. The *thyroid* and *parathyroid* glands are in the neck. Removal of the parathyroids is usually fatal. Removal or insufficient functioning of the thyroid produces the physical and mental symptoms of cretinism, including retarded growth, drying of the skin, loss of hair, accumulation

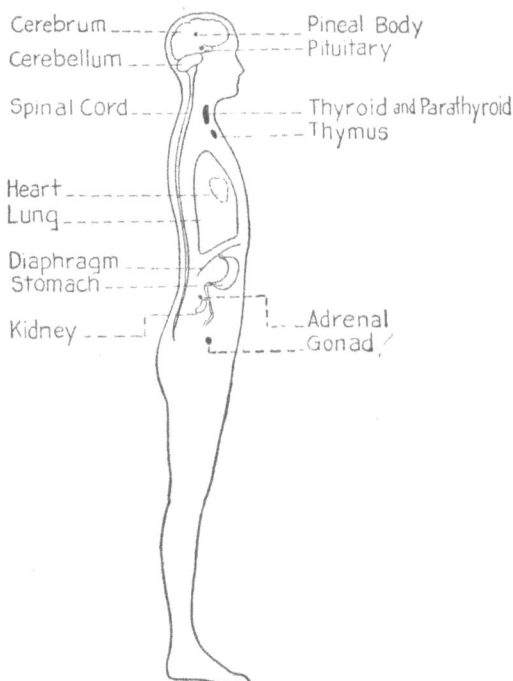

FIG. 12. — Diagram showing the approximate location of the endocrine glands mentioned in the text.

of fat, and mental deficiency. A tendency towards this condition in the adult, caused by a goitre, can be overcome by administering thyroid substance. Hyperfunctioning of the thyroid produces the nervousness, protruding eyeballs, rapid pulse, increased perspiration, and other symptoms of exophthalmic goitre. The physiologist Crile (1) points out that these are the characteristic fear symptoms. The active principle of the thyroid autacoid was isolated recently and named *thyroxin*. It contains 60 per cent iodine, and it is administered to patients suffering from thyroid deficiency. The *adrenal* glands are two small pea-shaped bodies situated above the kidneys. Each is divided into two parts, the cortex and the medulla. The cortex is little understood but the medulla secretes an autacoid, adrenin, that liberates stored sugar in the blood and produces increased blood pressure. The physiologist Cannon pointed out that these conditions prepare the organism for violent physical exertion, and that they prevail, as the result of increased adrenal function, during the emotions of fear and rage. The *sex* glands in the male secrete an autacoid that is responsible for the appearance of secondary sex characteristics — the masculine voice, the beard, etc. When administered at the onset of senescence this autacoid seems to produce temporary rejuvenation. The sex glands are functionally related to some of the other endocrines. In fact, the functions of the various endocrines overlap and modify each other in ways not yet clearly understood.

References

1. CRILE, GEORGE W. The Origin and Nature of the Emotions, 1915.
2. FRANZ, SHEPHERD IVORY. I. Symptomatological Differences Associated with Similar Cerebral Lesions in the Insane. II. Variations in Distribution of the Motor Centers. Psychological Review Monograph Supplements, 1915, 19, 1–161.
3. FRANZ, S. I., AND LASHLEY, K. S. The Retention of Habits by the Rat after Destruction of the Frontal Portion of the Cerebrum. Psychobiology, 1917, 1, 3–18.

4. HERRICK, C. JUDSON.   An Introduction to Neurology, Second
      Edition, 1918.
5. ——Neurological Foundations of Animal Behavior, 1924.
6. HOWELL, WILLIAM H.   A Text-book of Physiology, Seventh
      Edition, 1919.
7. LASHLEY, K. S.   Studies of Cerebral Functions in Learning.
      Psychological Review, 1924, 31, 369–375.
8. LASHLEY, K. S., AND FRANZ, S. I.   The Effects of Cerebral
      Destruction upon Habit-Formation and Retention in the
      Albino Rat.   Psychobiology, 1917, 1, 71–139.
9. LASHLEY, K. S.   Studies of Cerebral Function in Learning, No.
      III.   The Motor Areas.   Brain, 1921, 44, 255 ff.
10. SHERRINGTON, CHARLES S.   The Integrative Action of the
      Nervous System, 1906.
11. STILES, PERCY GOLDTHWAIT.   The Nervous System and Its
      Conservation, Second Edition, Revised, 1917.
12. STRATTON, GEORGE M.   Some Preliminary Experiments on
      Vision Without Inversion of the Retinal Image.   Psycho-
      logical Review, 1896, 3, 611–617.   Report continued in sub-
      sequent numbers of the Review.
13. TITCHENER, EDWARD BRADFORD.   A Text-book of Psychology,
      1919.

CHAPTER III

THE PSYCHOLOGICAL FOUNDATIONS OF BEHAVIOR

Having outlined the biological principles underlying behavior, we shall now apply these principles to the actual, observed facts of behavior. Inasmuch as our discussion has been concerned largely with biological facts a point previously made should be stressed; namely, that the psychologist is interested in anatomy, physiology, and other biological sciences only in so far as they contribute to his knowledge of human or animal nature. In a similar way he is interested in certain phases of chemistry and physics. But the physical and biological sciences as they are now defined will never solve *psychological* problems.

Historical Explanations of Behavior. Since our present task is to analyze the psychological foundations of behavior we might note by way of introduction some ancient views on the subject. The first attempts at psychologizing about men and animals totally ignored the possibility of a naturalistic explanation. All higher organisms were supposed to possess spirits or demons, many of which were evilly disposed. Thus epileptic and insane people were possessed of evil spirits. These unfortunate victims of disease were frequently flogged or otherwise tortured so that the wicked spirits would be driven from their bodies. In certain cases, however, the spirits commanded respect and awe. People who now would be recognized as hysterical patients were thought to speak in unknown tongues and to possess transcendental knowledge. Occasionally they were hailed as prophets. Today such patients are treated by physicians with psychological training. The doctrine of the transmigration of souls is another variety of spiritism or demonology. According to this belief, the death of the organism liberates the spirit to seek another, newly-born organism, as its home. The souls of animals as well as human beings transmigrate into human bodies, thus accounting for real or fancied resemblances between men and animals. All of these beliefs grew out of the attempt to explain certain facts of behavior.

When scientific psychology came into being, less than a century ago, it turned to biology for its fundamental principles. It sought an explanation of human abnormal behavior in neurology rather than demonology. Of course this move did not preclude the development of many erroneous notions, for the simple reason that biology itself was still under the spell of spiritism. For instance, some psychologists taught that conscious states or memories are inherited, and that they are passed on from one generation to another. Dreams of falling or of gliding through the air without physical support were explained as vestigial memories going back to our animal ancestors. The modern biological standpoint in psychology was adopted when this doctrine of innate ideas was discarded.

The Complexity of Stimulus-Response Relationships

The essential items in the biological standpoint are the systems of receptors and effectors, together with their neural connections. But a description of sensori-motor mechanisms does not satisfactorily account for the behavior of higher organisms. As the following considerations show, both aspects of these mechanisms, namely, the stimulus and the response aspects, present particular psychological problems:

(1) We have not explained as yet what determines the response made to a given *stimulus*. The same stimulus presented to an organism on different occasions by no means arouses identical reactions. We cannot always predict whether a stone thrown at a strange dog will stir it to fear or to a threatened or real counter-attack. In the realm of human responses we note that individuals show surprising and seemingly unaccountable differences in their likes and aversions. All normal human beings are capable of exhibiting fear; but why do they exhibit such striking differences in their responses to high places, wild animals, darkness, thunderstorms, water, blood, fire, open spaces, closed spaces? In fact, we have not fully explained how any given stimulus, affecting either man or animals, arouses any particular response at all.

(2) So far in the discussion little attempt has been made to analyze the *response*. Certain responses, such as breathing, coughing, sneezing, crying, winking, grasping, and moving the arms and legs, are called reflexes. They are relatively simple, and since they appear in infancy without formal drill or practice they are assumed to be hereditary. As compared with these, other responses are quite complex, in the sense that they involve more muscle groups and consume more time. Although many complex activities are usually assumed to be of hereditary origin, this bare statement is practically meaningless; it fails not only to explain but to describe the facts involved. As applied, for example, to the nest-building activity of birds, it gives us little information about the activity itself. Is building the nest a series of reflexes? Is it as independent of habit and experience as some would have us believe? Does it involve intelligence? Does it involve consciousness? Many other questions just as per-

tinent could be asked of this and of similar types of behavior.

The Integration of Behavior Units. The questions just asked illustrate further the distinction between psychological and biological science. As we explained in the preceding chapter, psychology begins where biology ends, for psychology is concerned with the stimulus-response relationships manifested by the human or animal organism in adjusting to its environment. Relatively few of these adjustments are effected by simple, independent reflexes; and in fact, such reflexes are seldom found in the normal, intact organism. Most of them are organized or integrated into complex responses. Even the few that escape complete integration, such as the pupillary reflex, the wink reflex, sneezing, coughing, and the various pain reflexes, vary according to the changing condition and experience of the organism. The new-born infant is decidedly something more than a mere bundle of reflexes.

Integrations of simple, stimulus-response mechanisms are known as patterns, or pattern reactions. They are broadly classified as *simultaneous* or *successive*. Fear is primarily a simultaneous pattern reaction. This pattern consists of certain characteristic unit reactions, such as cold perspiration, staring eyes, trembling, "goose-flesh," shrinking, palpitation of the heart, turning pale, and various other autonomic reflexes. Successive integrations are illustrated by such activities as running, typewriting, and talking. The distinction between simultaneous and successive responses is relative, since the majority of patterns show both characteristics.

The chief factor responsible for the integration of simple responses into patterns is the tendency of many responses to bring additional stimuli in contact with the receptors. In the *chain reflex* a response automatically furnishes the stimulus for a succeeding response. An illustration is found in the food-getting activity of animals. When an insect alights a foot or so in front of a lizard, the eyes of the reptile are stimulated, causing it to advance toward the source of the stimulus. This act intensifies the visual stimulation by increasing the size of the retinal image. When this image attains a certain size it elicits a new response: the lizard's tongue darts out and captures its prey. This response provides new stimuli for the lizard, namely the tactile and gustatory stimulation on its tongue. The latter arouse the swallowing reflex and in turn the act of swallowing furnishes the stomach with food. As the food is being digested it is forced through the alimentary canal, stimulating the digestive reflexes in sequence. Thus the entire series of responses, including the digestive reflexes, constitutes a chain of reflexes displayed successively.

The *circular reflex* or circular response is a special type of chain reflex in which the proprioceptive afferent impulses started by a muscular act travel to the central nervous system only to be redirected back as efferent impulses which reinforce or maintain the original act. In the act of holding a pencil while writing, the proprioceptors of the hand and fingers are stimulated by the tense condition of the muscles involved, and this stimulation automatically tends to perpetuate the act. Frequently a circular response directs exteroceptive stimuli upon itself. As Allport (1) explains, this phenomenon is illustrated by the young child learning to talk. Each time the child says " da," its ears are stimulated by its own voice; and this auditory stimulation, combined with the circular proprioceptive stimulation from the vocal apparatus, prompts it to repeat the syllable indefinitely. In stuttering, this tendency is manifested to an abnormal degree. Since the proprioceptive system functions in all somatic activity, integrations of the circular type are component parts of all adjusting processes.

Correlation and Behavior. Ordinarily various receptors

coöperate in mediating responses. The neurological basis for this fact is found in the mechanism of correlation, described in the preceding chapter. The pianist reads the musical score, hears the selection as he plays it, and utilizes the kinaesthetic and tactual factors furnished by the receptors of his hands and arms. A base-ball player relies chiefly upon visual and proprioceptive stimulation. A dressmaker, in turn, depends upon tactual discrimination as well as visual and proprioceptive sensitivity. In all forms of behavior, however, the proprioceptors play an essential rôle, since they are directly concerned in muscular activity. As the previous chapter disclosed, the proprioceptive system functions in connection with all other receptorial mechanisms.

To some extent, certain forms of behavior place a premium upon fineness of receptorial discrimination rather than dexterity shown in the response. The traditional profession of wine-tasting is a case in point. Again, the conductor of an orchestra necessarily possesses a good " ear." But behavior of this sort involves the effectorial systems more than is ordinarily assumed. The wine-taster must have a distinguishing verbal response for each discrimination he is capable of making. In fact, lacking an adequate vocabulary, it is doubtful if he could make the discrimination at all. The conductor is enabled to detect minute qualities and intensities of musical sound by virtue of his musical training. That this training involves response factors cannot be doubted. In general, the principle of " learning by doing " applies to the receptors as well as the effectors.

Selection and Attention. The organism is the constant recipient of numerous stimuli. Even the individual alone in a sound-proof, pitch-dark, odorless room cannot escape from the sound of his own breathing and the activity of his cutaneous, proprioceptive, and interoceptive systems. But the organism can react overtly to relatively few stimuli at a time; hence these in some way must be *selected,* and the remainder ignored. Reverting to the pianist, we note that most of the afferent impulses generated in his nervous system are not essential to his performance. In so far as they affect him at all, some help and some hinder his playing. The presence of an audience may serve as a general stimulation, or " inspiration "; but on the other hand, noises emanating from his audience may distract him. Lower organisms too, the amoeba for example, must act selectively to their environmental influences.

In order to behave adaptively, an organism must " select " the stimuli directly involved in its movements. Sometimes this phenomenon is known as *attention,* but *selection* is the preferable term because it is less suggestive of conscious choice. We cannot ascribe any mysterious power or faculty of attention to animals in general when organisms as low as the amoeba react as efficiently to their environment as man does to his. Selection, therefore, is a fundamental psychological phenomenon manifested by all organisms according to their biological composition. It cannot be explained in terms of consciousness.

To a large extent selection is determined by purely objective conditions. An individual responds to a sudden and intense sound, to a blinding flash of light, and to a nauseating odor whether he wills it or not. This principle has been stated in the form of several laws, usually called the *objective conditions of attention.* Thus, the intensity, extensity, duration, and movement of stimuli are selection factors. All four of them find illustration in the electric signs displayed in cities. The characteristic of extensity is limited to visual and cutaneous stimuli, while that of duration applies to all. As every naturalist knows, animals react to movement, so that a carnivorous animal must stalk its prey. Occasionally the prey escapes destruction by feigning death. Movement is shown by cutaneous as well as visual stimuli. Even auditory stimuli change in a way analogous to movement: a melody " flows " or " moves." According to Hunter (10), " movement is the fundamental objective condition of attention." [1]

But the factors which determine selections are found primarily in the organism itself. We have already stated that behavior is determined basically by morphology or structure. Birds fly, fishes swim, snakes crawl, and men walk because of their respective structural characteristics. Obviously the stimuli responsible for these activities are selected by receptors structurally adapted for such functions. The bird's receptorial as well as its effectorial system is responsible for its flying. The organism is prepared by virtue of its structure to respond in certain ways to certain stimuli.

Original versus Substitute Behavior. For purposes of convenience we may call some stimuli *original* and some responses, *native*. Hunger is an original stimulus effective in producing the native response of crying. A bright light is an original stimulus which causes the eyes to move. Such stimulus-response relationships take effect without specialized training or experience. As is well known, however, both training and experience tend to modify these relationships. This modification is seen both on the response side and on the stimulus side. For example, a week-old baby will not respond with a movement of its lips when it *sees* the nursing bottle, but at the age of a year the same visual stimulus will cause a decided response of the mouth parts. The original stimulus that produced the mouth-opening response was *tactual* in character — bringing an object in contact with the lips; but now a *substitute stimulus*, the *sight* of an object, serves to bring about the same native response.

[1] *Op. cit.*, p. 130.

In a similar fashion it can easily be shown how in the course of time the character of the native responses is changed. Objects originally grasped with the whole fist come to be grasped with the fingers alone. We may refer to such changes as *modified responses*. At present we shall be concerned with a study of the nature of substitute stimulation, reserving the problem of modified response for later consideration. In reality every case of substitute stimulus may also be studied as a case of substitute response and vice versa. It is only a difference in emphasis and viewpoint which distinguishes them.

Some Examples of Substitute Stimulation. In order to crystallize the nature of the problem in question it will be advantageous to consider a few additional examples of substitute stimulus. A young colt will run if struck with a whip, but for the full-grown horse merely cracking the whip suffices to make him run. An auditory stimulus has been substituted for a cutaneous one. The youngster's mouth waters when he tastes a piece of chocolate. Later the sight of the candy, or even the sight of the printed word " chocolate," is adequate to bring about the same sort of salivary response. Here a visual stimulus has been substituted for a gustatory one. Another child is given a dose of castor oil mixed with orange juice. The mixture is so distasteful that the child struggles against being made to swallow it; that is, it responds to the castor oil with avoiding movements. Before that time it always relished its orange juice. After this experience with the mixture of oil and orange juice, it responds to orange juice when given " straight " with avoiding movements or with a response of rejection. Here we have the response of avoidance originally attached to the castor oil stimulus also tied-up with the orange juice stimulus. Again it is a case of one stimulus substituted for another. It is relatively easy to multiply these examples, but the ones given are adequate to illustrate the nature of the problem. As psychologists we want to know how one stimulus can be substituted for another in evoking the same response. What is the nature of the underlying mechanism? Is the range of stimuli capable of being substituted for a given response limited? Can any stimulus at all be made to serve in this vicarious fashion? These are some of the questions the psychologists raise in connection with the problem.

What is the Mechanism of Substitute Stimulus? The examples of substitute stimulus that have just been given show that the matter is not new, although this way of describing it may be novel to the non-psychologically trained person. Examination of psychological literature shows that the solution of the problem has tended to take two principal forms: one, the older explanation, is subjective in form; and the second, the more recent, is objective in character. To state it differently, the first explanation is in terms of consciousness and the second is in terms of physiology.

Let us first examine the nature of the older explanation. According to this view the substitution comes about as a result of the mechanism of association of ideas. Postponing for the time being a discussion of the second or physiological explanation, we may at this point digress somewhat and briefly consider the nature of the principles of association.

The Laws of Association

It is well known that when we observe introspectively the passage of ideas which comes to us while reflecting or idly thinking, they seem to come in no systematic order. We may be walking along a country road and at the sight of a cow the idea comes to mind that it is a stupid-looking animal. This may be followed by the idea that our dog at home is much more alert than any animal we have ever seen. Then we recall that we forgot to tell the maid to let the dog out in the yard for his afternoon exercise. This idea in turn may remind us that we have certain Latin exercises to do when we get home. Upon which the thought comes to mind that our Latin teacher once told us he disliked dogs. Then the idle speculation as to whether dogs like Latin teachers flits through the mind, etc. In other words, we find one thought or idea giving way to the next in a more or less random fashion. Ever since the time of Aristotle scholars have been interested in this random, kaleidoscopic shift of ideas. Why does thought A give rise to thought X and not thought Y? Is there any cause and effect principle at work which determines the sequences of ideas? This is the problem of the association of ideas. As a result of their study of such sequences, psychologists have formulated several so-called laws of association. In reality they have elaborated one fundamental law and several subordinate laws of association.

The Fundamental Law of Contiguity. According to this law, whenever two experiences have occurred together, the subsequent return of one will tend to recall or reinstate the other. Hearing the word pipe makes us think of tobacco; Ellis Island makes us think of immigration; the word baseball induces us to think of bat, and so on. Since we have experienced these matters *together*, they become more or less united in our experience. Because of this " togetherness " or contiguity the law is referred to as the law of contiguity. This law, like all other scientific laws, summarizes an observed relationship. The matter is rendered somewhat more difficult by the fact that a given experience may be connected with a diversity of experiences. Under such circumstances we want to know which particular one of the many possible experiences will be revived on a latter occasion.

For example, the word pipe may be connected with tobacco as suggested, or with the idea of plumber, or with the word gas, or dream, or meerschaum, or briar, or lead, etc. In order to account for the particular one of a great many *possible* associations that actually comes to mind, several subordinate laws of association have been formulated. These are the laws of frequency, recency, intensity, emotional congruity, and the mental set or the *Aufgabe*. We shall briefly consider these in order.

The Law of Frequency. The law of frequency states that if two or more events have been experienced together with a third one, and if on a subsequent occasion the latter is re-experienced, then, all other factors being constant, of all the associates with that experience, the one that has occurred most *frequently* will more likely be reinstated than any other. Warren (21) explains the principle of frequency as follows: " An experience which has been repeated many times tends to be suggested in form of a memory or thought more readily than an experience which has occurred in the past only once or a few times. We recall the name or looks of a friend much more readily than we recall a stranger. The same phenomenon appears in language; we recall and repeat far more readily phrases which we have memorized than those which we have read or listened to a few times only." [2]

Because of this factor of frequency of association, an habitual pipe-smoker upon hearing the word pipe is more likely to think of his own pipe, rather than anybody else's; or rather than any one of the other possible associates of the word that we mentioned.

The Law of Recency. It may be, however, that if our hypothetical pipe-smoker just had a leak in his gas pipe repaired an hour before, his association will be different. If

[2] *Op. cit.*, p. 341.

he should happen to be in a psychological laboratory and volunteer to act as a subject in an association experiment, then when the psychologist speaks the *stimulus word* " pipe," he may respond with the words " gas pipe " and not " my briar pipe." In other words the *recency* of the gas pipe experience gives it the advantage over the frequency of the other. Apart from other factors, this factor of recency enables us to recall more completely and more readily what we read in this morning's paper as opposed to what we read in last month's paper. Accordingly, we can formulate the *law of recency* to state that if two or more events have been experienced with a third one, and if on a subsequent occasion the latter is re-experienced, then, all other factors being constant, of all the associates with that experience, the one that has occurred most *recently* will more likely be reinstated than any other.

The Law of Intensity or Vividness. Let us assume that last month's paper contained a picture of our father with a detailed account of his appointment to an ambassadorship by the president. Under such circumstances, because of the intense and vivid nature of that experience, the stimulus word " newspaper " may evoke a memory of that experience rather than the sensational murder story which appeared in the morning paper. The factor of intensity will outweigh the factor of recency. Similarily, if ten years ago our habitual pipe-smoker lost his child as a result of asphyxiation due to a leak in the gas pipe, then the stimulus word " pipe " is apt to evoke the response of " gas pipe," because of the intense nature of the tragedy connected with it. Here the factor of frequency is not strong enough to overcome the effect of the factor of *vividness* or intensity. Phenomena such as these are incorporated in the law of intensity or vividness. According to this law, if two or more events have been experienced together with a third one, and if on a subsequent

G

occasion the latter is re-experienced, then, all other factors being constant, of all the associates with that experience, the one that has occurred most *vividly* or most *intensely* will more likely be reinstated than any other.

The Laws of Emotional Congruity and Mental Set. The foregoing laws of frequency, recency, and intensity refer to the history of the associated experiences. In addition to such determining factors reaching back into the past, introspective analysis has revealed two others whose influence is more fleeting and momentary. One of these factors is concerned with the influence of emotions on our associations, while the other refers to the influence of definite intellectual problems or goals. The former factor is summed up in the law of emotional congruity and the latter is formulated in the law of mental set. We may take these up in order.

It is a familiar experience for most people when they are feeling depressed or " blue " to have most of their thoughts limited to matters that are depressing and discouraging. On the contrary, when in a happy or exalted frame of mind our associated ideas tend to be pleasant, joyous, and encouraging. In fact it is difficult to switch voluntarily the emotional trend of our ideas under the circumstances. The student who tries to refrain from giggling in chapel by endeavoring to think of " sad " things is an example of this. Another example is the difficulty we have of breaking up a train of worrisome associations by deliberately resolving to think only pleasant things. In other words, our emotional state at a particular instant of time acts as a directive factor in influencing the sequence of our associations. At the time of a quarrel with our best friend we find ourselves thinking only hateful thoughts about him. Similarly the lover when dominated by his emotion cannot associate unpleasant or unlovely things with the object of his affection. Consideration of such familiar facts as these has given rise to the *law of emotional congruity*. This law states that if two or more events have been experienced together with a third one, and if on a subsequent occasion the latter is re-experienced, then, all other factors being constant, of all the associates with that experience, the one that is most in line with or most *congruous* with the emotional trend of the moment will more likely be reinstated than any other.

As has already been stated, the factor of mental set is similar to the factor of emotional congruity in that it is a present rather than a past controlling factor. A few examples will readily illustrate the sort of thing referred to by this factor. If we hear the digit seven spoken, and immediately after it the digit six, we might think of 76, 13, 42, etc., depending on whether we react to the stimulus words as calling for the reaction of perceiving a simple whole number, or the reaction of addition, multiplication, subtraction, etc. All these associates with the two numbers have been built up in the past and all are possible of re-arousal. However, if before the stimulus words are spoken we should hear the word " multiply," then only one response will take place and we will be forced to think of " 42." The instruction to multiply acts as a controlling or directive factor determining the precise association that comes to mind. In the same way if we are asked to give the opposite of the word black, we think of white immediately, because of the directive influence of the instruction. Without such direction we might have thought of dog, negro, yellow, a man by the name of Black, or any other experience we had at any time with the meaning conveyed by the word. The instructions given may be said to give a certain set to the mind, called a *mental set,* which determines the exact association that will be evoked by the stimulus words. Such associations as are guided along more or less predetermined channels or directed toward a definite end or goal are called *controlled associations*. Opposed to controlled associations are those which are more or less spontaneous and undirected, such as those that take place when we indulge in reverie or day-dreams. These are known as *free associations*. The words that come to mind when we are engaged in solving a cross-word puzzle illustrate the nature of such restriction. If we are searching for a four-letter word only short words tend to come to mind. Long, polysyllabic words are for the time being shunted off. In technical language we might say that the mental set facilitates responses in line with its goal and inhibits or wards off all others. Sometimes the German word *Aufgabe* is used to designate this mechanism of the mental set. This word means " task," " problem," or " assignment." The *Aufgabe* or mental set has to do with the particular task or problem governing the associations which come to mind. The assignment or *Aufgabe* is what makes the difference between free and controlled associations. We can thus formulate the *law of mental set* to state that if two or more events have been experienced together with a third one, and if on a subsequent occasion the latter is re-experienced, then, all other factors being constant, of all the associates with that experience, the one that is most in line with the *Aufgabe* of the moment will more likely be reinstated than any other.

The Mechanism of Association. The various laws of association make an immediate appeal to common sense and the beginning student of psychology usually has no trouble in accepting them. That one idea should be associated with another seems perfectly obvious to him. In fact, for centuries the reality and utility of the principle of association was practically unquestioned. But with increasing knowledge regarding the part played by the brain in mental experience difficulties in the way of accepting these laws at their face value began to present themselves. Very few, if any, psychologists to-day believe that ideas *as such,* or thoughts conceived of as separate entities, are ever associated. We may speak of them as associated only in the interests of descriptive convenience. The actual association — the real connection — takes place between the neural elements of the brain cortex. " . . . the brain associates . . . ," writes Titchener (20), one of the leading exponents of the introspective method.[3] It is instructive to consider his treatment of what we have called the fundamental law of association. In this connection he says: " . . . let us call the brain-processes that are correlated with mental (conscious) processes ' psychoneural ' processes. Then we may say: *When a number of psychoneural processes, all of which are reinforced and all of which stand alike under the directive influence of a nervous disposition, occur together under certain favorable conditions, then associative tendencies are established among them, such that the recurrence of any one tends to involve, according to circumstances, the recurrence of the others.*"[4] In a similar vein Hunter reminds his readers that when " we speak of a *function* of a conscious process it is only for convenience. It is the underlying nervous activity which has the function."[5] It is important to remember this fact of the neural basis of our conscious experiences. To speak of association of ideas is permissible only as a matter of economy of description.

Substitute Stimulus Explained in Terms of Association. Bearing in mind the main points of this brief survey of the nature of ideational association, we are in a position to return to our main problem of explaining the mechanism of substitute stimulus. It will be recalled that two types of explanation were referred to, the subjective and the objective. The explanation in terms of association of ideas is subjective. According to this explanation the reason the

[3] *Op. cit..* p. 149.   [4] *Ibid.,* p. 164–165.   [5] *Op. cit.,* p. 297.

full-grown horse begins to trot at the *sound* of the whip is because he associates the sound with the earlier painful cutaneous experience. We also asked why the youngster's mouth waters at the *sight* of a piece of chocolate. This too is explicable in terms of association. The taste of the chocolate has become associated with its appearance. Experiencing the latter recalls the former and the original response of salivation takes place. In everyday language we might say that the sight of the chocolate reminds the youngster of its taste, and thinking of its taste causes his mouth to water. Let us consider one more example. If an individual without much psychological training is asked to justify his fear of lightning, he is apt to reply that the flash reminds him of the destruction and death caused by electrical storms, and that this thought precipitates his fear. He would be explaining his reaction in terms of association of ideas. It would be a case of substitute stimulus; for originally the fear response was made to the idea of destruction and death, whereas now it is evoked by the sight of lightning.

Until comparatively recent times most psychologists accepted such explanations of the way in which one stimulus or situation comes to take the place of another. Even today, so far as human experiences are concerned, many psychologists do not hesitate to invoke the principle of ideational association as an adequate explanation. However, other psychologists regard it as an inadequate or outworn principle. At best, as has been intimated, they regard it as a convenient, figurative way of describing a more fundamental and actually causative process. Before giving an account of what they regard as the better explanation, it will be advisable to consider some of their objections to the older and still popularly prevalent explanation in terms of association.

Criticisms of Ideational Association as an Explanatory Principle. Psychologists object to this older view not only as it is held by the man in the street, but as it is advanced by some of their brother psychologists. If we include their objections to the former as well as the latter at least four criticisms are directed against it.

In the first place, it is clear that so far as any particular case of substitute stimulus is to be accounted for, we cannot find out what specific association of ideas will explain the case unless we resort to the introspective technique. It should be remembered that in the case of the mental life of animals introspection cannot be used at all. To say that the horse behaves at the sound of a whip as he does because of ideas recalled by such a sound is either a matter of guesswork or sheer *anthropomorphism*. (By the latter term we mean that the thinker is reading human experiences into non-human events, or reading human nature into animal nature.) In the second place it is difficult, if not impossible, to understand how " ideas " can influence the functioning of bodily parts. How can the " idea " of pain make the muscles of the horse's legs move more energetically? [6] Of course, as has already been stated, the psychologist in using the word " idea " has in mind the physiological mechanisms that represent the neural basis of our conscious experiences. But if that is the case, then the most complete explanation will call for an investigation of the nature of these physiological mechanisms. In the third place, the explanatory value of the principle of association of ideas is weakened by the fact that it is difficult to subject the principle to experimental verification in the case of individuals without training in introspective analysis, and impossible in the case of ani-

[6] See the discussion of pleasure-pain theory in Chapter V for a more detailed analysis of this difficulty.

mals, and young children. In the fourth place, the principle does not apply at all in those cases where the subject reports that he experiences no " associated idea " that will account for the specific reaction. This is illustrated in the case of a person who fears something, but is unable to say why he fears it.

THE CONDITIONED REFLEX

As a result of these limitations of the older subjective explanation many psychologists have either abandoned or modified it in favor of the objective and more physiological explanation. This is usually described as the *conditioned reflex* explanation. It originated in the laboratory of the Russian physiologist, Pavlov, about twenty years ago. Our understanding of the new explanation will be clarified by a brief review of Pavlov's original investigation, now classic in the history of science.

Pavlov's Conditioned Reflex Experiment. In the course of a comprehensive investigation of the part played by various glands in the process of digestion, Pavlov centered his attention on the functioning of the salivary glands. The original normal or adequate stimulus for the functioning of these glands seems to be the presence of food in the mouth. Food placed in the mouth of an animal increases the flow of saliva. Pavlov found that the smell or sight of food produces a similar effect. For the time being we may regard the taste, smell, or sight of food as adequate stimuli that normally elicit the salivary reflex. Any other stimulus, such as the sound of a bell, fails to influence the salivary mechanism. However, Pavlov found that if conditions are properly arranged such an auditory stimulus can be made to provoke a salivary reaction. This is consequently known as a *conditioned reaction;* that is, when by appropriate control of the conditions of stimulation, a stimulus originally inadequate to provoke a given reflex is rendered capable of doing so, we have *a conditioned reflex*. Under such circumstances the substituted stimulus is referred to as the *conditioned stimulus*, while the original or naturally effective stimulus is referred to as the unconditioned stimulus. For example, powdered meat placed in the mouth of a dog represents the unconditioned stimulus for the salivary reflex, while the sound of a bell that subsequently brings about a similar reflex represents the conditioned stimulus.

The nature of the technique employed by Pavlov is illustrated and described in Figure 13. By referring to this figure the student will see how the technique described enables the experimenter to measure the amount of saliva secreted during any period of time. Using apparatus of this sort, Pavlov measured the amount of saliva secreted by a dog when food is placed before it. He found that when a bell is sounded at a time when no food is before the animal there is no measurable increase in the flow of saliva. If, however, the stimulating conditions are deliberately changed so that on repeated occasions when the dog is fed the bell sounds simultaneously with the feeding, sounding the bell alone will evoke the salivary reflex. A conditioned reaction to the sound of the bell will have been established. Assuming that the unconditioned response to the bell was merely a perking of the dog's ears, we can indicate the essential aspects of Pavlov's experiment in the following schematic way:

Before Training

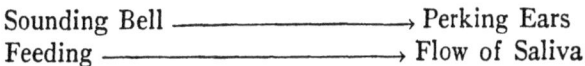

Sounding Bell ⟶ Perking Ears
Feeding ⟶ Flow of Saliva

After Training

Sound of Bell ⟶ Flow of Saliva

According to the usual explanation of this phenomenon, the process of simultaneous stimulation establishes a connec-

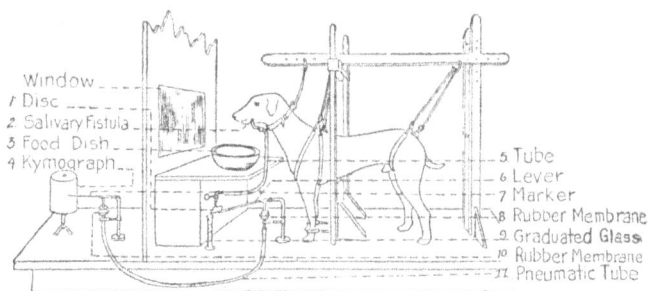

FIG. 13. — Diagram illustrating Pavlov's method of establishing the conditioned salivary reflex.[1]

The dog is presented with the unconditioned stimulus of the food in the small dish *3*. The food is introduced automatically through the window. Just prior to the presentation of the food the conditioned stimulus of the bell is started and usually continued through the feeding reaction. In order to secure an objective record of the flow of saliva an incision is made in the dog's cheek to the salivary gland. This is called a salivary fistula *2*. The opening of the fistula is connected with tube *5*. As the saliva trickles through this tube it falls on disc *1*. From the disc it drips into the graduated glass *9*. In this way the total quantity secreted can be measured. However, in striking the disc the drops of saliva depress lever *6*. This downward movement of the lever is transmitted to the rubber membrane *8* and as a consequence the air pressure in the pneumatic tube *11* is increased. As a result the rubber membrane *10* is made to bulge outward. This last movement causes marker *7* to move upward. A record of this movement is automatically made on the rotating smoked paper of the drum *4*. Such a recording device is called a kymograph. In this case the kymographic record tells the experimenter not only the number of drops of saliva secreted, but also the regularity of the flow. Additional markers are often employed to indicate the time or rapidity of secretion. It is also of interest to note that the harness works no hardship on the animals. After a little experience with the apparatus the dogs often become so conditioned to the experimental situation that they leap into the harness quite spontaneously as soon as they enter the room.

[1] Taken from Yerkes and Morgulis (23).

tion between the brain center for hearing and the center that regulates the salivary secretion. It is further held that this conditioned connection, like the unconditioned one, is reflex in nature. This is another way of saying that it is a relatively simple neural connection between the auditory receptor and the salivary effector. Reflexes, it will be remembered, are native neural bonds between receptors and effectors, involving a receptor, afferent neuron, usually a central neuron, an efferent neuron and an effector. While we shall have occasion to criticise this explanation, it should be pointed out that it dispenses with the need for explaining the change in terms of " ideas " or other subjective factors. This pioneer experiment of Pavlov prepared the way for an objective, experimental approach to problems hitherto inaccessible to such treatment. It furnished psychologists with a new instrument and in many respects with a new point of view. However, before taking up some of the more distinctly psychological implications of the conditioned reflex principle, it will be profitable to consider in some detail a few of the characteristics of the conditioned reflex that have been revealed by studies on the part of Pavlov and his pupils.

Some Characteristics of Conditioned Responses. The amazing adaptability of the conditioned reflex technique is revealed in the number of investigations carried on in Pavlov's laboratory in Russia. Some of these have recently been summarized in English by Pavlov's pupil, Anrep (2). Unless otherwise stated we shall be following this summary in our account of the work.

According to Anrep, " the method of conditioned reflexes is a method of experimental formation of new reflexes "; by " new " he means acquired as opposed to native or inborn. All reflexes acquired by an animal as a result of experience are to be regarded as conditioned reflexes. The con-

ditions under which the animal lives determine the formation of these reflexes. Since this is the case the experimental
work has to be carried on under particularly stringent control of conditions.[7] All of the work is carried on in a sound-
proof room. Furthermore, the animal is isolated from the
experimenter who is in an adjacent room and who employs
automatic devices during the entire course of the experiment.
A periscope is used to observe the animal's behavior. In this
way the possible influence of the presence of different people on the conditioning process is eliminated and the experimental conditions are rendered relatively constant. All stimuli which might affect the animal save the ones actually
being used in a given experiment are thus kept constant.

One fact revealed by this careful technique is the importance of controlling both the sequence and duration of stimulation. With respect to the sequence there are three general
possibilities:

(1) The unconditioned may precede the conditioned stimulus.

(2) The two stimuli may be presented *simultaneously*.
The part played by duration of stimulation will be pointed
out as each of these possibilities is discussed in order.

(3) The conditioned may *follow* the unconditioned stimulus.

There are three such combinations mentioned by Anrep:

(1) The unconditioned stimulus is applied first and then
followed by the conditioned stimulus. This combination
was carefully studied by Krestovnikov in 1920. He employed a tactile stimulus as the conditioning factor; that is,
he first presented the unconditioned stimulus of the food and
after a short interval of a few seconds he stimulated the
dog's skin by scratching it. Although this precise combina-

[7] An article by Morgulis (17) contains a detailed description of the
painstaking control of conditions in Pavlov's laboratory.

tion and sequence of stimuli was presented over 1,000 times in the course of the experiment, Krestovnikov was unable to build up a conditioned reflex.

The possible application of this finding to the problems of controlling human and animal behavior by means of reward should be noted. If Krestovnikov's result is applicable to such problems, it is clear that rewards should never precede the execution of the desired act.

(2) The conditioned stimulus is given first and is instantly followed by the unconditioned, or else while it is still being applied the unconditioned stimulus is given. Such a combination calls for a primary application of the conditioned stimulus (touching or scratching the skin) and then for the presentation of the unconditioned stimulus of the food. When this sequence is used, 20 to 30 trials will suffice to establish a conditioned reflex.

It has been found that varying the interval of time separating the *beginning* of the conditioned stimulus from the instant the food is presented makes for a definite variation in the final result. Considerable freedom may be exercised in the control of this time factor: the first stimulus may be applied from a few seconds to five minutes or more before the second. In any event, irrespective of the exact time interval, there is no actual pause between the cessation of the first and the application of the second. The two stimuli are made to operate *simultaneously* for at least a brief period in every trial. In other words, the first stimulus is not withdrawn until after the second has been introduced. Frequently it continues without a break throughout each trial and is even made to outlast slightly the second stimulus.

In connection with such variations of the time factor it has been found that if a very short interval, such as a few seconds, separates the conditioned from the unconditioned stimulus during the training series, the resulting conditioned reflex will be characterized by a similar time interval. For example, the tactual stimulus is applied for three seconds; then the food is presented and after the salivary response to the food has been made, the tactual stimulus is withdrawn. With this time interval characterizing the trials, the conditioned reflex will not be evoked until three seconds after the application of the conditioning stimulus. If a two-second interval was maintained during the trials, the same interval will prevail after the conditioned reflex is established. Two seconds will have to elapse from the instant the tactual stimulus is applied until the saliva flows. In the same way, by appropriately controlling the time interval, it is possible to build up a conditioned reaction that will not be elicited until the lapse of several minutes after the conditioned stimulus is given. Although there is no sharp line of distinction, in general, those reactions taking place after a very short interval are called simultaneous conditioned reactions, while those requiring a longer interval are called delayed conditioned reactions.[8]

(3) The conditioned stimulus is first applied and only after its withdrawal is the unconditioned stimulus introduced. This sequence of stimuli is the same as the foregoing combination with the exception that the unconditioned stimulus is not given until after the conditioned stimulus has ceased to act. There is always a gap between the two. Simultaneity of stimulation is not permitted to take place. Despite this fact, the conditioned reaction is readily estab-

---

[8] Anrep refers to these as simultaneous and delayed conditioned reflexes and actually uses the term, "latent period," in referring to the reaction times. Since such usage does violence to the usual meaning of the term reflex, it is better to refer to them as conditioned reactions. See section below under heading, "Is the Conditioned Reflex a True Reflex?"

lished. However, since under the training conditions the food is not administered until after the tactual stimulus has been removed, " it is not the actual conditioned stimulus, but merely its trace left on the central nervous system, that is combined with the unconditioned one." The resulting conditioned reaction is consequently termed a *trace reflex*. In this type as in the previous type the time of reaction is equal to the time intervening between the beginning of the conditioned and the onset of the unconditioned stimuli. According to Anrep the longest time of reaction for trace reflexes that so far has been obtained is half an hour. This means that during the entire training period the tactual stimulus was first administered for a brief interval and then removed. After a delay of 30 minutes the dog received the food. By repeating this sufficiently often, a conditioned trace reflex was established. In this instance the *immediate* effect of applying the tactual stimulus was nil, but after the expiration of thirty minutes the saliva flowed just as if food had been administered.[9] In trace reflexes it is not the duration of the conditioned stimulus that is significant, but rather the length of the pause separating the cessation of the latter from the application of the unconditioned stimulus.

These discoveries regarding the sensitivity of the nervous system to time intervals may be of importance in explaining many common problems. Among them we may note the regularity of digestive functions, the seeming ability of some people to control their hour of awakening by " making up

[9] This interpretation may appear so exaggerated that the following statement of Anrep is given by way of justification:

" The longest latent period hitherto obtained was 30 minutes, with an accuracy of somewhat less than a minute." (*Op. cit.*, p. 407.) Anrep gives the dissertation of Feocritova (Petrograd, 1909) as the authority for the finding. This dissertation is summarized on page 376 of Morgulis's article previously mentioned.

their minds," and the changes in mood that often take place " for no reason whatsoever." In the latter case it may be that a conditioned stimulus experienced several hours earlier is responsible for the sudden emotional change.

The Specificity and Irradiation of Conditioned Reflexes. As has already been emphasized, in the conditioned reflex work the experimental conditions are kept as uniform as possible. This applies with particular force to the control of the conditioned stimulus. For instance, if the latter is of the tactile variety, it is always applied to the same spot on the animal's skin and with the same amount of pressure and for the same length of time. The resulting conditioned reflex is usually conceived of as representing the establishment of a new neural pathway extending from the point stimulated to the salivary center in the medulla. Since there was no salivary response obtained from tactual stimulation before the training, it is usually held that no pathway conveying the tactual impulse to the salivary center exists at first. The conditioning process creates one. The term, " new pathway," must be interpreted in this sense. A problem arising out of this conception is that of the *specificity* of the new path. Is the reflex elicited only when this particular spot is stimulated, or will other portions of the skin surface give equally effective conditioned reactions? This is the problem of the spread or *irradiation* of conditioned reflexes and the answer to it varies depending upon whether the reflex in question is of the trace variety or of the simultaneous type.

As a result of a long series of experiments Coopalov showed that there are two phases of irradiation characteristic of the simultaneous and delayed types of conditioned reflexes. In the first place, when the reflex is still in process of being established, stimulation of any spot on the skin, even one that was never before combined with the feeding, will suffice to elicit the reflex. Some secretion will be obtained, thus showing more or less irradiation of the reflex. The second phase is revealed after the reflex is more firmly entrenched. With the onset of this second phase the amount of irradiation becomes less and finally only a small area immediately adjacent to the stimulated spot is potent to arouse the reflex. There is practically no irradiation; the reflex is specific or localized. So far as the development of these two phases is concerned, it seems to be immaterial whether the reflex is of the simultaneous or the delayed type. In both cases the end result is *specificity of reaction*. The only difference will be in the time of reaction, which will be short in the case of the simultaneous and longer in the case of the delayed reflex.

The nature of the spread of trace reflexes was studied by Pimenov. It differs from the foregoing in that the second phase (specificity of reaction) is never established. The initial irradiation continues even after the final establishment of the reflex. Stimulation of any spot on the skin will produce the salivary reaction. Pimenov found this reaction to be identical with the one obtained from the original spot during the training series. It was the same in force and in time of reaction. Furthermore, it appears that if during the training a long time interval prevailed, the irradiation will extend beyond the boundary of touch receptors and embrace other cutaneous receptors, such as those for cold and warmth. If the interval is made still longer the degree of irradiation will become correspondingly larger so that other receptors, such as the visual and the auditory, will be linked with the salivary center. In other words, the longer the time interval employed in the process of setting up the trace reflex the greater will be the extent of irradiation. In a special series of experiments Anrep demonstrated that the precise degree of irradiation and the strength of the response

H

can be regulated by adjusting the time interval appropriately.

The Conditioned Reflex in Animal Psychology. The conditioned reflex method is particularly important in animal psychology. By means of it the psychologist can secure an understanding of certain phases of animal mentality which have hitherto been incapable of direct solution. A good illustration of this matter is to be found in the study of the dog's auditory sensitivity. So far as humans are concerned this problem has been approached by asking the subject to indicate whether or not he can hear a particular sound under given conditions of stimulation. It is obvious that such an approach is impossible in the case of the dog. As a consequence, it was only by conjecture that the animal psychologist could say whether an animal was able to hear a given sound. To-day he can settle the question by means of the conditioned reflex technique.

In order to do this it is necessary to establish what is known as the *differential conditioned reaction*. This method is explained below. Suffice it to say at this point that the dog is first made to respond to a given auditory stimulus with a flow of saliva according to the regular conditioning procedure. A different sound is then introduced and if the flow takes place as before, it is assumed that the animal fails to perceive the difference. The sound is varied until the animal fails to respond to the variable sound while still responding to the original conditioned stimulus. In other words a differentiation between the two sounds has been revealed. By this method of differential conditioning it has been shown that the dog's hearing is more sensitive than man's. According to Morgulis (16), a tuning fork of 1012 vibrations is distinguished from one of 1000 vibrations. A metronome beating at the rate of 100 strokes is reacted to, while one of 94 is not. It has also been demonstrated that the dog will not only perceive a difference as small as one-eighth of a tone, but that he can also perceive tones that are inaudible to humans.[10]

Conditioned Inhibition. Such findings as these naturally raise the question as to whether the animal is actually sensitive to the stimulus to which he fails to respond; that is, may not the failure of the salivary secretion be indicative of the functioning of an indifferent stimulus? How can we be sure that it represents a genuine differentiation between the two stimuli? In order to answer this question it is necessary to consider the actual manner of setting up a differential reaction. The ordinary procedure is to feed the dog after sounding a particular note and to omit the food after sounding another; that is, one note is followed by the unconditioned stimulus, the other is not. Repetition will soon suffice to bring about a conditioned reaction to the sound that was followed or accompanied by the food stimulus. The other sound will fail to evoke a salivary secretion. In technical language, the latter sound is then said to exert an inhibitory effect on the salivary center. Inhibition, the opposite of excitation, refers to any neural process that retards, slows down, or brings about the cessation of some other neural activity. But physiologically or functionally it is just as much an *activity* as stimulation or excitation. One way of demonstrating that the failure of the secretion to take place represents a case of genuine inhibition and not merely the action of an indifferent stimulus is to sound the conditioned stimulus immediately after the inactive one. When this is done no secretion ensues, showing that the inhibition has not completely worn off. As Anrep puts it, " the inactive stimulus has always a certain inhibitory after-effect." [11] When this after-effect has disappeared, the conditioned stimulus once more evokes the secretion. Some-

[10] *Op. cit.,* p. 144.   [11] *Op. cit.,* p. 415.

times the inhibition, instead of putting a stop to the secretion when the active stimulus is presented, merely decreases its amount. This shows that the inhibition may be partial or complete. There are thus two kinds of conditioning, active and inhibitory. As will soon be shown, the latter is particularly important in training the animal or child *not* to do a certain thing.

Is the Conditioned Reflex a True Reflex? Beritoff (3, 4) has shown that the Russian physiologists regard the brain cortex as the chief mechanism responsible for the establishment of conditioned reflexes. This conception is in harmony with a traditional psychological view which regards association of ideas as but the conscious accompaniment of cortical processes. In the second chapter the latter view was criticised on the ground of its failure to give due weight to the part played by the afferent and efferent neural impulses, which connect the cortex with the periphery. Recently the conditioned reflex conception has been subjected to a somewhat similar criticism. It will be to our advantage to consider the nature of this criticism; for if it is valid, it will necessitate a radical revision of present-day conceptions of the conditioned reflex mechanism. In fact, as will presently be demonstrated, this recent criticism tends to cast serious doubt on the applicability of the term " reflex " to conditioned reactions.

Ordinarily it is assumed that as a result of the establishment of a conditioned reflex a new and relatively independent nervous pathway has been brought into operation. According to this assumption, the new pathway functions independently of the original one. To take the salivary reaction as an illustration, the original pathway extends from the receptors in the mouth to the salivary centers in the medulla and back from there to the salivary gland. Then, in consequence of the conditioning process, an auditory stimulus can be made to act on the same gland. This new pathway extends from the auditory receptor first to the hearing center in the brain cortex and goes from there to the salivary center in the medulla and thence by means of an efferent neuron to the salivary gland. We may indicate this view by means of the diagram (Fig. 14). In this diagram the

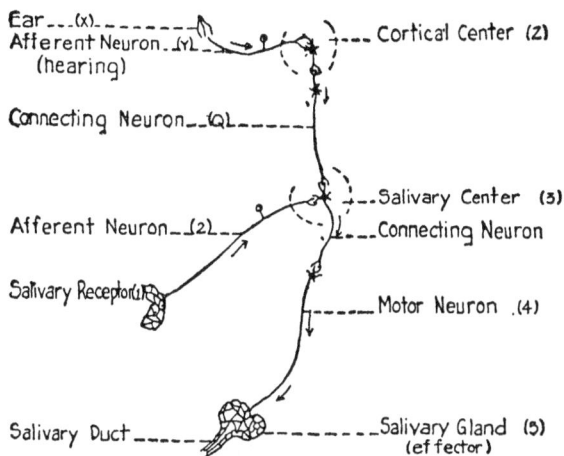

FIG. 14. — Scheme of neurological connections presumably operative in the establishment of the conditioned salivary reflex through auditory stimulation.

original pathway is made up of elements 1, 2, 3, 4, and 5. The new pathway consists of elements, X, Y, Z, Q, 3, 4, and 5. Inspection of these connections indicates that once the conditioned reaction has been set up, stimulation of the auditory receptor will produce a salivary secretion even though the original connection from 1 to 3 be destroyed. This is the usual conception of the conditioned reflex mechanism. It is representative of what the term reflex involves; namely, a receptor, an afferent neuron, a central connection, an efferent neuron, and an effector. The time required for a neural impulse to go from the receptor to the effector is spoken of as the *latent time of the reflex*.

This interpretation concerning " new pathways " was subjected to experimental proof in 1923 in one of the Canadian laboratories by Lang and Olmsted (13). Their results showed the interpretation to be erroneous. While their work was not along lines of the conditioned salivary reaction, we may at this point apply their findings to the latter before giving a short account of their experiments. If their results hold true for the experiments of Pavlov, it means that the " new " pathway will not function unless the old is intact. Stated otherwise, if upon the establishment of the conditioned reflex, the old or original connection is destroyed the new one will cease to operate. In terms of our diagram, if after we secure a salivary secretion upon merely sounding a given note, neuron number 2, the afferent salivary nerve, is cut across so that no impulses can traverse it, the conditioned reflex will be abolished. In other words, for a conditioned reflex to function both the new and the original pathways must be intact. To the extent, therefore, that the conditioned reflex requires two dissimilar afferent pathways (in this case an auditory and a salivary neuron going to the salivary center) it differs from the ordinary " native " reflex. Just to this extent, furthermore, it can not be regarded as a true reflex.

Lang and Olmsted's Experiment. Although Lang and Olmsted worked solely with conditioned motor reflexes, their results call into question the tenability of the traditional view with regard to all conditioned reflexes. Consequently it may prove instructive to consider the nature of their experiment.

As the unconditioned stimulus they employed an electric

shock applied to the left hind leg of a dog. This produced the native response, withdrawing the leg. Such reflex bending of the leg in response to a painful stimulus is spoken of as a flexion reflex. By combining the electric shock with the simultaneous sounding of a buzzer, the conditioned stimulus, they soon succeeded in securing a flexion reflex to the sound alone. This is what is meant by a conditioned *motor reflex*, since it calls for the movement of striped muscle tissue. (The salivary reflex is glandular.) After the conditioned reflex was well established in this manner, Lang and Olmsted operated on the spinal cord of the animal in such a way that the pain nerve going from the skin of the hind leg to the brain was severed, while leaving intact the nerve coming from the brain to the muscle of the leg.

Such an operation is possible because the nerves in question follow different routes to the spinal cord. The afferent nerve acted on by the electric shock ascends to the brain in the right side of the cord while the efferent nerve going to the muscles of the left leg is located in the left side of the cord at the point where the incision was made. This point was in the lumbar region, corresponding to the level of the small of the back in humans. Instead of making the incision all the way across the spinal cord, it was made only half way across on the right side. The technical name for this operation is a right hemisection of the cord. So far as its effects are concerned it leaves the muscles of the right hind leg paralyzed, while those of the left remain relatively unaffected. However, the operation also cuts off all afferent impulses conveyed by nerves in the right half of the cord below the level of the incision. This means that the afferent neuron originally activated by the electric shock can no longer transmit impulses to the brain.

According to the Pavlovian conception, the latter neuron

should not be necessary to evoke a conditioned reflex once it is established; for the connections from the auditory receptor to the effector are not disturbed by the operation. But despite this fact the conditioned reflex was destroyed by the operation. Needless to say, Lang and Olmsted, by appropriate control experiments, demonstrated that the destruction of the reflex could not be attributed to the influence of the shock resulting from the anaesthesia and the incision. It would carry us too far afield to describe the nature of these control experiments and the rest of their work.

It is of more immediate concern to note that their results render it necessary to enlarge the scope of the mechanism operative in conditioned reactions. Such enlargement carries with it the further necessity either of revising the usual meaning of the term " reflex " or of describing cases of substitute stimulus in some other way. Under the circumstances it may be best to refer to them as conditioned reactions, rather than reflexes. Incidentally, the extremely long " latent times " characteristic of some of the delayed and trace " reflexes," suggest the possibility that we are dealing with more complex functions than reflexes are assumed to be. Certainly, as we have stated earlier in this chapter, to speak of a latent time of 30 minutes, as Anrep does, is utterly at variance with what we know of the time relations of " pure " reflexes. These usually take place so rapidly that they have to be measured in thousandths of a second, never in minutes. It seems safer, therefore, to employ the term conditioned reaction or conditioned response. In this way we avoid committing ourselves prematurely to any definite view concerning the precise mechanism by means of which substitute stimulation is achieved. However, since the term conditioned reflex has obtained such extensive usage, it would be somewhat pedantic to scrap it entirely. We may regard it as referring to a *technique* rather than a neurological mechanism. It is in this sense that we have employed and shall continue to employ the term.

The Conditioned Reflex in Human Psychology. Experimental investigations carried on both in this country and abroad have shown that the conditioned reflex method with the advantages of its objectivity can be used for solving problems of human as well as animal psychology. Substitute stimuli have been successfully introduced for glandular responses, for striped muscle reactions, and for smooth muscle reactions. In other words all types of effectors are susceptible of having their afferent connections modified. Without any attempt to give a complete account of these experiments,[12] we may well turn our attention to a few of the more outstanding ones which help explain the general subject of substitute stimulation in humans.

The Conditioned Salivary Secretion in Humans. As an example of the establishment of conditioned salivary reactions in human subjects we may cite the work of Lashley (14). Of course in the case of humans it is impossible to make an incision to connect the measuring tube with the salivary gland. Lashley circumvented this difficulty by constructing a piece of apparatus which could be placed in the subject's mouth for the purpose of collecting drops of saliva and conducting them out of the mouth. In this way the amount of saliva normally secreted and the amounts secreted under stimulating conditions could be measured. Burnham (6) cites the following results secured by Lashley in his experiment with a child:[13]

---

[12] For a very readable and semi-popular account of the significance of conditioned reflexes in human psychology together with an excellent and simple summary of the chief experimental researches, the reader is referred to the text by Burnham mentioned in the bibliography.

[13] *Op. cit.*, p. 88.

Normal rate: about one drop per minute.

Chocolate placed in subject's hand:

1st minute	4 drops
2nd minute	3 drops
3rd minute	4 drops
Subject smelled chocolate	5 drops
Brought chocolate to lips but kept mouth closed	9 drops

The increased flow of saliva resulting from the contact of the chocolate with the subject's hand is in some respects comparable with results Anrep secured in his tactual conditioned reflexes in dogs. Our earlier example of the child who came to dislike orange juice because " it tasted like castor oil " is seen to be a case of conditioning similar to the above instance of having the child smell the chocolate. In both cases we have olfactory conditioned reactions.

Watson (22), referring to this experiment of Lashley, makes the following statement: " Unless this method had been employed, we would not have known that the mere sight and touch of food had such a stimulating effect. The subject's own report is worthless, because the food might have inhibited swallowing, even though the fluid came at a normal rate. He probably would have told us that his mouth watered. Some situations as we have experimentally determined do actually inhibit swallowing; then the mouth fills with fluid, even though the stimulus actually produces glandular inhibition. . . . It is quite possible that all the glands of the body are subject to stimulus substitution." [14]

The Conditioned Motor Reflex in Humans (Striped Muscles). Conditioned motor reflexes involving the striped muscles have been established in humans by several phys-

[14] *Op. cit.*, pp. 31–32.

iologists and psychologists.   Krasnogorski [15] succeeded in applying the conditioned reflex technique to infants less than a year old and to very young children.   He selected the reflex of opening the mouth as the response to be conditioned.   After quieting the youngster to be experimented upon, the child was blindfolded and the spontaneous movements of the mouth and throat were recorded for purposes of securing a control record.   When the child was given a taste of a bit of candy (unconditioned stimulus) a bell was sounded.   After a few repetitions of this combination of stimuli, sounding the bell alone brought about an opening of the mouth.   This was a conditioned auditory motor reflex.   In the course of his work Krasnogorski also established tactile conditioned motor reactions, differential reactions, and trace reflexes.   It is evident that the various kinds of conditioned reactions secured in animals can also be established in humans.   This pioneer application of the conditioned reflex technique to humans was modified and improved by the American psychologist Mateer (15).   She found that the speed with which conditioned reflexes can be established in children may be developed as a means of measuring intelligence.   Feeble-minded children are not conditioned as readily as youngsters with normal mental endowment.

Conditioned motor reactions for the muscles of the fingers, analogous to the flexion reflex in the case of the dog, were obtained by Watson,[16] Hamel (9), and others.   Another striped muscle mechanism that psychologists have succeeded in conditioning is the winking of the eye.   This was accomplished by Cason (8).   As is well known, winking can take place both voluntarily and involuntarily.   Cason not only succeeded in provoking the wink reflex by a substitute stimulus, but he was also successful in making the resulting

[15] Burnham, *op. cit.*, pp. 92–97.   [16] *Op. cit.*, p. 33.

conditioned reaction take place more quickly than the voluntary wink response. Such a result means that the mechanism of the conditioned reaction is very likely different from the mechanism by means of which the same reaction is brought about voluntarily.

The Conditioned Motor Reflex in Humans (Unstriped Muscles). In another experiment Cason (7) showed that unstriped muscle tissue can be acted on by indifferent stimuli as a result of conditioning. He selected the pupillary or iris reflex as the mechanism for investigation. The fundamental or adequate or unconditioned stimulus provoking this reflex is a change in the intensity of the light striking the eye. When a brilliant light is flashed into the eye the smooth muscle fibers located in the colored part of the eye, the iris, contract and the pupil becomes smaller. On the contrary, when the conditions of illumination are poor, as in dim light, certain radial muscle fibers in the iris contract and the pupil is dilated. In other words the unconditioned responses characterizing the iris reflex are as follows:

Stimulus of Bright Light ⟶ Response of Pupillary
                                                   Contraction

Stimulus of Dim Light ⟶ Response of Pupillary
                                               Dilatation

In his experiment, Cason tried to condition these pupillary responses to a sound stimulus, the sound of an electric bell. In a preliminary experiment, however, he found that his proposed substitute stimulus without training caused a slight dilatation of the pupil.[17] He also found that in order to obtain the best results from the conditioning process it was necessary to give the auditory stimulus *while* the pupil was changing in size. Giving the bell stimulus *after* the

[17] *Op. cit.*, p. 110.

response of the iris had taken place rendered the establishment of the conditioned reflex impossible. This finding confirms the previously mentioned investigation of Krestovnikov. It will be recalled that he also reported the impossibility of obtaining a conditioned reaction if the conditioned follows the unconditioned stimulus.

In the endeavor to bring about a conditioned contraction Cason increased the intensity of light being flashed into his subject's eye. At the same time the bell was sounded. After approximately 400 repetitions of this combination of increase in light intensity plus the bell, the conditioned reaction was set up. Now sounding the bell alone caused a contraction of the pupil. This was a clear-cut case of conditioning, since the original effect of the bell on the pupil was to cause a slight dilatation. In other words, the effect of the simultaneous stimulation was not only to bring about a substitution, but even to reverse a pre-existing response.

However, in those experiments designed to make for conditioned dilatation his results were not quite so clear-cut. Cason himself evidently interprets his results as showing the establishment of conditioned dilatation; but his data are not altogether convincing. In conditioning for dilatation, the bell was sounded along with a decrease in light intensity. In order to establish an unmistakable conditioned reaction, the final response to the bell alone should show a dilatation greater than that taking place normally upon sounding the bell. Cason does not make this claim, but he concludes nevertheless that a conditioned dilatation was established, for after the training, the combined stimuli of the sound and the decrease in light intensity resulted in a greater dilatation than the combined stimuli had produced in the beginning. To interpret such a result as a conditioned reflex is to distort the meaning of the term. It is better interpreted as an example of facilitation or re-enforcement. At all events, though, Cason has certainly shown in the case of the pupillary contraction that substitute stimuli may be connected with smooth muscle mechanisms in accordance with the requirements of the conditioned reflex concept. In the case of the pupillary dilatation he has at least demonstrated the influence of co-acting exteroceptive stimuli on the functioning of involuntary or smooth muscles.

Conditioned Emotional Reactions. An important theoretical and practical application of the conditioned reflex principle is seen in the modern method of studying the genesis of our likes and dislikes. Traditionally, such affective or feeling reactions have been accounted for either on the basis of reason in those cases where the individual was able to state definitely why he liked or disliked certain things or people, or else they have been explained on the basis of ideational association. When neither of these principles could be applied to the particular affective reaction it was accounted for on the basis of inheritance. Watson paved the way for a new line of approach to this question by employing the genetic method. He conducted his investigations in a maternity hospital and used as his subjects infants whose entire emotional history was known. They were from 170 to 200 days old. He found that such stimuli as cats, rabbits, and a pigeon in a paper bag failed to evoke fear responses either when the babies saw them or touched them. Similarly a baby held by a stranger in a faintly illuminated room showed no fear when a dog jumped upon the couch near it. A barking dog at the end of a leash and various animals seen at the zoo likewise proved ineffective as fear stimuli. All these frequently-assumed " native fear stimuli " gave negative results.[18]

Before giving a summary of Watson's results, it might be

[18] *Op. cit.*, Chapter VI.

well to point out some of the implications of the problem under consideration. Before we can indicate the actual development of our emotional reactions to various situations it is necessary to determine the original stimuli which evoke emotional reactions. Any stimulus resulting in an emotional response may be spoken of as an emotional stimulus. The term emotional stimuli refers to any source of exteroceptive excitation that is the immediate antecedent of an emotional reaction. For the present we may disregard the possibility that emotions are either modified or initiated by such internal stimuli as endocrine secretions or other metabolic factors. In this discussion we are limiting ourselves to the exteroceptive phases of stimulation. Accordingly, the burglar who terrifies his victim, the infant that elicits love from its mother, and the crawling insect that fills some sensitive individual with disgust represent the stimulus aspects of these situations.

Such examples of emotional stimuli and reactions are readily found. The question that confronts us in each case is the problem of deciding whether the particular emotional stimulus represents the unconditioned stimulus for that emotional response, or whether something akin to a conditioned stimulus is responsible for the emotional display. The possibility of conditioned emotional reactions is a relatively recent conception.

Emotional responses to specific stimuli were formerly explained in terms of heredity. For instance, both the color red and the smell of blood were supposed to excite cattle to anger. Tradition also claims that animals have hereditary enemies. Cats, it is said, inherit a fear of dogs; and birds, in turn, inherit a fear of cats. Furthermore, particularly intense emotional experiences are presumed to leave such an indelible impression on the animal or human organism that the effect of the experience is passed on to the succeeding generations of the species. Such an explanation is, of course, based on the now practically discarded theory of the inheritance of acquired characteristics.[19] In the older psychological literature the inheritance of the vestiges of ancestral experience, accepted as a fact, was frequently used to explain many cases of emotional reaction. We find, for example, that even so astute a psychologist as James explains the fright of a puppy thrown into a panic by a fur rug in terms of the emotional experiences of its ancestors. Similarly, human beings are supposed to fear darkness, blood, water, confinement, wild animals, and other natural objects and situations because of vestigial ancestral experiences. A case in point is the familiar explanation that our dreams of falling through space reflect the arboreal habits of our pre-human ancestors. Such an explanation is often given in all seriousness and by way of confirmation it is further alleged that since our actual line ancestors were evidently not killed by falls, we consequently never dream of being killed in this way. According to such theories not only our fears but our loves hark back to prehistoric times.

Are Emotional Stimuli Inherited? While the view that emotional experiences are inherited may appeal to our romancing proclivities, it is scientifically weak in two important respects. In the first place, as has already been implied, it runs counter to modern biological concepts of the mechanism of heredity. In the second place, all carefully controlled experimental investigations argue against it.

With respect to the first objection we may call attention to the fact that biological inheritance is limited to morpho-

[19] For an excellent summary of the present status of this theory with particular reference to Pavlov's contention that conditioned reflexes are inherited see T. H. Morgan's article entitled "Are Acquired Characters Inherited?" It is to be found in *The Yale Review* for July, 1924, pp. 712–730.

logical characteristics. It is difficult to conceive of a psychological trait being inherited except in so far as that trait rests upon a structural basis. Broadly speaking, the puppy mentioned above inherited its receptors or sense organs, its effectors or muscles and glands, and presumably, certain of its neural connections. In other words, it inherited a fear mechanism. But this is very different from saying that it inherited a fear of a particular external object. All perceptual reactions, as such, are thus acquired through experience. They are never inherited. A puppy viewing either a tiger or the latest sedan for the first time will find them equally unfamiliar and equally little calculated to arouse fear. Nor can it be convincingly argued that the odor of the tiger as opposed to the odor of gasoline, is more calculated to elicit fear responses from the naïve puppy. Evidence in support of this statement is given below. Odors are effective stimuli for organic reactions, such as hunger and nausea, but even these reactions are developed largely through experince. The basic consideration is that the exteroceptors are sensitive merely to forms of physical energy, not to traditions or historical associations. The environment carries with it no ancestral prejudices.

With respect to the second objection, examination of the available experimental evidence makes the case against the inheritance of emotional or instinctive stimuli even more convincing. While our experimental literature does not dispose of the case of James's puppy, it does throw light upon a related psychological issue. Stratton (18) tested the common belief that cattle become angered when a red object is made to stimulate them. Experimenting on a range near Berkeley, California, Stratton exposed about 40 cattle to strips of white, black, red, and green cloth, each 2 by 6 feet, by urging them toward the strips that had been conveniently suspended just above the ground. Although the red and green colors were both vivid, the cattle actually paid more attention to the white. They exhibited a mild distrust of all the colors, but they manifested no emotion that could possibly be called anger. These results hold for both wild and tame cattle. Incidentally, Stratton found that his experimental findings were corroborated on the whole by the judgment of California cattlemen.

The results he obtained by using blood as an emotional stimulus were even more convincing (19). Here he found the testimony of the cattlemen, obtained independently of his experiment, quite favorable to the tradition that blood has a direct, exciting effect upon cattle. Generous amounts of blood obtained from horses and cattle were placed in front of the animals. The blood was presented in open vessels and on several thicknesses of white cloth. In one test the blood was covered by a layer of straw to render it invisible. Again the results were definitely negative. There was little excitement, no pawing or horning the ground, and no sign of panic. Like any other unusual stimulus, the blood merely caused a mild curiosity and distrust that was soon satisfied. Some of the cattle actually licked the blood, showing no aversion to blood of their own species. As in the previous experiment, Stratton tried this test on both wild and tame cattle.

However, to infer from these experiments that no cattle react emotionally to bright visual stimuli or to blood would be altogether fallacious. All that Stratton demonstrated was that cattle do not inherit these specific reactions. When they are found, they are to be attributed to some experience lived through by the particular animal. Stratton's data are not concerned with this problem, of course; but on the basis of evidence obtained from other sources it is fairly certain that such specific emotional reactions are due to some conditioning process. There is no necessity or justification for explaining them on the basis of inheritance, reasoning, or association of ideas.

Watson's Experiments with Infants. We are now in a position to resume our account of Watson's investigation of the emotional responses of infants. As has already been stated, he got negative results when he confronted the babies with a variety of stimuli that are frequently alleged to be " naturally " fearsome. Some of the animals belonged to species that are often classed as man's " natural " enemies. Accordingly, if there is any basis in fact for the common theory of the inheritance of the traces of our ancestors' oft-repeated emotional experiences, Watson's tests should have resulted in some definite emotional responses. Since he failed to secure them, his experiment certainly lends no support to the idea of the existence of vestigial traces in the infants' brains.

In all instances where emotional responses were elicited from infants Watson found that the stimuli were distinctly physiological. They were explicable in terms of direct sensori-motor connections, rather than ancestral memories. For example, he found that the situations evoking fear were the sudden removal of support, loud sounds, a push or a shake, or a sudden pull on the blanket on which the infant was sleeping. Watson found no evidence in support of the belief that infants are instinctively afraid of the dark. In the case of anger or rage he found that the one adequate stimulus consisted of hampering the infant's movements. A response which Watson designates as love was called out by tickling, patting, and stroking parts of the body, and by rocking or dandling the infant. Since these three emotions of fear, rage, and love were the only forms found by Watson in young infants we may assume that his list of adequate unconditioned emotional stimuli is fairly complete.

although future experiments may necessitate minor revisions.

Watson's results lead to the conclusion that the majority of emotional responses made by children and adults were originally conditioned by experience. In terms of the conditioned reflex principle, almost any stimulus presented concurrently with one of the adequate physiological stimuli a sufficient number of times should, of course, itself become effective in eliciting the same emotional response. In order to test this hypothesis Watson selected an eleven-months old infant that had displayed no fear of a white rat and subjected this infant to the combined stimuli of the rat and sudden noise. As was expected, the infant subsequently showed marked fear when the rat alone was presented. Moreover, further experimentation showed that this fear was transferred to a rabbit, a fur coat, and with less intensity, to a dog and to cotton wool.[20] We might note incidentally that while this experiment was somewhat detrimental to the infant's emotional welfare, it is exceedingly mild as compared with the treatment frequently accorded infants by mothers and nurses.

The Unconditioning of Emotional Reactions. According to modern psychiatrists, mental disturbance is more a matter of distorted emotional life than of illogical or irrational thinking. Control of emotional reactions is thus of great importance in the preservation of mental health and the attainment of personal efficiency.

Watson's experiments have demonstrated the vast majority of our specific attitudes of aversion, hostility, and affection to be the result of conditioning experiences. This is particularly the case in infants and children where presumably emotional conditioning occurs so readily.

[20] This possibly accounts for the fear of the rug manifested by James's puppy.

Unfortunately, however, unfavorable conditioning cannot always be avoided. In daily life it is well-nigh impossible to shield the infant from all conditioning circumstances. While the baby is out for an airing a dog may bark suddenly and loudly. The auditory stimulus provokes a fear reaction and since the visual stimulus of the dog is simultaneously experienced, the sight of a dog may thereafter suffice to make the child afraid. It may now be said to be conditioned against dogs. Is it possible to detach or uncondition such a fear?

The experiments of Jones (11) were concerned with this problem. In connection with a study of children's fears this investigator developed a technique whereby negative, avoiding reactions of fear were replaced by positive, approaching reactions. Her method was to confront the child with the fear-object during its meal. She first determined how far the fear-object had to be removed before the child would eat. This distance gave a rough measure of the initial strength of fear. While the child was eating the object was brought close until it produced an avoiding response. This procedure was continued on successive days until the object could be brought directly up to the child. This method depends for its effectiveness on the strength of the child's hunger. By way of illustrating the method concretely, Jones cites the case of Peter, a boy of 2 years, 10 months, who was one of her most difficult cases. Two months of daily or twice daily treatment was required before his particular fear was eliminated. The following laboratory notes describing the first and last days of experimentation serve to summarize the method and indicate its effectiveness:

"March 10, 10:15 A.M. Peter sitting in high chair, eating candy. Experimenter entered room with a rabbit in an open meshed wire cage. The rabbit was placed on the table four feet from Peter who immediately began to cry, insisting that the rabbit be taken away. Continued crying until the rabbit was put down 20 feet away. He then started again on the candy, but continued to fuss, 'I want you to put Bunny outside.' After three minutes he once more burst into tears; the rabbit was removed.

"April 29, 9:55 A.M. Peter standing in high chair, looking out of the window. He inquired, 'Where is the rabbit?' The rabbit was put down on the chair at Peter's feet. Peter patted him, tried to pick him up, but finding the rabbit too heavy asked the experimenter to help in lifting him to the window sill, where he played with him for several minutes." [21]

As Jones points out, this method must be delicately handled. " Two response systems are being dealt with: food leading to a positive reaction, and fear-object leading to a negative reaction. The desired conditioning should result in transforming the fear-object into a source of positive response (substitute stimulus). But a careless manipulator could readily produce the reverse result, attaching a fear reaction to the sight of food." [22]

The Instinct Hypothesis

We have discussed the psychological foundations of behavior without introducing the term, " instinct." In fact, the considerations so far advanced in this chapter are at variance with the instinct hypothesis. They are concerned with principles governing all behavior, whereas instincts are alleged to be specific forms of behavior determined by inheritance. The latter view has long enjoyed popular favor, but at present it is being subjected to vigorous criticisms. A number of contemporary psychologists have re-defined the term, " instinct," and many of them would eliminate it altogether from scientific literature. They assert that the word, " instinct," is merely a verbal tag which fails signally to explain any activity so designated. More constructively, they

[21] *Op. cit.*, p. 389.   [22] *Ibid.*, p. 389.

argue that the so-called instincts are really habits, originating doubtless in the inherited response mechanisms of the body, but so subject to conditioning processes that their innate qualities are of minor significance in the adult organism. Because of their complexity, they are often called habit-complexes. In short, these psychologists regard the term, " instinct," as misleading and scientifically useless.

Instinct Not an Explanatory Term. The first criticism may be considered briefly. According to the traditional statement, the food-getting instinct drives the organism to seek and devour food, the sex instinct provides for its reproductive functions, the nest-building instinct prompts the bird to construct its home, and the gregarious instinct draws members of the same species together. It will be noticed that each of these statements is purely descriptive and not explanatory. Each is tautological. For instance, the last statement merely tells us that individuals of the same species flock together because they flock together.

If this criticism is well taken, " instinct " is open to the objection which all psychologists urge against the term " intuition." The latter has been dropped from scientific psychology because of its implication that the experience which it designates is *unanalyzable* as well as unanalyzed. Thus, a person is alleged to read the character of another individual by " intuition "; that is, by employing some unanalyzed and mysterious power or gift. As a matter of fact, his judgment is likely to be a blind prejudice, possibly a response transferred from some individual whom he has previously known. In many instances it can be accounted for, and in any event it is presumably the product of experience. In much the same way instinct usually refers to an activity which, as we show below, is actually capable of analysis. The psychologist Kuo (12) has voiced this criticism by charging that the instinct hypothesis makes for a *finished* psychology. In other words, by substituting verbal labels for detailed analyses it discourages inquiry and investigation.

Instincts Are Not Inherited Responses. The criticism that the alleged instincts are habit-complexes is particularly pertinent to the assumption of instincts in human beings. When we approach the study of human nature from the genetic point of view we see that the *original* activity of the individual can be most accurately described as the functioning of reflexes. Consider the alleged food-seeking instinct: Why does the organism eat? Is it in order to preserve life? What is the provocative stimulus and what is the motive of the original feeding response? As is explained more fully in Chapter IV, the native stimulus is a change in the physiological condition of the organism that results in rhythmic contractions of the stomach. Nerve impulses initiated by these contractions constitute the physiological basis of hunger sensations. In the absence of this condition in some degree, the feeding response does not take place. Anyone who has ever attempted to force an infant to finish its bottle of milk will testify that the feeding movements cannot be coerced. Note that the stimulus from the physiological side is a series of reflexes; and on the response side also we find nothing that is not recognizable as a reflex or a chain of reflexes. This response is not evoked until food is brought into contact with the mouth parts. In mammals this includes sucking movements, also reflex in mechanism. Consequently, the only part of the total feeding behavior which can be described as native is of this reflex sort. To recapitulate: as regards the stimulus we have the organic state of hunger and the presence of food in the mouth; and on the response side we have the series of chain reflexes which constitute the processes of swallowing, digesting, assimilating, and eliminating the ingested material. All else ordinarily associated with feeding is learned. The infant does not possess an instinct that drives him to seek his mother's breast: he is put there and conditions are so arranged for him that suckling ensues.

When in the appropriate physiological condition the infant will indulge in the same movements as soon as *any* tactual stimulus not particularly disagreeable or painful in character is applied to the lips. For instance, so far as any instinct is concerned, he will respond to a finger or a rattle. The fact that on a future occasion he relinquishes the rattle in favor of the bottle is due to his experience and not to his instinct. In other words, the only part of food-getting that is truly instinctive, so far as impulse is concerned, is the tendency to swallow when food is in the mouth. All else is learned and consequently not instinctive.

Furthermore, we have no evidence to support the popular notion that instinct informs the organism what kind of foods to take. A young chick will peck at any small object indiscriminately — an insect, a piece of red pepper, its brother's eye. As we have just said, the human infant is notorious for putting anything in its mouth. In the adult human or animal such habits as have survived through training and experience determine what is eaten. Because we feel like eating something salty is not necessarily proof that our physiological supply of sodium chloride is below par. In fact, as drug fiends prove, acquired tastes are sometimes far stronger than innate or " natural " tastes.

We have considered the alleged food-seeking instinct in detail because the criticisms directed against it are representative of the criticisms now being levelled at the other instincts. So far as the human being is concerned, a careful study of the genesis of feeding behavior seems to show that what is inherited and therefore instinctive is limited strictly to the series of metabolic or physiological reflexes already mentioned. In addition, the inherited nervous connections make for a display of random movements of a restless sort, plus vocalizing responses whenever the internal stimulus asserts itself. Even the early combination of these random movements into the act of grasping the nursing bottle is learned. And in the human adult, food-getting activities are so governed by habit and convention that no traces of any instinct save the reflexes are discernible.

Nor is there any point in designating the functioning of food and hunger reflexes by such a term as the " instinct of self-preservation." Psychologically an infant cannot be said to seek food instinctively in the sense of responding to some inborn urge to maintain life. His physiological constitution impels him to indulge in restless movements whenever his nutritive equilibrium, or the state of balance in his digestive system between food needs and food supply, is disturbed. These movements persist until the equilibrium is re-established as a result of the administration of food by others. In the course of time a complex series of feeding habits is built up. Even the definite recognition that the hunger disturbance calls for food is a learned and not a native factor of the individual's nature. To say that the starving man steals a loaf of bread because of the instinct of self-preservation or the food-getting instinct is psychologically false. He may, so far as the facts are concerned, actually prefer not to preserve his life. He steals the bread because he has *learned* that bread will restore his gastric equilibrium. The only part of this completed act that is instinctive is what takes place from the moment the bread reaches the mouth; all else is acquired.

Many So-Called Instincts are Social Habits. The considerations just advanced can be applied directly to many human practices usually assumed to be instinctive. In short, they suggest the possibility that these practices are products of culture, tradition, and convention. To state the issue negatively, the mere fact that a human (or animal) mode of behaving has been manifested universally and uniformly for generations in no respect establishes it as an instinct. The fact does not even argue for its instinctive basis. No human practice is more universally followed than the employment of language, yet no informed individual believes in an instinct either for articulating or for writing words. Articulate language undoubtedly originated in primitive vocalizations, just as gesture language originated in bodily postures and arm reflexes, but this is far from saying that the specific elements in spoken or "deaf and dumb" language are instincts or even instinctive. The inherited structural organization of the human body makes the development of human articulate language possible and perhaps inevitable; and the fact that human beings live in organized societies insures the perpetuation of language through successive generations. The instinct hypothesis is entirely superfluous in accounting for the origin or use of spoken language.

This hypothesis is likewise unnecessary in explaining most if not all human practices. For instance, beliefs and practices with respect to modesty vary so exceedingly among different races and different generations that this human trait can scarcely be called an instinct. As anthropologists have pointed out, some savage tribes have regarded covering the body as an immodest act. Again, Bernard (5) has subjected many alleged human instincts to a critical analysis and found that their basis is largely traditional. Thus the group concerned with family relationships, comprising the maternal, paternal, and parental instincts, contains two groups of factors, the physiological and the cultural. While Bernard employs the term instinctive, he restricts it to what we have designated as physiological. As regards the mother as well as the child, nursing is a physiological process involving reflex and glandular functions. Consequently, the emotional attitude manifested by the mother toward the child *begins* as a physiological process. We explained how it can become attached to or conditioned upon the child. As such it is shared, of course, by the higher mammals below man. But the psychologist is the first to point out the gap between human and animal maternal love. The human maternal response is determined by the accumulated knowledge and experience of the race, hence it is the result of social rather than biological inheritance. In much the same way such assumed human instincts as play, fighting, curiosity, and construction are products of the two groups of factors. Their natural basis is found in the anatomical and physiological equipment of the organism; their specific forms are determined by education, custom and tradition. To designate them as instincts is merely to confuse these two groups of factors.

The Yerkes and Bloomfield Experiment. A study of one alleged instinct in a higher animal will show that the " instinct " in question can be analyzed into simpler response units which become organized as the result of the animal's experience. Yerkes and Bloomfield (24) were interested in ascertaining whether or not kittens instinctively kill mice. Though they answered this question affirmatively, their experimental evidence does not prove the existence of an inborn, integrated tendency to kill mice. On the contrary, this evidence indicates the activity of separate reflexes which were organized, not innately, but in consequence of the stimulus-situation to which the animals were exposed. According to the results, kittens whose eyes had not opened showed no particular response to the odor of live mice. Their reaction to this odor differed in no essential respect from their reactions to weak ammonia, sour yeast, leather, and the experimenter's hand. Though the kittens were physiologically immature, they were able to react to the odors named, including the mouse odor. After their eyes were opened the kittens were placed near the mice, but at first they paid them little attention. Only after the mice *moved around* did the kittens notice them. Moreover, the responses of the kittens were exceedingly varied and changeable, including the withdrawing or " fear " reaction. Other responses were clawing, growling, tail-switching, ear-twitching, spitting, crouching, sheathing and unsheathing the claws. During its second contact with a mouse one of the kittens caught the animal and devoured it. As the authors say, it became transformed from a playful kitten into a beast of prey. Yerkes and Bloomfield also stress the fact that the kittens invariably caught the mice by their heads, arguing that this act implies an inborn purpose in that it protects the kittens from being bitten. However, since no facts to the contrary are adduced, we can better believe that the head was seized because of its superior potency in attracting attention. The eyes, nostrils, vibrissae, and mouth of the mouse are exceedingly mobile structures.

Everything considered, the outstanding results of the experiment are (1) the practice period through which the kittens went before they manifested an " instinctive " killing response, and (2) the variety of components in the response itself. During the practice period the stimuli represented by the mice became conditioned upon the hunger and feeding responses of the kittens. The latter learned to devour mice, just as they might have learned to eat bread and milk. The responses aroused by the stimulus-situation included practically the entire repertoire of reactions which kittens are capable of showing. It will be observed that many of these reactions are involved in other activities of kittens. Among the responses displayed by the kittens, Yerkes and

Bloomfield make specific provision for an *instinct to chase moving objects;* but having gone this far, they might have included specific instincts for moving the eyes, running, pouncing, spitting, clawing, biting, masticating, swallowing food, digesting food, and many other elements in the total behavior. If each of these is an instinct, the alleged instinct to kill mice evidently consists of numerous specific instincts. According to our interpretation, unit responses of this kind are reflexes determined by the structural equipment of kittens. At best, the alleged " instinct to kill mice " is a term used to describe the total behavior of kittens involved in the act of catching and devouring edible objects which move. The term " instinct " is misleading when applied to such habit-complexes. It suggests a simple, innate unit of behavior when the facts point to a complex and acquired integration of responses.

References

1. ALLPORT, FLOYD H. Social Psychology, 1924.
2. ANREP, G. V. The Irradiation of Conditioned Reflexes. Proceedings of the Royal Society, Series B, 1923, 94, 404–426.
3. BERITOFF, J. S. On the Fundamental Nervous Processes in the Cortex of the Cerebral Hemispheres. Brain, A Journal of Neurology, Part 2, Volume 47, 1924, 109–148.
4. —— On the Fundamental Processes in the Cortex of the Cerebral Hemispheres. Brain, A Journal of Neurology, Part 3, Volume 47, 1924, 358–376.
5. BERNARD, L. L. Instinct: A Study in Social Psychology, 1924.
6. BURNHAM, WILLIAM H. The Normal Mind, 1924.
7. CASON, HULSEY. The Conditioned Pupillary Reaction. Journal of Experimental Psychology, 1922, 5, 108–146.
8. —— The Conditioned Eyelid Reaction. Journal of Experimental Psychology, 1922, 5, 153–196.
9. HAMEL, J. A. A Study and Analysis of the Conditioned Reflex. Psychological Monographs, 1919, 27, 1–66.
10. HUNTER, WALTER S. General Psychology, Revised Edition, 1923.

11. JONES, M. C. The Elimination of Children's Fears. Journal of Experimental Psychology, 1924, 7, 382–390.

12. KUO, ZING YANG. How are Our Instincts Acquired? Psychological Review, 1922, 29, 344–365.

13. LANG, J. M., AND OLMSTED, J. M. D. Conditioned Reflexes and Pathways in the Spinal Cord. American Journal of Physiology, 1923, 65, 603–611.

14. LASHLEY, K. S. Reflex Secretion of the Human Parotid Gland. Journal of Experimental Psychology, 1916, 1, 461–493.

15. MATEER, FLORENCE. Child Behavior: A Critical and Experimental Study of Young Children by the Method of Conditioned Reflexes, 1917.

16. MORGULIS, S. The Auditory Reactions of the Dog Studied by the Pavlov Method. Journal of Animal Behavior, 1914, 4, 142–145.

17. —— Pavlov's Theory of the Function of the Central Nervous System and a Digest of the More Recent Contributions to the Subject from Pavlov's Laboratory. Journal of Animal Behavior, 1914, 4, 362–379.

18. STRATTON, G. M. The Color Red, and the Anger of Cattle. Psychological Review, 1923, 30, 321–325.

19. —— Cattle and Excitement from Blood. Psychological Review, 1923, 30, 380–387.

20. TITCHENER, E. B. A Beginner's Psychology, 1917.

21. WARREN, H. C. Human Psychology, 1919.

22. WATSON, J. B. Psychology from the Standpoint of a Behaviorist, Second Edition, 1924.

23. YERKES, R. M., AND MORGULIS, S. The Method of Pavlov in Animal Psychology. Psychological Bulletin, 1909, 6, 257–273.

24. YERKES, ROBERT M., AND BLOOMFIELD, DANIEL. Do Kittens Instinctively Kill Mice? Psychological Bulletin, 1910, 7, 253–263.

CHAPTER IV

THE MOTIVATION OF BEHAVIOR [1]

The psychology of motivation undertakes to explain *why* the organism acts in a given way on a particular occasion. A few hypothetical illustrations will clarify this statement and relate the general problem of motivation to the problems previously discussed. On being taunted with an insulting remark an individual flares up and strikes his enemy in the face. Two men of equal wealth contribute identical sums of money to a charitable organization, yet we suspect that one gives cheerfully and the other reluctantly. A dog and a cat manifest friendly interest and fear respectively when confronted with another dog. Without apparent cause a circus elephant noted for its amiable disposition suddenly turns savage and morose. An insane patient who refuses to eat palatable food insists, unless restrained, upon swallowing chalk, bits of wood, or even metal objects. Or perhaps an individual whose moral conduct has been blameless embezzles money. As we pointed out in our introductory chapter there are internal causes for these types of behavior, over and above the exteroceptive stimuli which are their immediate antecedents. Motivation is merely the general term that denotes such internal causes.

An excellent introduction to the study of motivation is furnished by Woodworth's conception of drive and mecha-

[1] Some of the theoretical considerations discussed in this chapter appeared in an article by one of the writers in the *Psychological Review*, 1923, 30, 176–191. They are here reproduced by the permission of the editor of the *Review*.

nism (28). The drives of an organism explain *why* it does certain things; its mechanisms explain *how* such acts of behavior are accomplished. To use Woodworth's illustration, the drives of a baseball pitcher account for his interest in the game and the zeal with which he pitches against any particular batter, while his mechanisms are responsible for the skill which he displays. Woodworth also uses the analogy of machinery to explain his distinction. The drive is the motive power — the steam, the electricity, or gas, while the mechanisms of a machine include its gears, levers, and pulleys. It goes without saying that drives and mechanisms are mutually interdependent, so that any discussion of drives presupposes the existence of mechanisms.

In the present chapter the terms drive and motive are synonymous. To appreciate the nature of drives we should think of such varied factors in behavior as a toothache, the pain caused by a whipping, hunger, boredom, the craving for cocaine, disgust, anger, affection, emotional hypersensitivity, chagrin, jealousy, and delight over a compliment. It will be noticed that these are states of the organism that modify and direct its behavior. Moreover, while some of these states are apparently physiological and others mental or psychological, they are all ultimately physiological in character. The student will find it profitable at this point not to attempt to distinguish too closely between physiological and psychological phenomena.

Although the term *motivation* is ordinarily restricted to human psychology, the factors which it includes are found in the higher animals. Emotions constitute one important group of motivating factors shared in common by man and beast. The *physiological* drives discussed in this chapter likewise characterize both human and animal behavior. The higher organisms behave as they do because they are equipped with the physiological mechanisms for fear, anger,

x

sexual love, hunger, pain, and the like. On the other hand, man is far removed psychologically from the apes, his nearest prototype. As the following considerations show, the distinctive features of his psychological composition are nowhere more clearly reflected than in his motives.

Two Groups of Factors in Human Motivation. There is no denying the fact that man is a creature of flesh and blood. This fact has been sufficiently stressed, but upon analysis human motives are found to be highly intellectualized and socialized. Since the term *socialization* really involves the process of intellectualization, it can be used conveniently to designate both processes. This enables us to describe two groups of factors in human motivation; namely, the physiological and the social. Both groups are found in practically all motives.

By way of illustration we may consider the hunger drive. At the first glance nothing would seem further removed from psychological interest than the activities involved in securing and preparing food. The topic seems to belong to physiology and economics rather than psychology; and at best the pleasure of eating would seem to be " purely physical." The truth of the matter is, however, that a surprisingly large part of human conduct is motivated by the hunger drive. Moreover, it is a highly socialized function. For the majority of people a meal eaten in solitude is a dismal affair.

The conditioning process described in the last chapter operates in two different directions in assimilative functions: digestive reflexes become conditioned upon stimuli associated with eating, and aesthetic responses seem to be derived in part from the satisfaction of food desires. It is generally recognized that immaculate linen, shining silver, flowers, music, and agreeable conversation are conducive to good digestion. We have sound experimental evidence for believing that these factors act as conditioned stimuli for gastric movements and secretions. Conversely, the pleasures of eating become attached by the conditioning process to extraneous objects and situations. According to tradition, the wife should broach the delicate question of buying an expensive set of furs to her husband just after she has regaled him with a satisfying meal. Perhaps on strictly logical grounds few things are more disgusting than the act of masticating and swallowing food, but so intense is the resulting enjoyment that " good taste " has become synonymous with aesthetic appreciation. It seems clear that the conditioned responses associated with the hunger drive are responsible for the degree of socialization attained by this drive.

In a very significant way the activities involved in securing and preparing food are intellectualized. People *think* about good things to eat; intelligent and cultured people indulge without shame in pleasurable anticipations of hunger satisfaction. Both the dog and the human enjoy their meal; but unlike the animal, the human being *remembers* his last meal and *plans* the next one. It seems generally true that in the development of the race the chief function of intelligence is to provide for the fundamental biological needs.

The sex drive in human beings affords a still better example of the socialization of motives. Since sex functions provide for the race rather than the individual, they are of necessity regulated by society. In this respect they present an interesting contrast to the food drive: for instance, even though gluttony is personally disgusting, it is scarcely to be thought of as immoral. Sex motives have been socialized and regulated to the extent that their physiological basis is frequently not introspectively recognizable; that is, people often refuse to acknowledge sex motives when these motives actually dominate their behavior. The Freudians, a school of psychologists named after its leader, Sigmund Freud, have used the term *repression* to designate extreme cases where individuals, from idealistic reasons, flatly and indignantly disavow sex motives unmistakably responsible for their conduct. The extent to which sex drives enter into human behavior may be surmised from the perennial interest in love themes manifested by the normal run of human beings. From poetry to moving pictures all forms of art attest to this fact.

The process of socialization has been carried so far that some of the most powerful human motives apparently have lost their biological affiliations. This fact requires explanation. It is easy to see how physiological drives in human beings become ends in themselves, since they originate in known anatomical mechanisms. Just why, however, should people be so greatly concerned over the various forms of social recognition? As a matter of pure enjoyment, the average individual might prefer a compliment on his good looks to an excellent meal, although he possesses no elaborate system of organs for the former as he does for the latter. So far as we know, the various forms of social motivation, centering around the fundamental *prestige* motive, are practically unknown in animal behavior. But since they are derived from the basic physiological drives, their analysis must be deferred until these drives are given more consideration.

Rationalization. The process whereby human physiological drives have become intellectualized and socialized has produced one curious human trait. We have already pointed out that human beings often refuse to acknowledge their sex drives. As a matter of fact, however, they refuse to acknowledge many of their motives, and prefer to endow themselves with purely fictitious ones. This process is called *rationalization.* Examples of this trait are not far to seek:

it is found in all of us. People are notorious for finding reasons why they should do agreeable things, and why they should postpone disagreeable tasks. No sooner does the student sit down to the irksome task of translating a Latin assignment than he thinks of the letter that must be written home without delay. Again, we excuse faults in people we like, and criticize these same faults in those not so favored. Another way in which we rationalize our motives is to substitute righteous indignation for what is actually jealousy or envy. As the term suggests, rationalization is one form of the process of intellectualizing motives. In most instances the physiological drives and the basic emotions are the motives which are rationalized.

PHYSIOLOGICAL DRIVES

The foregoing considerations suggest that the psychology of motivation should start with physiological mechanisms and then proceed to the more purely social factors involved. The physiological mechanisms concerned are by no means limited to the digestive and reproductive systems. Man requires moderate degrees of thermal stimulation, comfortable physical surroundings, opportunity for physical exercise, health; and by virtue of his capacity to acquire tastes he frequently demands narcotics and stimulants. His intellectual and social activity is largely devoted to the satisfaction of his physiological drives.

The Autonomic Functions and the Personality. Perhaps the most complete theoretical explanation of what we have designated as physiological drives is found in E. J. Kempf's analysis of autonomic functions as related to human personality (16). According to Kempf the behavior of human beings and the higher animals is *motivated* by the autonomic nervous system and *executed* by the cerebrospinal. This means that the former system is responsible for the " why " of behavior and the latter system for the " how." The cerebrospinal nervous system, therefore, is subordinate to the autonomic. Through its system of exteroceptors it guides the organism about in the environment in a way physiologically satisfactory to the autonomic system. While Kempf does not employ the term, he regards drives as states of tension in the autonomic system that demand relief. In any one case the desired relief can be obtained by presenting the appropriate stimuli to, or by eliminating unwelcome stimuli from, the exteroceptors. In brief, the cerebrospinal system moves the exteroceptors in the environment for the purpose of adjusting stimuli to the needs of the autonomic system. In practice, of course, the entire organism moves in the environment, but it moves with reference to the needs of the autonomic system.

The facts upon which Kempf bases his conclusion are rather well known. As we show in more detail below, hunger is a craving caused by certain characteristic contractions of the stomach. This craving is relieved when the appropriate food stimuli are placed in contact with taste receptors, provided that the food is subsequently swallowed and digested. If, however, no food is available, the exteroceptors are required to do scout duty until it is found. The organism moves about until its visual, olfactory, and even auditory receptors locate the desired food objects. In much the same way sex cravings caused by glandular activities and smooth muscle contractions prompt the mating activities of animals and the courtship of man. In the cases just mentioned the cravings are caused by visceral stimuli, but in other cases, as when a human being smells putrid flesh, the stimuli are somatic. But the reaction involved, namely, the state of nausea or disgust, is, like hunger, a change in the tonicity of visceral muscles. In the majority of situations visceral and somatic stimuli combine, either to arouse or to satisfy a craving.

Kempf's theory is hedonistic in that he practically regards pleasantness and unpleasantness as the determining factors in motivation. Unpleasantness is due to, or identified with, a spastic, tonic condition of a given smooth muscle segment — that is, a condition of marked contraction in which some position of a visceral muscle is maintained more or less spasmodically. Pleasantness results when the muscle returns to its state of normal contraction or tension. The nerve impulses generated by the visceral condition associated with unpleasantness and demanding relief, discharge into and control the cerebrospinal neurons, and the organism acts accordingly. According to Kempf's theory a hypothetical organism, either animal or human, that is completely deviscerated would be utterly lacking in motives and consequently incapable of moving about. It would have no emotional life, no capacity for experiencing pleasantness or unpleasantness.

In viewing emotions as autonomic or visceral tensions Kempf again is merely emphasizing a general view that long antedates his theory. But Kempf's definitions of the specific emotions in terms of his theory are somewhat unique. Each emotion he defines functionally, with reference to the stimulus-response situation that affects the autonomic system. The fear response tends or attempts to remove the exteroceptor from a painful stimulus. It is, therefore, a withdrawing reaction that relieves an unpleasant condition of the visceral muscles by getting away from the stimulus responsible for this condition. The proverbial ostrich complies with the letter if not the spirit of Kempf's definition of fear behavior. In contrast to fear, anger tends to remove a painful stimulus from the receptor. In the case of the small boy who, bent on stealing a watermelon, invades a field only to be discovered and chased out in a state of terror by its irate owner, we find excellent illustrations of Kempf's definitions. According to his theory, sorrow or grief is a form of fear due to the loss of a pleasure-giving stimulus. Joy is a pleasant state caused by the disappearance of a potential pain-stimulus or the acquisition of a pleasure-stimulus. Kempf furthermore states that certain emotions are derived from others. Disgust contains elements of fear and anger. Jealously and envy are even more complex. All emotions necessarily possess a feeling-tone — that is, they are either pleasant or unpleasant.

Experimental Studies of Animal Drives. When we turn from theoretical to experimental literature we find that drives or motives can not only be described but also measured. Two investigations, conducted by Moss and Simmons respectively, will show how the psychologist approaches this problem. Incidentally, although it was necessary for both investigators to subject the animals to painful stimuli, their treatment on the whole was milder than the educational discipline often meted out to children.

(1) Moss (22) based his experiment upon the following thesis: " The behavior of any animal is the resultant of his drives to action and the opposing resistances." In order to measure these factors he devised a box, divided by two partitions into three compartments. The first compartment contained the animals to be tested; the second, which opened from the first, had a floor constructed of metal plates so arranged that they could be charged with varying amounts of electricity; the third, opening in turn from the second, contained the stimuli designated to arouse the drives. In order to go from the first compartment to the third, the animal was forced to traverse the metal plate and receive a series of electric shocks.

In one series of tests Moss measured the strength of the

hunger drive. After his rats had been " taught " that the plate was painful, four of them were placed in the first compartment and kept there 12 hours without food; but none of them during this period crossed the plate, which was charged with a 20 volt current, in order to secure the tempting food placed in the third compartment. A second group of 4 rats was tested for 24 hours, with the result that one crossed the plate and satisfied his hunger. A third group of 4 was kept for 48 hours, but this time 3 of them crossed. A fourth group of 4 rats was kept for 72 hours, and all of them finally crossed. In a variation of this test Moss discovered that a 72 hour hunger drive is stronger than a 28 volt resistance. Thus Moss measured the hunger drive in hour quantities in terms of an electrical stimulus graded in volts.

In a second series of tests Moss measured both sex and maternal drives in female rats. Contrary to popular belief, sex was found to be inferior to hunger in driving force. Still weaker was the maternal drive, for of a group of mother rats placed in the first compartment only one braved the metal plate to reach her squealing offspring on the other side. Moss discovered, however, a considerable amount of individual difference among the animals.

A third series of tests was concerned with relative differences of intensity in the driving forces studied. For one thing, Moss measured the relative efficacy of ice water compared with the electric shock as a stimulus. He also established permanent conditioned inhibitions for particular kinds of food by associating this food with shocks — in much the same way that a cat is kept by punishment from jumping up on the dinner table. Finally, Moss studied the ancient question of punishment versus reward by forcing his rats to learn to escape from an intricate series of pathways. He found that both food and sex incentives are superior to punishment under the conditions of the experiment.

What Moss did with white rats under controlled conditions is attempted in haphazard fashion by all human beings
who attempt to control their fellows. People responsible for
the supervision and care of the feeble-minded, the insane, or
the inmates of jails and penitentiaries could well afford to
study this and similar experiments with the purpose of applying the ideas and suggestions contained to their particular problems. Parents and teachers by so doing would place
the management of children on a level at once more scientific and more humane. While scientific psychology is primarily concerned with facts, its applications are in many
instances self-evident.

(2) Simmons (25) was interested in the problem of controlling incentives in animal learning. As she points out,
the incentive is a factor which has been neglected in most
studies of habit formation or learning in animals. One device frequently employed in studies of this sort is the maze,
a complicated series of pathways with one true path leading
by a devious route from entrance to exit, and with many
branching culs-de-sac or blind passages. A diagram of a
maze is given in the following chapter of this book. The
typical animal maze is constructed of wood, and, when designed for the white rat, its pathways are approximately 4
inches wide and 4 inches high. The length of the pathways
varies from several inches to several feet. The animal, mod-
erately hungry, is placed in the entrance and left to discover
the food at the exit. As one can readily imagine, its initial
behavior consists of random, exploratory movements. It
usually finds a way to the food, as the result of its persistence, but it is permitted to eat only a few bites. This performance constitutes one trial. Subsequent trials differ
from the first in one important respect — the animal has
been given a more definite incentive for learning the maze.
And with a sufficient number of trials the animal will

" learn " the maze; that is, it will require the ability to go from entrance to exit with no errors. Time and errors are recorded for each trial, so that the experimenter has a quantitative record of the learning process.

In Simmons' experiment groups of white rats learned two mazes under conditions of varying incentives. In order to control the factor of difficulty, one of the mazes was relatively simple and the other decidedly more comp This enabled the experimenter to ascertain whether res obtained from the easy and from the difficult learning lems were comparable with respect to incentive. Th lowing rewards were used as incentives: bread and sunflower seed, temporary freedom or escape from the m return " home " (to the cages), sex attraction and mate appeal. The bread and milk reward was the standar comparison. The effect of delaying the bread and mil also studied.

Simmons found that the various incentives produc s-tinctive effects upon the learning process. The bre d milk incentive turned out to be the most effective, showing that so far as the conditions of her experiment are concerned, a favorite food is a more effective incentive to learning activity in a white rat, than freedom, " home," or sex. Furthermore, the relative effectiveness of the different incentives was constant for the two mazes. The effects of delaying the reward were somewhat contradictory, but on the whole they were relatively insignificant as compared with the kind of incentive used and with the degree to which the impulse aroused by the incentive was satisfied. For instance, complete satisfaction of hunger was more effective than partial satisfaction. An additional result is that the differences among the various incentive groups were more marked for time records than for error records; that is, the time consumed in going through the maze was a more exact indication of the kind of incentive used than the number of errors made in the same trial. With certain incentives the rats tended to waste time by stopping to scratch themselves and to wash their faces.

The Hunger Drive. In experiments of the kind just described the chief factors controlled are the external stimuli, and the objective responses made by the animal. Our knowledge of physiology enables us to say that these external stimuli exercise specific effects upon certain internal mechanisms, such as the digestive and reproductive organs. These were indirectly controlled in the experiments just summarized. That they can be directly controlled is shown by some experiments which we shall now review.

It is possible to study the inner mechanisms responsible for the specific drives by means of the proper physiological technique. In this way hunger has been studied by Cannon (8), Carlson (9), and Wada (27). The student should not regard studies of this sort as " mere " physiology. It happens that of the three investigators just mentioned, the first two are physiologists and the third a psychologist; but the classifications are inconsequential. Quoting Cannon, Wada states that " on the same plane with pain and the dominant emotions of fear and rage as agencies which determine the action of the organism, is the sensation of hunger." Wada further explains how hunger as a motive is of tremendous interest in history, sociology, and social psychology. It plays an important rôle in explaining why men do what they do, hence it is a factor in human behavior.

The technique employed by both Cannon and Carlson in investigating hunger involved the use of a rubber balloon which was swallowed in a collapsed condition, with a connecting tube leading out of the mouth, and afterwards inflated with air until it filled the cavity of the stomach. The free end of the tube was connected with a recording device, a pointer that made a tracing on smoked paper placed on a revolving drum. By means of this apparatus stomach contractions were registered graphically by fluctuations of the pointer.

Using this apparatus Cannon made the discovery, subsequently verified by Carlson and others, that the conscious pangs of hunger are accompanied by contractions of the stomach. In fact, all available evidence points to the contractions as the cause of hunger, or as the immediate condition for the arousal of hunger sensations. According to Cannon, these contractions cease after a few days of absolute fasting with the result that the fasting individual then experiences no hunger. Under normal conditions hunger contractions begin three or four hours after eating, and continue at intervals as long as the stomach is empty. Hunger contractions differ from the digestive movements of the stomach. The former start at the cardiac opening of the stomach and spread in peristaltic waves to the pylorus, or the opening from the stomach to the duodenum (the beginning of the small intestine) ; whereas the digestive contractions begin at about the middle of the stomach and run to the pylorus.

The most extensive investigations of hunger contractions from the psychological standpoint were made by Wada, who used the balloon method. Among the phenomena which occur simultaneously with the contractions are, according to Wada, the flow of saliva, bodily movements during waking and sleeping states, dreaming, increased strength of handgrip, and greater efficiency in mental work. Hunger thus acts as a tonic upon mental activity. Wada also discovered that while hunger rhythms cannot be controlled voluntarily they are inhibited by reading interesting stories, particularly those with an emotional appeal. Other investigations referred to subsequently would seem to corrobo-rate this result.

Cannon reports a variety of experiments concerned with the digestive process that have an important bearing upon psychology. By an operation upon a dog's stomach he pro-duced a gastric fistula, similar to the salivary fistula of Pavlov's dog, mentioned in the previous chapter. This en-abled him to measure directly the secretion of gastric juice in the stomach, and to show that the smell or sight of a favorite food will cause this juice to flow. As he says, " The stomach as well as the mouth waters." But anxiety or em-barrassment inhibit both gastric and salivary secretion. In the " ordeal of rice," a practice once prevalent in India, an individual accused of some crime was forced to chew and spit out rice, and if it was dry, the accused was adjudged to be guilty.

That the actual presence of food in the stomach is not a prerequisite for the secretion of gastric juice Cannon proves by his experiment in " sham " feeding. Animals were oper-ated upon in such a way as to cause food when swallowed to drop to the ground through an opening in the esophagus and thus never reach the stomach at all. In such instances, however, the gastric juice begins to flow after an interval of five minutes and continues after the sham feeding ceases. To all intents and purposes the animals enjoy eating under such circumstances; and they have the advantage of being prepared physically to eat indefinitely.

In another series of experiments with the fluoroscope, the instrument that utilizes the X-ray for purposes of direct ex-amination, Cannon demonstrated the inhibitory effect of un-pleasant emotional stimuli upon gastric and intestinal peri-stalsis. When the food given a cat is rendered opaque to the X-ray by bismuth or barium the normal peristalsis of the animal can be observed. It is ordinarily continuous; but let a dog be brought into the room near the cat and the peristalsis ceases abruptly. All of Cannon's studies of hunger show how intimately this physiological function is associated with psychological activities.

Drives, Adrenin, and the Autonomic Nervous System. Kempf and others have definitely explained drives in terms of visceral tensions and endocrinal activities, but few investigators have attempted to ascertain the exact rôle of the autonomic nervous system in behavior. This is another way of saying, of course, that the physiology of the autonomic nervous system is little understood. Of the views concerning this system that have been advanced, Cannon's is perhaps the best known and (provisionally) the most generally accepted. It at least possesses the merit of being based upon experimental evidence.

In calling attention to Cannon's view of the autonomic system it is necessary to note certain anatomical details of this system not yet mentioned. The sympathetic nervous system is that part of the autonomic which consists of the chain of ganglia near and parallel to the thoracico-lumbar portions of the spinal cord. In addition to the sympathetic, the autonomic system includes (1) the cranial ganglia, located in the head, and (2) the sacral ganglia, located near the base of the vertebrae. Anatomically, therefore, the sympathetic nervous system is interpolated between the cranial and the sacral divisions of the autonomic. Figure 15 indicates these divisions and their functions.

On the basis of function the cranial and the sacral segments taken together are distinguished from the sympathetic, for reasons that will appear presently. In brief, the sympathetic segment dilates the pupil of the eye, accelerates the heart, inhibits the activity of the alimentary canal, inhibits digestive secretions, reduces the flow of the blood in the alimentary canal, causes pallor and " goose-flesh," excretes sweat, and secretes adrenin. As opposed to this group of activities, the cranio-sacral segments of the autonomic retard heart action, contract the pupils, accentuate salivation, increase the activity of the alimentary canal, provide for the excretory functions of the digestive system, and,

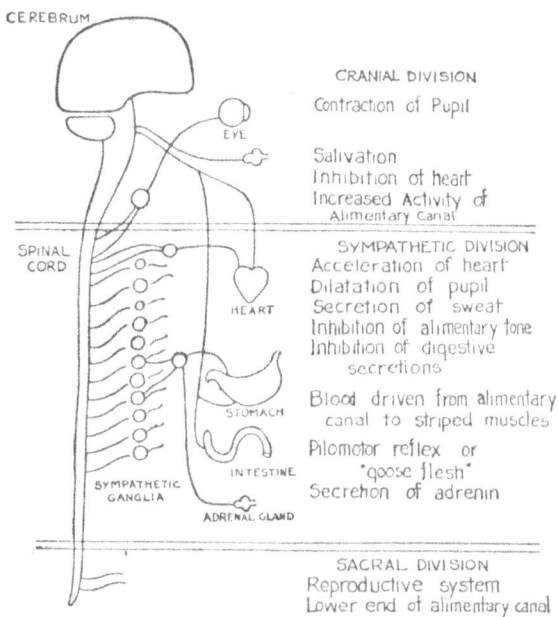

CEREBRUM

CRANIAL DIVISION
Contraction of Pupil

EYE

Salivation
Inhibition of heart
Increased Activity of
Alimentary Canal

SPINAL
CORD

SYMPATHETIC DIVISION
Acceleration of heart
Dilatation of pupil
Secretion of sweat
Inhibition of alimentary tone
Inhibition of digestive
secretions

HEART

Blood driven from alimentary
canal to striped muscles

Pilomotor reflex or
"goose flesh"
Secretion of adrenin

STOMACH

INTESTINE

SYMPATHETIC
GANGLIA

ADRENAL GLAND

SACRAL DIVISION
Reproductive system
Lower end of alimentary canal

FIG. 15. — Diagram showing the divisions and presumed functions of the autonomic nervous system. (Modified from Cannon.)

in part, innervate the reproductive organs. Experimental evidence shows, according to Cannon, that the two sets of functions just enumerated are definitely associated with the two divisions of the autonomic system.

This functional distinction can best be understood by noting that the sympathetic activities considered as a whole show the organism in a state of physical and emotional excitement, whereas the cranio-sacral functions picture the organism in a state of vegetative tranquillity. The sympathetic functions, for example, are elicited in states of pain, fear, and rage; the cranio-sacral activities predominate when the organism is quietly feeding or resting. Thus the sympathetic portion of the autonomic system has an emergency function in that it is aroused during a crisis. On the other hand, the cranio-sacral portion acts as a conserver of bodily resources. Bodily excitement and bodily calm are perhaps the two opposed terms that most concisely express the antagonistic effects of the autonomic nervous system.

Cannon finds that the adrenal glands function in connection with the sympathetic portion of the autonomic system. Adrenin, the hormone secreted by these glands, primarily functions by liberating sugar from the liver into the blood stream. Such an increase in blood sugar makes a larger supply of energy available. When more sugar is released than the body can consume the resulting effect is glycosuria, or the condition which, when chronic, is directly responsible for the disease, diabetes. Cannon discovered that glycosuria developed in cats that had been confined in the presence of dogs for a time, in football players on the eve of a crucial game, and in some medical students just before a hard examination. Grief and anxiety result in glycosuria, hence individuals who suffer from some prolonged emotional strain, such as soldiers on the battlefront, are subject to diabetes of emotional origin.

Adrenin produces some further effects. It drives blood from the abdominal viscera into the heart, lungs, body, and the central nervous system, or into those regions of the body where it is needed in a crisis. Adrenin also increases arterial pressure and coagulates blood. Its most immediately

L

useful effect, however, is to abolish or relieve muscular fatigue. Evidence indicates that it does this by neutralizing fatigue toxins in the blood.

That the effects of adrenin are comparable with the action of the sympathetic segments of the autonomic system is obvious. The sympathetic nerve impulses that produce visceral changes also stimulate the adrenals, and some of the symptoms of sympathetic activity are due to adrenal activity.

Emotions

As we have stated, all emotions are motives. Just as hunger impels the organisms to obtain and devour food, so fear prompts it to flee from danger and anger spurs it to belligerent activity. While certain emotions are depressing or inhibitory, their effects upon behavior are none the less immediate and marked; hence they are true motives. Woodworth (29) has the motivating aspect of emotion in mind when he writes of its *impulsive* phase. By this he means that each emotion is in part a tendency to *act* in some characteristic way. In general, emotions are motivating factors in behavior to the extent that they are strong or intense. To reverse the statement, strong emotions are those which exercise marked effects upon behavior.

Since modern psychology stresses the physiological approach to the study of emotion, attention should be called to the intimate relationships that exist between emotions and physiological drives. Closely associated with the sex drive is the emotion of love. The latter is undoubtedly derived from the former. In many respects such organic states as hunger, pain, and weariness possess features in common with the emotions. Frequently it is difficult to decide whether boredom is an emotion or an organic condition. The view is advanced in this chapter that emotions are physiological drives upon which many different kinds of stimuli have become conditioned. So far as the nature of the response is concerned, hunger is as truly an emotion as love. It differs from love primarily in the fact that its stimuli are limited in scope. If physiological hunger could be aroused and satisfied by landscapes, flowers, animals, novels, and motion pictures, it would in truth be an emotion.

The James-Lange Theory of Emotion. From the historical standpoint at least the greatest theoretical contribution ever made to the psychology of emotion is an explanation of its general nature formulated about 1884 by Carl Georg Lange, a Danish physician, and by William James, an American psychologist. Since these men working independently arrived at the same general conclusion, their combined contribution is known as the James-Lange theory of emotion.

In order to appreciate the significance of this theory we must note the fact that at the time of its formulation few scientific attempts had been made to place emotion upon a definite physiological basis. Emotions were popularly regarded as vague, ethereal states of mind or consciousness totally incapable of scientific analysis. As a result of the prevailing view that distinguished sharply between the spirit and the flesh, emotions which possessed a high social value were regarded as essentially spiritual or mystical, while other emotions, of questionable moral worth, were classified as base, physical passions. In short, the emotions primarily interested poets and mystics. Nor was the psychological treatment of that period much more scientific, for it was concerned largely with extensive and formal classifications of (assumed) emotional entities. Moreover, this so-called psychological treatment strongly reflected the popular views just mentioned.

In reality the ancient Greek thinkers rather than the

writers of the last few centuries anticipated the James-Lange theory of emotion. The fact that they recognized the physiological nature of emotion is disclosed by their belief in " humors," or substances which were supposed to circulate in the body and cause the various emotions. A vestige of this belief is found in the expressions, " good " or " bad " humor. But it must not be inferred that the Greek philosophers thought of psychological problems from the modern standpoint, or even that they had a differentiated science of psychology. Their writings merely indicate a realization of the physiological correlates of emotion.

In essence the James-Lange theory explains emotions as conscious states directly caused by physiological activities. More specifically, it regards emotions as fusions of bodily sensations that are aroused, like other groups of sensations, by the stimulation of sense organs attached to sensory nerves. In terms of modern nomenclature, both James and Lange identified the emotions chiefly with interoceptive sensations. Lange emphasized the vasomotor or circulatory system as the source of emotions, while James included the entire viscera and the striped musculature. They agreed on the physiological nature of emotions, differing only in the specific physiological mechanisms involved.

The physiological activities responsible for these sensations are, according to James and Lange, nothing more than the so-called expressions of the emotions. Thus, the human expressions of fear include in part a cringing bodily posture, trembling and partial paralysis, wide-open or protruding eyes, " gooseflesh," spasmodic and vigorous heart action, labored breathing, marked vasomotor changes and an altered tonicity of the alimentary canal. Anger, love, jealousy, and other emotions show other typical expressions or physical symptoms. While James and Lange were sure only of such expressions as are readily observable, they were con-

smooth muscle tonicity and endocrinal activity. In this sense control merely means repression or restraint. On the other hand, it is quite likely that when the inner as well as the outer physiological expressions of an emotion disappear, the emotion ceases to exist. One method of quelling an emotional condition is to neutralize it by engaging in some physical activity. Whistling to keep up courage is a familiar instance. Certainly the facts of every-day observation can be interpreted in favor of James's standpoint.

(3) Two physiologists, Sherrington and Cannon, have criticized the James-Lange theory. (a) Sherrington transected the spinal cords of some dogs in the lower cervical region in the attempt to eliminate visceral sensations from the emotional responses of the animals. He found, however, no alteration in the subsequent emotional behavior, and concluded that organic sensations (or processes) are not necessary components of emotion. In another experiment, using two of the same dogs, he cut both of the vagus nerves, thus eliminating possible sensations from the stomach, lungs, and heart. Again the dogs growled when teased and displayed as many apparent signs of emotion as their condition permitted. And to prove that his animals did not react with emotional habits acquired through experience and " stored " in the brain, where sensory-motor connections were still intact after the operation, Sherrington repeated his experiment upon puppies nine weeks old and obtained similar results.

But the majority of psychologists regard Sherrington's results as inconclusive. He merely established the fact that certain elements in the total emotional response, namely those unaffected by the operation, can be elicited after the nerve connections between the viscera and brain have been severed. In other words, he did not prove that the dogs really experienced emotion.

vinced that these manifestations could account for the coarser emotions. As regards their analysis of the emotions they were directly indebted to Darwin, who had published in 1872 his *Expressions of the Emotions in Man and Animals*. Darwin elaborated a theory of the origin of emotional expressions, but it remained for James and Lange to explain the psychology of emotion in terms of these expressions.

In addition to its emphasis upon the physiological nature of emotion, the James-Lange theory reverses the commonly accepted notion that emotion is a cause and its manifestation an effect. On the contrary, it definitely regards the emotional consciousness or " feeling " as a result of the physiological disturbance. It assumes that the steps involved in emotion are, in logical sequence, (1) the stimulus or exciting situation, (2) the physiological changes, and (3) the consciousness of these changes, or the emotion itself. In the case of an individual terrified by the sudden discovery of a rattlesnake at his feet these steps are represented by his perception of the reptile, his physiological expressions of fear, and his state of consciousness resulting directly from his physical commotion. In other words fear consists of certain characteristic " creepy " feelings on the skin, the sensations aroused by trembling muscles, and the disagreeable feeling-tone of the viscera. To the extent that they involve physical manifestations, all emotions likewise consist of typical groups of sensations. Emotion is the conscious result of bodily *commotion*.

James epitomizes his theory in the following words: " Our natural way of thinking about these standard emotions is that the mental perception of some fact excites the mental affection called the emotion, and that this latter state of mind gives rise to the bodily expression. My thesis on the contrary is that the bodily changes follow directly the perception of the exciting fact and that our feeling of the same changes as they occur is the emotion."

In another passage James explains his position in terms of an illustration that is commonly cited and usually misunderstood. In spite of the usual assumption that a man runs because he is afraid — so James states it — the truth is that he is afraid because he runs. The point is merely that the act of running represents the total physiological series of fear disturbances that cause the feeling or the emotion. James does not mean that the sensations from the legs of the runner alone constitute his fear.

Nor does James imply that there is a perceptible time interval between the physiological disturbance and the emotional consciousness. Although retinal stimulation actually precedes visual consciousness, no introspector can detect the time interval involved; and by the same token the emotion apparently occurs simultaneously with its cause, the physiological changes. In stating that the bodily change comes first and the emotion second James clearly is stressing the *logical,* not the psychological, sequence of the two events.

James bases his theory primarily upon real and hypothetical introspective evidence. His argument is as follows: " If we fancy some strong emotion, and then try to abstract from our consciousness of it all the feelings of its characteristic bodily symptoms, we find we have nothing left behind, no ' mind-stuff ' out of which the emotion can be constituted, and that a cold and neutral state of intellectual perception is all that remains . . . purely disembodied human emotion is a nonentity." According to this argument, intellectual apprehension of danger differs from the emotion of fear. The fireman, for instance, entrapped in a burning building, may be more keenly aware of the danger and at the same time less fearful of the consequences than an occupant whom he has just discovered. To put the case another way, if we can imagine some drug in tablet form, endowed with properties that restore all disturbed physiological functions to their normal operating level, we can readily believe that its specific effect would be anti-emotional. James finds additional evidence for his theory in the emotional behavior of many insane patients. Although this behavior is outwardly violent, James maintains that it is devoid of the inward commotion that is the essence of a genuine emotion. His point is that lacking the actual physiological disturbances, such emotional behavior, while apparently violent, is actually superficial and shallow.

James also advances the argument that the assumptions of the relationships that obtain between brain activity and conscious states corroborate his explanation of emotion. Since all brain centers directly associated with consciousness are sensory, emotion is either located in sensory centers or in other centers that have escaped discovery. And since the surface of the brain cortex, containing the known sensory centers, has been carefully explored, James believes that the existence of specific centers for emotion is highly improbable. We should note that while this conception of definite cortical centers is scarcely in accord with modern interpretations of cerebral functions, it was, in James's day, the accepted view. His argument, therefore, is extremely plausible in the light of his knowledge.

Criticisms of the James-Lange Theory. In spite of its tremendous influence upon psychological doctrine, the James-Lange theory has been subjected to severe criticisms from its first appearance to the present. These criticisms are of three sorts, based respectively upon (1) logical, (2) introspective considerations, and (3) direct experimental evidence.

Arguments of the first type may be summarized as follows: (1) It is urged that an emotion consists of factors other than the kinaesthetic and organic sensations stressed by James and Lange. This is the argument so frequently advanced in other connections; namely, that a given theory is correct so far as it goes, but that it does not go sufficiently far. Concerning the fact involved there is little question if we can trust the observations of most psychologists. Hunter (15), for instance, finds in every emotion, in addition to its core of bodily sensations, an affective element of pleasantness or unpleasantness, and "an awareness of some thought or object as the arouser of the emotion."[2] But as Hunter points out, this fact does not argue against the James-Lange theory as interpreted by James himself, for James claims that the sensation-element is the determining, rather than the sole, factor in emotion. And it should be remembered that James consistently restricts his theory to the "coarser" emotions.

(2) Many psychologists, including those who are generally sympathetic with the James-Lange explanation, find that the theory fails to indicate the differentiating factors in the specific emotions. They note that many diverse emotions are manifested by the same bodily disturbances, and conversely, that the same emotion subjectively analyzed shows a variety of physiological expressions. For instance, running and some of its accompanying physiological activities characterize either fear or joy; and grief is expressed either actively or passively, with marked differences in the respective bodily disturbances. As we note below, Cannon voices this criticism on the basis of experimental data. That the James-Lange theory is entirely inadequate with respect to this issue can scarcely be questioned, but it does not follow that the discovery of the differentiating factor or factors will militate against the theory. In the first place, the answer to the first criticism made against James and Lange is

[2] *Op. cit.*, p. 199.

equally applicable to the second. Granting the existence of specific differentiating factors in emotion, it may still be true that the factor common to all emotions is the background of kinaesthetic and particularly organic or visceral sensations. In the second place, we cannot assume that a scientific classification of emotions, when it is properly elaborated, will correspond at all with our present conception of the different emotions. On purely introspective grounds we seemingly experience emotions for which we have neither verbal designations nor accurate descriptions. It might be better, as Watson, Max Meyer, and others have implied, to designate the specific emotions as x, y, and z, and to avoid popular dictionary terms altogether. Furthermore, the characteristic physiological changes that underlie the various emotions have not as yet been described. It is futile, therefore, to criticize the James-Lange theory for its failure to differentiate among the specific emotions when the emotions themselves have never been adequately distinguished. It is conceivable, for instance, that there are only two kinds of emotion, pleasant and unpleasant, and that all other distinguishing features are really differences in the objective or ideational setting.

According to a somewhat popular objection to the James-Lange theory, also based upon alleged introspective evidence, an emotion is really intensified rather than weakened by a suppression of its physiological manifestations. It is argued, for example, that silent, controlled grief is much more poignant than this same emotion violently expressed. Although superficially plausible, this objection is rather pointless in that it does not take into consideration the ambiguity in the word *controlled*. In the majority of cases to " control " an emotion means merely to inhibit its outward, visible expressions, with no attempt to modify what well may be the important factors in the emotion — namely,

(b) A second physiologist who attacks James and Lange is Cannon, whose investigations of certain visceral functions have already been described. Cannon believes that the visceral changes involved in the emotions are determined by the intensity rather than the quality of the emotion. For instance, he cites a case where vomiting was stimulated in one highly nervous individual, upon the receipt of extremely good news. If Cannon is correct, intense joy, sorrow, and disgust all tend to produce the same physiological effect. His conclusion is that "the viscera are relatively unimportant in an emotional complex, especially in contributing differential features." But as Hunter points out, Cannon "wrongly interprets his facts as antagonistic to the James-Lange theory. On the contrary they support the theory strongly by indicating a very delicate and widespread bodily disturbance during emotional seizures."[3] It is certain that Cannon's investigations point to visceral activities as the probable location of emotional response.

The Expression of the Emotions. Whether or not the James-Lange theory is accepted in substance we are forced through want of a better term to designate the physiological signs by which an emotion is manifested as the *expressions* of that emotion. Furthermore, the term is somewhat ambiguous in that it is frequently limited to such manifestations of emotion as are externally observable, whereas it logically includes all physiological changes in the total emotional complex. As used in the latter sense, for instance, it includes endocrinal activity.

Unfortunately for the theoretical considerations involved, the specific forms of emotional expression have not as yet been fully ascertained. Our knowledge of emotions in animals is meagre for the simple reason that few people have taken the pains to observe such phenomena systemati-

[3] *Op. cit.*, p. 203.

cally. One might suppose that human manifestations of emotion, particularly bodily attitudes, gestures, and facial expressions, could be readily studied in the photographic laboratory or moving-picture studio, but for reasons explained below such is not the case. Although based primarily upon personal observation, Darwin's classic description of emotional behavior in men and animals is still accepted as reasonably authentic. At best systematic descriptions of emotional symptoms present composite pictures based upon numerous cases rather than individual pictures.

Among other descriptions of this sort Bernard (5), in his book on the instinct hypothesis, gives Thorndike's analysis of anger.[4] The analysis is in fact a symptomatology of anger, not wholly applicable to any particular individual. Thorndike's description includes the following: heartbeat and circulation affected, face reddens, face becomes purple, veins on forehead distended, falling down dead, respiration affected, chest heaves, nostrils dilate, nostrils quiver, muscles become stronger, will becomes more active, body held erect for instant action, body bent forward toward the offending person, limbs rigid, mouth closed with firmness, teeth clenched, teeth ground together, teeth grinding, arms raised, fists clenched, menacing gestures, striking objects, hurling objects to the ground, children rolling on the ground on their bellies, screaming, kicking, scratching, biting, trembling, lips paralyzed, voice sticks in throat, voice loud, voice harsh, voice discordant, mouth froths, hair bristles, frowning, eyes glare, eyes glisten, eyes protrude, lips protrude, lips retract, snarling, flow of tears, spitting, yelling, slapping, pulling objects, shaking objects, stamping, jumping up and down, hitting with the hand.

The symptomatology of the major emotions — anger, fear, and affection — is formulated in detail by Morrison (21), in

[4] Pages 382–383.

her investigation of the emotional behavior of mental defectives. Since they direct attention to all characteristic forms of emotional expression, arranged and classified systematically, Morrison's descriptions are germane to our present topic. They are as follows:

ANGER

1. Expression of the Face
    a. Brows contracted, eyes narrowed
       Brows raised, eyes wide and glaring
       Brows level, eyes fixed, glance cold and steady
    b. Mouth closed, lips thin, jaws set
       Mouth open (as in loud speech)
       Mouth opened slightly, lips curled, or twisted
    c. Nostrils distended
    d. Face flushed, pale, or of blotchy appearance
    e. Perspiration on forehead and upper lip

2. Vocal-motor Reactions
    a. Nasal and guttural sounds
    b. Cursing, sarcasm, insults, etc.
    c. Voice loud, hoarse, or low and threatening

3. Cardio-respiratory and Vaso-motor Reactions
    a. Very marked chest movements, deep and rapid breathing
    b. Increased strength and rate of heartbeat (seldom observed)
    c. Blood vessels of neck, face, and arms distended
    d. Color of skin, flushed or pale

4. Posture and Movements of the Body
    a. Erect, rigid
       Slightly crouched, and bent forward

   b. Trembling

   c. Running toward or throwing body against the offending object

     Spitting upon the object

5. Position and Movements of the Limbs

   a. Fists clenched

     Fingers claw-like

   b. Emphatic gestures of arms accompanying angry words

   c. Pulling hair, striking, kicking

6. General Attitude

   a. Unsociable

   b. Disobedient, resentful

   c. Irritable, sullen

FEAR

1. Expression of the Face

   a. Eyes staring, brows raised

   b. Mouth open, lips quivering

   c. Nostrils distended

   d. Face pale, or possibly flushed

   e. Cold perspiration

2. Vocal-motor Reactions

   a. Cries, screaming

   b. Words of distress, pain, etc.

     Prohibitive commands

   c. Voice husky, loud and high, hushed and low

3. Cardio-respiratory and Vaso-motor Reactions

   a. Very marked chest movements, deep and rapid breathing

   b. Increased strength and rate of heartbeat (seldom observed)
   c. Blood vessels of neck, face, and arms distended
   d. Color of skin, pale or flushed

4. Posture and Movements of the Body
   a. Body rigid, motionless
      Crouched
      Withdrawing
   b. Trembling
      Shivering
      Erection of hair
   c. Drawing or shrinking away
      Headlong flight

5. Position and Movements of the Limbs
   a. Hands clenched or shaking
   b. Arms thrust forward or thrown up toward face as if to push away or ward off the fearful thing
   c. Actually pushing away the fearful object
      Striking, kicking, fighting

6. General Attitude
   a. Of desire not to be alone
   b. Refusal to go to certain places
   c. Despondency, tearfulness

Affection

1. Expression of the Face
   a. Eyes bright, open, focussed on the attractive object
      Brows raised or level
   b. Mouth smiling, kissing
   c. Face flushed as in blushing

2. Vocal-motor Reactions
   a. Crooning, gurgling, etc.
   b. Pleasant, friendly speech
      Soothing and endearing words spoken to or about
      the object of affection
   c. Voice calm and low, clear and hearty

3. Cardio-respiratory and Vaso-motor Reactions
      (These responses are very difficult to detect in affec-
      tion, but we do get a hint of them in blushing)

4. Posture and Movements of the Body
   a. Posture relaxed, comfortable
   b. Leaning toward or against the attractive object
   c. Walking or running toward it

5. Position and Movements of the Limbs
   a. Hands relaxed, or spread out as in patting
   b. Gestures slow and gentle, as in stroking and patting
      Protective gestures
   c. Caressing, embracing
      Striking, kicking, even fighting to protect the be-
      loved object

6. General Attitude
   a. Friendly, sociable, talkative
   b. Desire to be near the beloved object
   c. Pain or distress (tears) when separated from the be-
      loved object
   d. Desire to do for and give to the beloved object

The Origin of Emotional Expressions.   Any discussion of the origin of emotional expressions logically begins
with Darwin's evolutionary theory, formulated in his *Ex-*

pressions of the Emotions in Man and Animals, a book that first appeared in 1872. Darwin's explanation takes the form of three principles that may be stated briefly as follows: (1) According to the *Principle of Serviceable Associated Habits* many forms of emotional expression are inherited vestiges of acts useful during an earlier period of racial history. For example, the snarl of anger shown by a dog and the corresponding scornful curl of the lips shown by human beings both date back to remote times when common ancestors exposed their teeth in fighting. (2) The *Principle of Antithesis* assumes that the emotions are arranged in pairs of opposites, and that an animal in any emotion tends to manifest expressions the opposite of its paired emotion. To quote Allport's example (3), " Thus the cringing and fawning of the happy, affectionate dog, together with his lowered ears and tail, and sinuous movements, could be understood only as the opposites of the erect and stiffened posture, and pricked up ears and tail, of the dog in anger." [5]   (3) The *Principle of the Direct Action of the Nervous System* assumes, something after the manner of present-day popular belief, that in strong emotion there is an overflow of nervous energy into the available motor channels. Trembling, for instance, is explained on this basis.

Darwin's principles, particularly his first, seem applicable to many familiar forms of expression. It is conceivable that we open our eyes in fear because our ancestors faced dangerous situations chiefly at night when the clearest vision possible was imperative. In the same way, disgust involves the expression of physical nausea. The individual who scathingly addresses the object of his scorn by the remark, " You make me sick," speaks better psychology than he realizes. A more far-fetched example of assumed survival value is found in the bristling attitude of a terrified cat. By

[5] *Op. cit.,* p. 211.

apparently doubling its size the cat inspires respect if not fear in its enemy. In addition to being somewhat negative, Darwin's second principle is open to the charge that emotions, as a matter of fact, do not show the paired arrangement that the explanation presupposes. It is of course obvious that his third principle is sufficiently elastic to cover any emotional expression of dubious practical value.

In essence at least, Darwin's theory of emotional expression has been adopted by many biologists and psychologists. It forms the basis of James's theory, for when confronted with the task of explaining the bodily disturbances that constitute the emotions James assumes their instinctive origin and their ancestral value. In more recent times the influence of Darwin is seen in the physiological studies of emotion made by Crile and Cannon. Both of these physiologists find survival values in visceral functions, and Crile (11) finds them in the conscious accompaniments of visceral functions. For instance, he states that pain due to lacerations of the flesh is almost unendurably unpleasant because it dates back to the experiences of our ancestors who coped with carnivorous beasts, while the pain that results from bullet wounds, having no evolutionary significance, is relatively mild. As we point out below, Cannon finds a biological purpose in the visceral accompaniments of emotion.

Nevertheless, Darwin's method of explanation has been criticized from two distinct points of view. In the first place, his basic assumption regarding the evolutionary process has been considerably modified by more recent biologists, and his specific theory of emotional expression has suffered accordingly. Allport has reformulated Darwin's principles in the light of modern biological doctrine. In the second place, as we show presently, Darwin's view does not square with all of the facts of human facial expression.

Taken together, the two criticisms probably represent the trend of modern views concerning emotional expression.

Allport believes that Darwin's principles should be reformulated rather than discarded. Referring to Darwin's idea of the origin of facial expression, Allport makes the following comment: He " demonstrated that facial expression, or communication, was not the original function of the facial muscles; but that such biological ends as mastication, dilatation of the nostrils for breathing, and shading the eyes were their proper functions. The purpose to express was therefore not the origin of this behavior." [6]

Allport then revises each of Darwin's three principles in conformity with present scientific knowledge. He substitutes for Darwin's first theory the explanation that emotional expressions have survived because they *become* important in the adaptation of the *individual* to the environment. In other words, they are acquired just as language is acquired. Allport revises Darwin's first principle as follows: " Darwin's formula was, ' The ancestor bites in angry attacks and the child instinctively expresses rage by baring his teeth! ' Our revision would read, ' The *child* bites and so acquires the habit of expressing rage by baring his teeth.' " [7] The principle of antithesis Allport modifies in terms of his emphasis upon the opposed affective states, pleasantness and unpleasantness, as the essential components of emotions. The principle of the direct action of the nervous system, according to Allport, can be retained by assuming that facial expressions are partly controlled by the autonomic system. For example, blushing is a vasomotor phenomenon which can be explained only in terms of a relatively widespread autonomic disturbance.

Studies of Emotional Expression. It will be remembered that, according to the second criticism, Darwin's view

[6] *Op. cit.*, p. 211.   [7] *Op. cit.*, pp. 214-215.

does not harmonize with the facts of emotional expression. The acceptance of Darwin's theory implies that various human emotions are represented by relatively fixed and characteristic facial expressions. Thus grief, love, anger, disgust, fear, and surprise should each, according to Darwin's view, conform rather closely to inherited emotional patterns. To the extent that facial expressions suggest an inherited, original purpose, they should conform to type.

On the other hand, two considerations argue against the assumption that emotional expressions are necessarily or even usually stereotyped. In the first place, these expressions are determined or at least modified tremendously by social convention. Current manifestations of grief in American polite society differ considerably from the custom, described in novels, which prompted the bereaved Russian peasant to wail audibly and publicly in front of his house. It can scarcely be argued that the latter custom, with its entailed publicity, is any more " natural " than our own. As a matter of fact, education and social progress tend to subdue all forms of emotional expression. Then, inasmuch as emotional expressions possess certain linguistic or communicative functions, they tend to become not only subdued but conventionalized. The moving-picture public soon accepts the artificial and conventionalized methods of registering emotion that it views on the screen. In fact, for reasons which need not detain us here, moving-picture actors have reduced their repertoire of emotional expressions to a minimum. A recent number of *Life* pokes fun at this tendency by caricaturing the actress in her attempt to register a series of emotions — all attempts resulting in identical, wooden expressions. It must be acknowledged that the conventionalized emotions seen on the screen or stage represent a very real trend in emotional manifestation.

Secondly, psychological investigations have shown that

judges have difficulty in identifying emotional expressions registered in photographs. In Feleky's study (12) a talented subject posed for numerous photographs of various emotions during a period of a year. Eighty-six of these photographs were finally selected and given to a group of 100 judges. They were able to agree upon certain expressions, such as aversion, contempt, and laughter, but they failed with others. Ruckmick (24) conducted a similar experiment, using a subject with considerable experience in amateur dramatics. Among other conclusions Ruckmick states that, . . . "as a rule the ' primary ' emotions, as love and hate, joy and sorrow, are much more uniformly interpreted than the ' secondary ' ones, like repulsiveness, surprise, distrust and defiance." Moreover, this investigator notes that judgments of facial expressions are modified by the moods of the judges.

Allport gives a summary of an investigation conducted and reported by Langfeld (18, 19). This experimenter obtained judgments of emotional expression based upon photographs posed for by an experienced actor. To quote Allport's summary: " In some of these tests five subjects were used, and in others, six. The subjects examined the photographs and named the expressions in their own words. A total of 525 judgments were obtained, of which only about 33 per cent were correct. If only the eight groups in the . . . table are selected (the others being unusually difficult or perhaps only ' projected ' expressions) the accuracy rises to 43 per cent, which is still surprisingly low. Laughter was the most readily identified, being correctly named in 64 per cent of the cases; anger the least readily (30 per cent accuracy). Pain was also readily seen (50 per cent); while disgust and fear were low (36 per cent each)." [8]

Using the same series of photographs, Allport conducted

[8] *Op. cit.*, p. 223.

a further test in which he asked his judges to underline one of eight titles for a given picture, only one of which was absolutely correct. Fourteen groups of names were used in all. In other words, the judges were furnished names from which they selected what they thought were the correct names. Under the conditions imposed by this method their judgments were 45–50 per cent correct.

Allport further gives the order of identifiability obtained by himself and by Langfeld. The two lists, containing the facial expressions ranked in the order in which they were correctly identified, are as follows:

(Langfeld)	(Allport)
6 subjects — 105 pictures	48 subjects — 14 pictures
Laughter	Laughter
Amazement	Bodily Pain
Bodily Pain	Fear (Horror)
Hate (Aversion-Hate Group)	Distrust (similar to Hate)
Fear (Anxiety-Fear-Terror Group)	Amazement
Disgust (Scorn-Contempt Group)	Anger
Doubt	Doubt
Anger (Anger-Rage Group)	Disgust

That the general conclusions just advanced apply to actual emotions is confirmed by the experiment of Landis (17). This investigator photographed people who were under the stress of various emotions. In order to obtain genuine emotional responses he was forced to administer rather heroic stimuli to his subjects. Some of the stimuli that proved to be really effective were jazz music, severe electrical shocks, pictures of loathsome diseases, touching live frogs concealed from vision, instructions to write and to read aloud (actually enforced) bits of embarrassing personal history, instructions (also enforced) to pick up a live rat with bare hands and decapitate it with a knife. The facial responses to these situations were photographed with extreme care. In one of his series black lines were drawn on the subjects' faces in order to make the facial expressions more visible.

From the standpoint of the present discussion the most significant result obtained by Landis was that individuals vary exceedingly in responding to the same emotional situations. As he states the result, " In no situation was the contraction of a muscle, group of muscles, or expression found to occur with sufficient frequency as to be significant. There is no expression typical of any situation in this experiment." [9] Moreover, each of the subjects manifested a tendency to use certain characteristic facial expressions in responding to stimuli, irrespective of the nature of the stimuli. In brief, facial expressions are determined primarily by the individual and not by the emotional situation. Landis also found little correspondence between verbal reports of emotional states and the facial expressions of these states. In other words, there was no facial expression typically associated with any verbal description of the emotion offered by the subjects. On the basis of his results Landis suggests that a distinction should be made between social and emotional expressions. Natural expressions of emotions are individual peculiarities, while the expressions that are ordinarily registered are highly conventionalized. The latter constitute the *language* of the face.

Physiological Manifestations of Emotions. The term, " *expressions of the emotions*," is really misleading. It reflects the old belief that the physiological disturbances which it includes are caused by subjective states or the

[9] Page 497.

" true " emotions. As a matter of fact, few contemporary psychologists, including even those who reject the James-Lange theory, accept this belief without considerable qualification. The term is ambiguous in its failure to distinguish between *all* physiological manifestations of emotion and merely those that are subject to voluntary control. In their courses of instruction schools of dramatic art naturally emphasize voice, gesture, bodily attitude, and other controllable elements in emotion, rather than smooth muscle tonicity or endocrinal activity. However, many psychologists seek an explanation of feeling and emotion in visceral functions. Inasmuch as these functions are included in the phenomena which theories of emotional expression attempt to explain, they are properly classified under this term.

Emotion and Gastro-intestinal Tone. While numerous investigators have assumed that the tonicity of the smooth musculature is closely related to emotional phenomena, the experimental evidence bearing upon this assumption is exceedingly meagre. In many strictly physiological investigations of visceral functions smooth muscle tissue is either exposed to direct observation in the anaesthetized animal or excised and studied while still living. But emotional phenomena are only manifested in the intact organism. Furthermore, even the trained observer has difficulty in studying his own visceral behavior.

One investigator, Brunswick (7), was able to study the effects of emotional stimuli upon the tonicity of the human alimentary tract, and to check his experimental results with introspective data. His results are of interest with respect to the physiological aspects of emotion, and they are related to the James-Lange theory. Using the rubber balloon technique, Brunswick obtained kymograph records of changes in tonicity in the lower end of the alimentary canal, and in the stomach. In addition he recorded fluctuations in breathing by means of a *pneumograph*. Changes in blood pressure were also recorded throughout the experiment. The subjects, 10 adults in the Johns Hopkins University, gave introspective testimony regarding their conscious reactions to strong emotional stimuli while their physiological responses were being automatically registered. Brunswick's conclusions are based upon both the physiological and the introspective findings.

A word should be said concerning the laboratory study of emotion. As our account of the experiment of Landis indicates, it is possible to elicit genuine emotions in the psychological laboratory, under conditions of controlled observation, provided that mature subjects are used. It is well known that certain emotional responses, disgust for example, can be provoked readily in the majority of human beings by appropriate pictures or verbal descriptions. The responses are none the less genuine even though they are deliberately aroused for purposes of investigation. In the psychological laboratory subjects are selected primarily on the basis of their interest in science, as shown by their willingness to act as subjects. When an experimenter undertakes the study of emotion, or any phenomenon requiring trained observers, he devises his technique, selects his subjects, asks them to report at certain periods, and gives them in advance such information about his experiment as seems advisable. Brunswick followed this general procedure, but as one might surmise, he did not inform the subjects regarding the stimuli which he had prepared for them. These stimuli included an unannounced turning off the light, an unexpected pistol shot, a threat to shoot a pistol aimed in the direction of the subject's head, an actual shot fired close to the head of the subject, dashing water into the face, the odor of decayed meat, a live snake that the subject was required to pick up, and an electrical shock. As his results show, some of these stimuli were exceedingly effective in arousing emotions.

Brunswick compared three chief factors controlled in his investigation; namely, the emotional stimuli, the changes in visceral tonicity, and the introspective reports. He found that the following emotions are characterized by relaxation or loss of tonicity in the stomach: fear, envy, disappointment, irritation, pain, and unpleasantness. As opposed to these, some of the emotions correlated with stomach contraction, or increased tonicity, are disgust, surprise, tenseness, wonder, anger, relief, pleasantness, interest, and amusement. His results, it should be said, were marked by a few discrepancies.

On the basis of these discoveries Brunswick concluded that tonic changes in the gastro-intestinal walls are actual factors in emotion. He is inclined to think that with better introspective technique and more sensitive apparatus such inconsistencies as he found would be eliminated. His records of tonic changes, however, are not sufficiently differentiated to explain the specific emotions. There was not a characteristic change for anger, another one for fear, and still another for surprise. On the other hand, he was able to correlate changes in tonicity with feeling-tone; for on the whole pleasant emotions were marked by contraction or increased tonicity and unpleasant emotions by relaxation or loss of tonicity. Brunswick suggests that the sympathetic system is responsible for unpleasantness while the parasympathetic (or the cranio-sacral) is, conversely, the agent of pleasantness. In addition to the foregoing results, Brunswick found evidence for compensating emotional reactions. Anger is a compensation for fear, hence its accompanying increased tonicity as contrasted with the diminution of tone in the latter emotion.

Brunswick's results and conclusions are of interest in several respects. They are fundamentally significant from a technical standpoint in that they bring experimental evidence to bear upon certain deductions previously arrived at by other psychologists. On the whole they support the James-Lange theory, for they tend to correlate emotion and feeling with bodily activity. They suggest that our popular ideas of the emotions stand in need of considerable revision. The traditional classifications of the emotions are entirely arbitrary, and our notions of the feeling-tone of emotions are extremely vague. In other words, it is possible that Brunswick's results fail to differentiate among the various emotions for the simple reason that they have never been adequately distinguished on introspective grounds. In conclusion it should be noted that Brunswick investigated only one phase of the physiology of emotions. Neither the influence of circulatory nor of endocrinal factors is incorporated in his report.

Blood Pressure Symptoms of Deception. Marston (20) and other investigators have found that changes in systolic blood pressure accompany the conscious attitude of deception so closely that they are fairly reliable objective signs of this attitude. Blood exerts a pressure upon arterial walls in much the same way that water exerts pressure upon a fire hose. By means of a suitable instrument, the *sphygmomanometer,* this blood-pressure can be measured. Marston took successive blood pressure measurements of subjects who were attempting to shield friends accused of hypothetical crimes or to deceive the experimenter regarding their own actions. His results indicate increased pressure during moments of attempted deception.

The Word-Association Method of Studying Emotion. In the opinion of many psychologists man is distinguished from the animals chiefly by his employment of language. As we will explain in Chapter VI, words are symbols that replace concrete, stimulus-response situations. Forms of fiction, the novel in particular, attest to the fact that human beings can live through experiences of the utmost physical and social complexity on a plane exclusively verbal. As any ordinary conversation between two people shows, words function both as stimuli and responses. But attention is called to the fact that the response to a verbal stimulus is in many cases not merely another word. It may be an overt act, as a movement executed by a soldier in response to a military command, or it may be an emotion. Frequently responses to verbal stimuli are quite complex, including emotional elements, overt responses, and other words.

The fact that verbal stimuli are exceedingly effective in arousing emotional reactions is utilized in everyday life. Our purely verbal responses are more or less mechanical and governed by habit. For example, practically the universal response to " black " is " white." But words associated with our emotional life, words that refer to people or situations that are sources of embarrassment, fear, hatred, jealousy, or love, produce mixed responses. Our verbal responses to such words are likely, for one thing, to " give us away," hence we inhibit them or seek other words as substitutes, and the net result is a *delay* accompanied with signs of confusion and embarrassment. Lawyers frequently apply this psychological principle while conducting cross-examinations; parents and teachers use it in controlling children.

In the psychological laboratory this principle is utilized under controlled conditions in the interest of scientific research. As the experiment is usually conducted, the psychologist prepares a list of stimulus words and pronounces each of them to his subject, who is required to reply orally to each by the first word that comes to his mind. Using a stop-watch, the experimenter records the time interval that elapses between each stimulus word and its response. He writes the actual response word and records any signs of emotional reaction.

Before the experiment is begun the stimulus words are carefully selected with reference to the desired responses. Normally such a list contains a number of *control* words; that is, words such as " up," " white," " table," " go," " sing," that are presumed to be relatively free from emotional connotations. The average time required in responding to such words, known as the normal verbal reaction time, varies considerably from one individual to another. It is separately ascertained for each individual subject, therefore, as a basis for comparison with his responses to supposedly *significant* words. Words of this sort refer to events that are common sources of worry, fear, shame, embarrassment, or perhaps guilt. Words which thus tend to arouse strong emotional responses are called " complex " words.

The term *complex* is a product of the psychoanalytical school of Freud and Jung. Taken literally, psychoanalysis means analysis of the mind, but the term has been appropriated by this particular school of psychiatrists to designate the method by which its members ascertain and study the personal, subjective life of their patients. The psychoanalyst endeavors to delve into the mind of his patient for the purpose of discovering memories of important experiences which the patient himself will not or cannot recall. These experiences have been put out of the mind of the patient because they are sources of embarrassment or shame. The process by which an individual refuses to think of his unpleasant experiences until he forgets them entirely is called *repression*. The chief contention of the psychoanalyst is that repressed memories, instead of disappearing from the life of the individual, may affect his dreams, his thoughts, and his everyday acts to the extent that he becomes neurotic and even mentally unbalanced. Only by resurrecting these forgotten experiences can a cure be effected.

The complex is the group of ideas or memories that has been repressed. According to the extreme psychoanalysts, the ideas composing the complex exist only in the " unconscious." It should be remarked, however, that this usage of the term *unconscious* is purely figurative. The unconscious refers merely to the individual's more or less successfully inhibited motives and impulses. If a child were taught that hunger is something to be ashamed of he would naturally refuse to acknowledge, to himself, his own hunger cravings; but his stomach rather than his " unconscious " would be the source of his unacknowledged desires. There is nothing particularly mysterious or metaphysical about complexes.

The *symptoms* of emotional disturbance recorded during a word association test are called *complex indicators*. In an article by Hull and Lugoff (14) the following complex indicators are enumerated: long reaction time, abnormally short reaction time, inability to respond, repetition of stimulus word, apparent misunderstanding of the stimulus word, defective reproduction of original response at second presentation of stimulus word, responding with the same reaction word to two or more different stimulus words, meaningless reactions, perseveration. Such complex indicators, together with the nature of the response word itself, are frequently significant.

The Psychogalvanic Reflex. The galvanometer is an instrument which detects weak electrical currents. One form of the instrument serves this purpose by reflecting a beam of light from a swinging mirror. Movements of the mirror change the angle of the reflected light.

Nerve impulses are known to generate electricity, hence

when the galvanometer is connected by wires with the human body it presumably responds to neural activity. It has been used successfully, however, only in the case of an emotional response. The resulting deflexion of the light is called the *psychogalvanic reflex*. This reflex has been studied under different conditions of emotional stimulation. For instance, the British psychologist Smith (26) compared psychogalvanic measurements with differences in verbal reaction time, and concluded that the galvanometer detects complexes when reaction time fails to do so. On the other hand, the extreme sensitivity of the instrument causes it to respond to many extraneous influences and therefore interferes with its usefulness in the psychological laboratory.

Other Devices for Detecting Emotion. Many of the physiological functions that constitute, or are correlated with, emotion are studied by means of special pieces of apparatus. The *plethysmograph* records changes in the volume of the blood in the hand or other parts of the body to which it is attached. It consists essentially of a rubber sleeve or glove into which the hand or part is fitted, surrounded by water which in turn fills a cylindrical vessel and communicates with a recording device. As the volume of blood increases or decreases, a tracing made on smoked paper goes up or down. The *pneumograph* measures changes in respiration by recording fluctuations in the circumference of the chest while breathing. The *automatograph*, the original form of the planchette or ouija board, records minute involuntary movements made by the arm. The *cardiograph* shows fluctuations of heart action. These instruments are exceedingly useful in studying emotion because they measure quantitative changes in the phenomena which they register.

Dream Analysis of Emotion. Freud and his followers maintain that dreams, when correctly interpreted, furnish unerring indications of emotional trends. The assumptions involved in this theory are briefly as follows: The basic human drive is sexual, and it is represented in mental life by the emotion of love. This drive, called the *libido,* frequently conflicts with the ideals of the individual who possesses it, in which case it may become repressed into his unconscious mental life.

But the repressed libido tends to assert itself whenever possible. Sleep furnishes such an opportunity because it is a state characterized by a diminished capacity for thinking and for making moral judgments. During sleep, therefore, the individual is morally off-guard, so that his repressed wishes appear in his dreams. Freud explains further that the libido or wish is disguised, even in the dream, for otherwise its true nature would be revealed to the dreamer. This necessity for disguise explains the fantastic character of dreams. Thus, according to Freud, all dreams are symbolic fulfillments of repressed sexual motives.

A critical evaluation of the Freudian hypothesis would be out of place in the present discussion, but we may point out, nevertheless, that Freud's theory of dreams has been subjected to severe scientific criticism. It certainly lacks experimental confirmation. On the other hand, Freud has rendered a possible service to psychology by insisting upon some sort of relationship between dreams and motives. It is possible to doubt his fundamental assumption regarding the libido and at the same time to utilize his technique for dream analysis in the study of motivation.

Moods. Not infrequently an emotion perseveres long after its immediate cause has disappeared. This characteristic of emotional behavior gives rise to the phenomenon of *moods.* In terms of the stimulus-response principle an emotion finds opportunity for continued expression by attaching itself to a succession of stimuli. Once his anger is thoroughly aroused, an individual may go about for some time seeking trouble. As we say, he is in an " ugly mood." Similarly, a state of depression caused by some trivial circumstance may color an individual's outlook for hours and even days. Fortunately, however, moods also characterize the happier emotions. The recipient of exceedingly joyful news at the breakfast table is likely to manifest considerable optimism throughout the day. The mood of an individual actually determines in part the stimuli to which he will react.

On the response side, an explanation of moods is found in the lethargy which characterizes visceral behavior, particularly with reference to the cessation of visceral activities. As compared with the skeletal muscles, smooth muscles begin to contract slowly and cease contracting with even more delay. Cannon tells of a cat under fluoroscopic observation that showed no gastric peristalsis for several hours after it had been confronted with a dog, although its only objective manifestation of nervousness was a slight twitching of its tail. Digestion is a leisurely process which is recognized as instrumental in determining human moods. In all likelihood, too, temporary changes in endocrine functioning affect the organism for hours. In general, the ancient Greeks were not misled in their notion of the " humors " circulating through the body.

Temperament. The factors responsible for moods are relatively stable in the life of the organism. They form certain habitual modes of response and thus constitute the basis of *temperament*. As one might suspect, differences in temperament can be described from several standpoints, depending upon the factors which seem most instrumental in shaping personality. Several theories of temperament have been advanced, three of which stand out as fundamental.

(1) According to one view, an individual's temperament is determined by his most characteristic mood or moods.

N

There are many temperaments, therefore, as there are habitual moods. Pronounced tendencies to display fear, anger, and love respectively are seen in the timid, irascible, and affectionate types of temperaments. Likewise, mixed or derived emotional reactions, such as jealousy, envy, and worry, are represented by as many temperaments. This basis of classifying temperaments is open to many objections, but at least it possesses the merit of simplicity.

(2) Berman (4) assumes that temperaments are almost exclusively the products of endocrinal activities. According to Bridges (6), Galen's ancient description of the sanguine, phlegmatic, choleric, and melancholic temperaments is the historical antecedent of Berman's view. In Berman's opinion, our present knowledge of the ductless glands justifies the description of a temperament for each gland, or for certain glands acting together. Thus, the restless and excitable individual belongs to the thyroid type of temperament. A person of the adrenal type is noted for his energy; or, if he shows a deficiency in adrenal secretion, he may develop into the neurasthenic patient who suffers from constant fatigue. The pituitary types are more complex, since they can be classified as masculine or feminine depending upon which lobe of the pituitary gland determines the personality. In general the two pituitary types conform to the popular ideals of masculinity and femininity. When the thymus gland continues to function during childhood and adolescence it gives rise to the "angel-child" personality. In a similar way all types of personality are accounted for in terms of balances among glandular activities.

(3) A third basis for the classification of temperaments is found in abnormal behavior. Psychopathic and insane people are literally *abnormal* in that they represent deviations from the normal. In other words, their traits are exaggerations of traits found in all normal humans. But there

are various kinds of insanity, just as there are different kinds of physical disease, hence it is theoretically possible to classify normal people on the basis of abnormal groups.

The psychiatrist Rosanoff (23) has elaborated one classification of abnormal people and described corresponding types of temperament. He recognizes four types; namely (a) the anti-social or criminal; (b) the cyclothymic, marked by periodic alternations of exalted and depressed moods; (c) the autistic, "shut-in," or self-centered type; and (d) the epileptic type, characterized by hypersensitivity, selfishness, and cruelty. As Rosanoff himself states, these distinctions are not sharply drawn in normal human beings. Like all type theories, they apply primarily to relatively extreme cases.

The psychoanalyst Jung has described two opposed types of personality or temperament by the terms *introversion* and *extroversion*. The introverted individual lives in a subjective world, whereas the extrovert prefers the outer or objective world. The introvert is the day-dreamer, or perhaps the poet or mystic; the extrovert is the " practical " man of affairs, the inventor, business man, or statesman. A list of introverted traits compiled by Freyd (13) includes, among others, the following: self-consciousness, hyper-sensitivity, moodiness, hesitancy in making decisions, tendency towards introspection, self-depreciation as regards abilities, habits of working by fits and starts, and reticence. The corresponding extroverted traits would be the opposites of these. The two tendencies are found in both normal and abnormal people.

Social Motives

In the first part of this chapter attention was called to the social aspects of human motives. In a subsequent section of the chapter it was further disclosed that human emotional responses, as well as stimuli, are determined largely by social influences. The two phases of human nature, namely the biological and the social, were found to be reflected in all human motives.

Our present and final problem is to analyze certain human motives in which the social factor predominates. That this is actually if not apparently the determining factor in many cases of human motivation has been repeatedly pointed out by a number of contemporary psychologists. Thus, during a charge on a battlefield more courage is required for a soldier to break ranks and flee to the rear than to " carry on " with his comrades. Again, it is not stretching the point unduly to say that fashions prevail in art, literature, and science just as they do in clothes and social etiquette. The standards are merely known by a more dignified term than fashion. While in the realm of music the standards of harmony are determined partly by the structure and mechanism of the ear, custom has not hesitated to violate these standards; so that frequently the discords of one generation become the accepted harmonies of another. The same can be said of color combinations. Classic art is based upon physiological principles; it employs such color contrasts, justified by the mechanisms of the retina, as red and green, blue and yellow, black and white. But let custom sanction such a violation of these principles, for instance red upon a purple background, and it becomes accepted as aesthetically pleasing. In science, government, and ethics, standards and modes of thinking develop and have their day. No intelligent individual could argue that they are determined by purely rational considerations. Everything considered, human nature itself is largely a product of society.

The Concept of Social Consciousness. One of the first writers to emphasize man's dependence upon his fellows for his thoughts, emotions, and modes of conduct was the sociologist Cooley (10). This fact Cooley formulated in terms of *social consciousness*, or the view that the consciousness of an individual is the consciousness of the various social groups to which he belongs. For example, consider the college freshman whose previous life has been spent in a small town far removed from a college atmosphere. His existence has been bound up in a number of overlapping groups or circles — his family, his church group, his high school group, his circle of intimate friends. These groups have given him his personal habits, mannerisms, taste in clothing, intellectual interests, religious and moral convictions — in short, the elements of his personality and character. Of course there may have been conflicts among the groups — as when his friends began the practice of surreptitious smoking. Cooley would say that individuality is possible only when group standards are in conflict. On leaving his home town to enter college, the prospective freshman is suddenly torn from his established groups, and of course homesickness is the inevitable result. His only sources of relief are letters, the home town newspaper, and his memories. Greater social and educational opportunities are awaiting him, but the process of transferring from one set of social groups to another is laborious and painful. In one word, he is " green." It goes without saying that the new groups into which he must fit himself are in many instances radically opposed to the old. But in the course of his four years at college the transition is made; and at the end of that period he is as reluctant to return home as he was originally to leave.

Of course many factors are discoverable in social motivation not provided for in our illustration. Many people avoid contact with actual, existing groups, preferring to live in fictitious groups. Indeed, many people seem to enjoy phantasy-building or day-dreaming. It will be noticed that day-dreams are highly socialized, and that the individual who indulges in them invariably enjoys in imagination a degree of prestige not accorded him by his real associates. Each individual is the hero of his own day-dreams. Cooley merely insists that all normal consciousness bears the imprint of the socializing process. A person may live entirely in the past, finding solace in memories of by-gone social standing and glory; or perhaps he prefers the future, and dreams of the time when his greatness will be accorded the recognition it deserves. So far as human motivation is concerned, Cooley has stressed the point that all normal human beings are motivated by the desire for *recognition.*

The Prestige Motive. A further analysis of this desire for recognition discloses the fact that it prompts each human being to assure himself of his superiority in some form over other human beings. In other words, all social motives reflect the fundamental *prestige* motive. Of the various specific social motives, the one most commonly manifested is the desire for notice or attention. Between the two evils of being utterly ignored or of being disparaged the latter is by all odds the lesser. The notice that one receives from his fellows is frequently a mere formal greeting, but even in this case its prestige implications are obvious. The pleasure which the greeting arouses in the individual recognized is heightened just to the extent that it issues from a worthy or estimable person — from a person capable of bestowing prestige. The servant is thrilled at some sign of recognition from his master, and immediately lords it over other servants less deserving of notice. To kiss the garment of a celebrity is an assertion of superiority as well as a token of subserviency. The same psychological effect is produced when one is recognized by a member of his own social group, for the recognition is accorded by one of a chosen or superior circle. While certain people boast of the fact that their circle of acquaintances is large, their boasting reveals anything but a democratic spirit.

When the desire for recognition takes a more active form than the desire to attract notice its underlying prestige motive becomes all the more apparent. Consider the instance mentioned in the introductory portion of this chapter; namely, the desire to be complimented or praised. There is no denying the fact that a compliment always proclaims the superiority of the individual so favored. When a genius is informed about his brilliant achievements, or a girl told that she is beautiful, the compliments are pleasing because they are *distinctive*. On the other hand, nothing irritates an individual more than to be classed with other individuals. To be called *common* is to be grossly insulted. In fact, it is to escape the level of commonness that most of our social efforts are directed. The social climber has his prototype in all classes of human beings; in some way or another all human beings are social climbers. The prestige motive is dignified by such terms as self-respect and ambition, but its nature is none the less in evidence.

The Inferiority Complex. The Viennese psychiatrist and psychoanalyst, Alfred Adler, has formulated a theory which explains behavior in terms of defeated or baffled prestige motives (1, 2). Adler was interested in the neurotic constitution — that is, in the characteristic symptoms displayed by patients afflicted with nervous or mental diseases. According to his statement, all such patients suffer, or originally suffered, from profound feelings or convictions of their own inferiority; and their attempts to escape from, or compensate for, these feelings gave rise to their neurotic symptoms. While Adler's primary concern was with abnormal motivation, his theory is equally adapted to explain normal human behavior. We have already pointed out the impossibility of distinguishing sharply between the two. In brief, Adler contends that all emotional complexes can be resolved into a general *inferiority* complex.

If Adler's observations are correct, neurotic patients are physically defective. They have weak eyes, hearts, or lungs; they are deformed, possibly just enough to handicap them socially; or perhaps they are afflicted with stammering or stuttering. This contention is significant, for Adler believes that the patient's abnormal nervous and mental symptoms are the physiological effects of his consciousness of physical inferiority.

We shall first examine the immediate effects of the feeling of inferiority, and then study the methods by which the individual obsessed by this feeling endeavors unconsciously to escape from it. Since the physical defects from which it springs as a rule go back to early childhood we should note the early stages of such pernicious influences. A child physically handicapped is forced to realize that he cannot compete successfully with his normal playmates. Through no fault of his own he is the loser or slacker in competitive games and sports. Moreover, he is the target for the thoughtless ridicule of his associates, and among other indignities, likely as not, he is given a nickname inspired by his deformity or weakness. As the result of all this he is profoundly unhappy. He becomes morbidly hypersensitive, distrustful, jealous, and envious. So far as he is concerned, the happiness of childhood is fiction and myth.

All of this tends to make him an *unsocial* human being, hence an abnormal one. By a logical and natural process, the traits just enumerated develop into vindictiveness and cruelty. Adler's theory bears out the statement frequently made that " catty " and hypercritical people are themselves unusually sensitive to personal criticism. Whether this holds or not the neurotic patient, according to Adler, is selfish and, when permitted to be, domineering. And it is but a step from these symptoms to others more serious in character. Jealousy and suspicion appear and prepare the way for delusions and hallucinations. Obsessions and fears become fixed in the patient. In extreme cases insanity is the final outcome.

The methods by which an individual convinced of his own inferiority endeavors to escape from the depression which it entails are called by Adler and other psychoanalysts *psychic* compensations. To illustrate, the domineering attitude mentioned above is an indirect effect of the inferiority feeling, or a compensation. Adler interprets this trait as an unconscious expression of the desire for superiority. The mark of superiority is authority and prestige, made known by the superior individual's ability to command and control others. The neurotic person attains this end by imposing upon his nurse and members of his family, or upon such playmates as happen to be weaker than he is. In other words he becomes the bully. His prototype is found in the typical factory " straw-boss," who, having a slight amount of authority bestowed upon him, proceeds to use it to the utmost. Thus Adler again substantiates a popular belief by pointing out that bullies and " hard-boiled " individuals are at heart cowards and weaklings. While it is unsafe to generalize too freely about the traits of human nature, Adler believes that his clinical evidence supports his theory.

In the examples of compensation just mentioned the individual escapes from his feeling of inferiority by the simple device of assuming superiority. Of course he does this unconsciously, in the sense that he is not aware of his own motives. Numerous instances of this method of compensating abound in both normal and abnormal motivation. The individual who has amassed a fortune by squeezing money out of others compensates by contributing generously to churches and other worthy institutions. This appeases his conscience and enables him to feel virtuous. Again, the mediocre student finds solace in the fact that he is not a " grind." Even if he does not make good grades, he is superior socially; and of course social superiority is the only kind really worth while. Curiously enough the " grind " himself, in all likelihood, is compensating by an identical method; he is interested in the " higher " things of life, and is really inferior in one particular respect. An interesting and common manifestation of this attitude is found in the way in which students account for their good and poor grades respectively: they " make " good grades, but the instructor " gives " them the poor grades. Doubtless the principle of compensating for inferiority by assuming superiority can be easily over-worked, but it seems applicable nevertheless to numerous acts of everyday behavior.

The terms *sublimation* and *transference* express methods of compensation which are recognized by Adler and by most psychoanalysts. Without attempting to analyze these terms in detail we may note that they involve the principle of conditioned responses. The classic example of the psychoanalysts is that of love which for some reason does not find a normal outlet. When so repressed it can be centered upon pets, novels, poetry, moving-pictures, gossip and scandal. Undoubtedly, many people derive a vicarious satisfaction of their sentimental emotions from such sources. Other people have imaginary love affairs with celebrated characters, especially moving-picture actors. Repressed impulses which are redirected upon socially accepted situations are said to be *sublimated;* those which are redirected from one definite object to another are *transferred*. While these facts are explained by the psychoanalysts in mysterious and metaphysical terms they are patently instances of substitute stimuli.

They are actually accounted for by the principle of conditioned responses. Adler differs from other psychoanalysts in viewing sublimations and transferences as expressions of the inferiority complex. As he would say, even love reflects the prestige motive, since the ideal lover is invariably *superior.*

The Motive of Doing Things for Their Own Sake. Several writers are in full sympathy with the popular view that an interest in *accomplishment* is very often the determining motive in conduct. The sociologist Veblen has stressed this view in his book, *The Instinct of Workmanship.* As his title suggests, he holds that the artistic impulse, or the desire to do things and to do them well, is a fundamental inborn human trait. And Woodworth (28) summarizes his discussion of the topic in the following statement: ". . . almost any object, almost any act, and particularly almost any process or change in objects that can be directed by one's own activity towards some definite end, is interesting on its own account, and furnishes its own drive, once it is fairly initiated."[10]   Whether it is called art for art's sake, the creative impulse, or something else the existence of the trait in question is quite generally recognized.

Before accepting this motive too unreservedly, however, we should examine some of its implications and test some of its applications. For one thing, it scarcely suffices to explain the creation of art forms. In painting, for instance, the artist observes the rules of color combinations and of composition. The juxtaposition of complementary colors is pleasing because it satisfies certain physiological demands in the retina of the eye. And composition includes the principles of balance and proportion, both of which make a direct appeal to our muscles. Moreover, it is reasonable to

[10] *Op. cit.,* p. 202.

suppose that the artist is interested in the theme which his picture expresses. If our analysis is correct, many motives and not merely a desire-to-create-something keep the artist at his task. It seems probable, too, that his joy when he inspects the completed task is due to several factors. The picture may impress him as better than his previous pictures, hence he is pleased at his progress; and he may be relieved because his task has been slightly irksome. In other words the motive of doing things for their own sake, like the "instinct" of self-preservation, is more complex than its name suggests.

It is also possible that this motive is socialized to a greater degree than is ordinarily assumed. Granting its existence in the artist, we may wonder if it would be effective without a social background. While he may genuinely shun publicity and abhor popular fame, the artist nevertheless expects his picture to be seen and appreciated by some individual or group of individuals. Again we must avoid hasty generalization, but we may well believe that the number of pictures that are painted and books that are written would be substantially reduced if they were doomed to total and permanent obscurity.

On the other hand, accomplishment for its own sake seems to be probable on physiological grounds just to the extent that the activity involved is relatively simple. In one sense of the term, muscular exercise is indulged in for its own sake. By the same token, people see, hear, and touch things for no reason save that the active functioning of the receptors is spontaneous. Such activities are most adequately explained in terms of physiological metabolism; when anabolism exceeds catabolism spontaneous activity is the direct physiological result; or in plainer language, an excess of energy means "pep," with its resulting spontaneous activity.

The Mutual Relationship Between Biological and Social Motives. In concluding our account of motivation we should state explicitly that no sharp distinctions exist between biological and social human motives. In any concrete activity, say the act of eating, the two are blended so intimately that they can be separated only for purposes of scientific analysis. All human physiological drives and emotions are socialized, and conversely, all social motives are ultimately biological. The first statement has been sufficiently explained throughout our discussion. The second becomes evident when we realize that social motives provide for the welfare of the organism in which they are manifested. Individual superiority is biologically useful, hence the prestige motive prompts the individual to make the adjustments necessary for his welfare. The biological significance of social customs is illustrated by the fact that in general they provide for the satisfaction of physical wants. The perfect host is indeed the one who makes his guest comfortable. It is true that fashion frequently dictates the wearing of uncomfortable shoes, but taken by and large, social custom sanctions cleanliness, physical well-being, and personal comfort.

References

1. ADLER, ALFRED. A Study of Organ Inferiority and its Psychical Compensation. Nervous and Mental Disease Monograph, 1917, 24.
2. —— The Neurotic Constitution, 1917.
3. ALLPORT, FLOYD HENRY. Social Psychology, 1924.
4. BERMAN, LOUIS. The Glands Regulating Personality, 1924.
5. BERNARD, L. L. Instinct: A Study in Social Psychology, 1924.
6. BRIDGES, J. W. Theories of Temperament. Psychological Review, 1923, 30, 36–44.
7. BRUNSWICK, DAVID. The Effects of Emotional Stimuli on the Gastro-intestinal Tone. Journal of Comparative Psychology, 1924, 4, 19–79, 225–287.

8. CANNON, WALTER B. Bodily Changes in Pain, Hunger, Fear and Rage, 1915.

9. CARLSON, A. J. The Control of Hunger in Health and Disease, 1917.

10. COOLEY, C. H. Human Nature and the Social Order, 1902.

11. CRILE, GEORGE W. The Origin and Nature of the Emotions, 1915.

12. FELEKY, A. M. The Expression of Emotions. Psychological Review, 1914, 21, 33–41.

13. FREYD, MAX. Introverts and Extroverts. Psychological Review, 1924, 31, 74–87.

14. HULL, CLARK L., AND LUGOFF, L. S. Complex Signs in Diagnostic Free Association. Journal of Experimental Psychology, 1921, 4, 111–136.

15. HUNTER, WALTER S. General Psychology, Revised Edition, 1923.

16. KEMPF, E. J. The Autonomic Functions and the Personality. Nervous and Mental Disease Monograph, 1918, 28.

17. LANDIS, CARNEY. Studies of Emotional Reactions. II. General Behavior and Facial Expression. Journal of Comparative Psychology, 1924, 4, 447–509.

18. LANGFELD, H. S. The Judgment of Emotions from Facial Expressions. Journal of Abnormal Psychology, 1918–19, 13, 172–184.

19. —— Judgments of Facial Expression and Suggestion. Psychological Review, 1918, 25, 488–494.

20. MARSTON, WILLIAM M. Systolic Blood Pressure Symptoms of Deception. Journal of Experimental Psychology, 1917, 2, 117–163.

21. MORRISON, BEULAH MAY. A Study of the Major Emotions in Persons of Defective Intelligence. University of California Publications, 1924, 3, 73–145.

22. MOSS, FRED A. Study of Animal Drives. Journal of Experimental Psychology, 1924, 7, 165–185.

23. ROSANOFF, A. J. A Theory of Personality Based Mainly on Psychiatric Experience. Psychological Bulletin, 1920, 17, 281–299.

24. RUCKMICK, C. A. A Preliminary Study of the Emotions. Psychological Monographs, 1921, 30, 30–35.

25. SIMMONS, RIETTA. The Relative Effectiveness of Certain In-

centives in Animal Learning. Comparative Psychology Monographs, 1924, 2, Serial No. 7.
26. SMITH, W. WHATELY. The Measurement of Emotion, 1922.
27. WADA, TOMI. An Experimental Study of Hunger in its Relation to Activity. Archives of Psychology, 1922, No. 57, 1–65.
28. WOODWORTH, R. S. Dynamic Psychology, 1918.
29. —— Psychology: A Study of Mental Life, 1921.

CHAPTER V

LEARNING BEHAVIOR

In the foregoing chapters various characteristics of human and animal behavior have been analyzed and described in terms of the stimulus-response program. Food getting, home building, manifesting anger, seeking approval and many other activities were shown to be reducible to the functioning of stimulus-response mechanisms. Some of these mechanisms, such as the anger-reactions of the infant when hampered in its movements, were found to be constituent parts of the new-born baby's repertoire of reactions. Others, such as the dog's salivary response to an auditory stimulus or the child's conditioned fear-response at the sight of a furry animal, were found to be dependent on the effects of previous stimulation to which the organism had been subjected. In ordinary speech we should say the dog has learned to regard the auditory stimulus in question as the signal for food, or that the baby has learned to be afraid of the rabbit. In thus saying the matter was *learned* we are stressing the fact that its essential characteristics are due to *changes* wrought by experience. In this sense learning is opposed to native or inborn behavior. Viewed from this angle, the popular adage " live and learn " emphasizes an important psychological fact; namely, that learning is bound up with having experience. To live means to have experiences. An inanimate object or a dead animal can have no experiences. This is the general import of the popular adage: to live means to react and to react means to learn.

In other words earlier behavior may influence later behavior. While this was incidentally brought out in the earlier chapters, it is of such tremendous importance for an adequate understanding of behavior that it will be discussed in systematic and somewhat detailed fashion in this chapter.

Scope of the Problem of Learning. Our specific task then is to study the influence of learning on behavior. Provisionally, learning may be defined as the modification of later behavior by earlier behavior. As has just been suggested, what we learn depends on the kinds of reaction we make or the kinds of experience we have. Some of our reactions, relatively speaking, may take place apart from experience and some as a result of it. The earlier chapters to a certain extent were concerned with an analysis of the former kinds of reaction. In the present chapter we shall be occupied more with the latter kinds of reaction. Both are essential for a complete description of behavior. At any one time the behavior of an organism is dependent on the following four factors:

(1) The nature of its bodily equipment
(2) The nature of the stimulus or situation
(3) The nature of the existing physiological condition
(4) The nature and influence of its previous experience

In order to get a clear grasp of the bearing of the previous chapters on the present problem, it will be advisable to discuss each of these factors separately.

(1) That our bodily equipment largely determines our reactions is readily illustrated by the fact that the reactions of the blind and lame differ from those with intact receptor and effector systems. As has been stressed in previous chapters, the dog's reactions differ from the bird's because of differences in inherited equipment. In other words the dog does not fly, not so much because he lacks the instinct or desire for flight, but because of the absence of wings. In

o

the same way we account for the bird's failure to bark on the basis of its morphological equipment. The dwarf reacts to the lurch of the trolley car by grabbing the seat handle, while the tall man reacts to the same situation by taking hold of the suspended strap. Other things being equal, the greater the similarity of physical endowment the greater the similarity of behavior. That is why, taken by and large, the behavior of a horse is more like that of a cow than it is like that of a frog. From this point of view it is evident why so much attention is paid to matters of bodily structure in the solution of psychological problems.

(2) As we explained at length in Chapter III, variations in the nature of the stimuli and situations to which the organism is subjected make for variations in response. A baby smiles at the sight of the rattle and cries as the bright light is turned out. Pat a dog on the head playfully and his tail wags: scold him and his tail behaves otherwise. As stimuli change, behavior changes and, conversely, as behavior changes, stimuli change. Life is an on-going process; stimulus A provokes response B; response B causes stimulus C to loom up; stimulus C precipitates response D, and so on. The kinds of stimuli we meet determine the kinds of reactions we make.

(3) It has already been pointed out that there are internal as well as external stimuli. A stomach ache is an example of an internal stimulus. That such internal stimuli influence behavior requires no extended argument. It should be kept in mind, though, that in addition to the kind of internal stimulus just mentioned, we have internal changes of a more diffuse sort that play tremendous rôles in determining behavior. A man may fail to respond to a sudden cry of " Fire! " not because he is deaf (influence of bodily equipment) or because the sound was too feeble to be heard (influence of the stimulus), but because he is too exhausted to

respond. Now weakness or exhaustion is due to the physiological condition of the individual. There are several changes in physiological status for which we have names in popular speech, such as hunger, thirst, fatigue, sleep, intoxication, and illness. It will be recalled that emotions are also related to physiological activities and that they too function as determining factors in behavior.

(4) A little reflection will show that there is still a fourth phase to consider in the analysis of behavior. An infant or a foreigner will fail to react comprehendingly to the cry of " Fire! " not necessarily because of the influence of any of the three factors just enumerated, but because of the absence of previous experience with the word. Experience determines behavior just as bodily equipment, stimuli, and physiological conditions do. It does so because the experience has brought about a change in the organism. The psychology of learning may be regarded as a study of the nature of this factor. To ask how we learn is to ask how the subsequent behavior of an individual comes to be changed or modified as the result of an earlier experience.

Of course this fourfold analysis of the principal factors determining reactions is really an abstraction of factors that actually coöperate and mutually influence each other. Except in a theoretic sense there is no such thing as one of them functioning without the others. This was implied in the statement that at *any one time* our reactions are dependent on these four factors. It is only in an abstract way that we can separate the factor of learning from the other three. From the instant of birth, if not before, the behavior of the organism is being conjointly influenced by all of them. The very first breath a baby draws is the resultant of its respiratory equipment, the stimulus of the air, its physiological condition and possibly its intra-uterine experience. The same is true of its first cry and the other reactions it manifests at birth. Some of these movements were made before the infant was born — spasmodic movements of the limbs — and to the extent that such movements are slightly modified in the way of being stronger as a result of the previous experience, we might maintain that they have been modified in the sense of having become different "through experience." Yet we should hardly say that these reactions were learned without doing violence to the meaning of the word. Learning refers to changes in inborn reactions, involving the organism as a whole, which are due to the modifying effect of the organism's experience.

It is difficult to draw a sharp and clear-cut line of demarcation between changes of the learned variety and of the non-learned. The distinction can readily be made when extreme cases are selected, but not when transitional cases are chosen. This is very much like endeavoring to differentiate between night and day in a formal definition. When it is dark outside, it is night, and when it is light outside, it is day. But what about twilight? For some purposes, such as kicking a football, it might be regarded as day; while for others, such as reading fine print, it is already night. Definitions must be pragmatic. In this sense, we can proceed to clarify our definition of learning. Speaking the word "meat" is a learned reaction, since it calls for a modification of the child's original vocal reactions as a result of its environmental experience. Furthermore this verbal acquisition involved the activity of the body as a whole to the extent of demanding, at the very least, changes in the tonicity of the striped musculature. On the contrary, although the child cannot digest meat at birth and yet succeeds in doing so a few years later, such a change in reaction is not of the *learned* variety. And this despite the fact that in popular speech we say the child has "*learned* to digest meat." Such a change is merely due to the spontaneous maturation of the digestive organs, and while the previous eating experience plays some part in influencing them, the organism as a whole does not control the process as such. Changes of this type belong more to the science of physiology than to psychology.

What Do We Learn? It should be clear that the term *learning* is a very broad one. It covers the multitude of acts, thoughts, meanings and habits the individual acquires in the course of a lifetime. We learn to dance, to manipulate tools, catch a ball, plant seeds, fire a gun, drive an automobile, and other acts of skill. We learn our native tongue or acquire language habits: to understand the meaning of words, to speak them, to write them, to read them, to arouse meaning in others by gestures and facial expression, and to understand the meaning of such gestures and expressions when stimulated by them. We learn the nature and properties of objects that surround us — the hardness of rocks, the softness of the turf, the painfulness of fire, the sweetness of candy, and the tonality of musical instruments. These are isolated instances of the content of learned behavior.

Learning and Memory. A perusal of the foregoing list of examples of learning shows that any acquired modification of behavior, as opposed to modification due to physiological maturation and growth, is to be classified as learning. From this point of view learning is a broader term than memory as that word is employed in daily speech, although they are frequently used interchangeably and with a variety of meanings. A man may have a splendid memory and yet not be a learned man, while another may have a poor memory and still be rated as learned. Used in this way the word *memory* refers to the ability to reproduce material more or less in its original sequence, and the word learning refers to the profundity and breadth of ideational acquisitions. We memorize a speech, but learn a dance-step. A violin selection is played from memory, but a drop kick is not executed from memory. The individual executes it because he learned it, not because he memorized it. And yet all of these uses of the two terms have one thing in common: the effects of experience persist over an interval of time and become observable through the changes they introduce in the individual's repertoire of reactions. This persistence over an interval of time is spoken of as *retention,* while the production of that which is retained is referred to as *reinstatement,* or in the case of verbalized material, it is referred to as *recall.* In general, whenever retention is mediated by verbal symbols we speak of memory, otherwise of learning and remembering. Or to state it more accurately, we use the words " to learn " or " to remember " wherever we also employ the words " memory " or " to memorize." But the reverse does not hold true. We do not " memorize " how to operate an automobile, although we may " learn " and " remember " how to do so. Yet if such learning were facilitated and controlled by means of words or language symbols, we should speak of memorizing the operation, just as we speak of memorizing a musical composition. Psychologically, all such acquisitions, whether involving muscular skill or verbal controls, are phenomena of learning. The supreme importance of language in the life of man is responsible for its separate consideration under the caption of memory. Psychologically there is no sharp break between learning as such, and memory as such.

Learning Experiments. For almost fifty years psychologists all over the world have been engaged in experimental attacks on a multitude of problems dealing with various phases of the phenomena of learning. As is to be expected when dealing with such complex and difficult phenomena, the problems are by no means completely settled. The solution of one automatically raises others and improvements in experimental technique bring about revisions of earlier results. Some of these problems are of a more general, theoretic type, while others are of a more specific, practical type. Such a differentiation is largely a matter of descriptive convenience, like the distinction between pure and applied science. In actual practice, of course, we cannot say where pure science leaves off and application begins. Theory modifies practice and practice modifies theory. With the understanding that there is no actual antithesis between the theoretical and practical in scientific experimentation the subsequent discussion of that which at first sight appears to be wholly " theoretical " should not be irritating to the student who is solely interested in the " practical."

The Mechanism of Learning. Of learning experiments that at first sight appear to belong to the category of " theory," the most fundamental are those having to do with the *mechanism of learning*. They are concerned with the basic problem of how learning takes place or how humans learn or animals learn. Stated differently, what changes take place in our bodily constitution when we learn a new language, break a bad habit, or learn to fire a rifle? What determines which acts shall survive and which shall be eliminated as we indulge in both correct and incorrect moves during the process of learning something new?

Much of our insight into the nature of such changes has come from studying learning in animals where the details of the process in many respects can be subjected to more rigid control than when working with humans. This applies particularly to the control of such factors as diet, environment, and the time of experimentation. Furthermore, the many studies of learning in humans can be compared and contrasted with analogous studies in animals.

ANIMAL LEARNING

One of the favorite experimental animals in this work is the white rat. Its normal life span is about three years and as a consequence it matures rapidly and in this way lends itself to facile control. Incidentally, the further fact that it is a prolific animal makes the study of the possible inheritance of learning capacity more amenable to experimentation. In connection with our discussion of the mechanism of learning, it will be necessary to give a somewhat detailed review of some of the work done on this animal. An understanding of this work is essential to an understanding of existing views of the nature of the learning mechanism. In the course of our review of experiments on the white rat we shall find it advisable to consider some of the experimental work in which other animals were employed. This preliminary survey of learning experiments with animals will not only serve the purpose of rendering the problem of the mechanism of learning intelligible, but will at the same time give a better and deeper understanding of the nature of learning itself. In addition it will fortify our grasp of the scientific method employed by the psychologist in the analysis of his problems and in the technique he devises in solving them.

When endeavoring to determine the manner in which an animal learns, psychologists place the animal in a situation that necessitates a realignment of inherited behavior mechanisms before particular organic needs can be fulfilled. For a rat to nibble at and swallow a piece of food placed in front of it does not indicate any learned reaction. The food response is inherited — manifested by the new-born animal. In reacting to the food it is supplying one of its organic necessities. If the meat, instead of being placed in front of the rat, is concealed in a compartment of the cage that can be reached only by means of an indirect and devious path, the animal must first solve the problem of finding the correct pathway before the particular organic need — in this case hunger — can be satisfied. A study of the consequent behavior furnishes an opportunity of examining the way in which organisms solve their problems. Learning is evident wherever an old situation is handled in a new way or where a situation that could not be handled in the beginning is handled at the end. By arranging such situations and systematically recording the resulting behavior of the animal, psychologists have amassed a large body of information concerning the nature of learning reactions.

The Maze Experiment. The psychologist Watson (36) has furnished us with an excellent and instructive example of the way in which such reactions are built up.[1] He placed white rats in a specially constructed box known as a maze. As has already been mentioned,[2] and as is indicated in Figure 16, the maze consists of a series of tortuous runways along the floor of the box, formed by inserting vertical partitions, that communicate with each other. Some of them connect up in such a way that when followed they lead to a central compartment in which food is placed. Others radiating out of those are in the nature of blind alleys or culs-de-sac. So far as the rat is concerned, the problem-situation is comparable to that which might confront a famished man shoved into a vast house built like a modern department store, except that the various rooms are arranged in helter-skelter fashion. The efforts of the starving man to find his way to the kitchen would be analogous to the efforts of the rat to find its way to the food box. We shall revert to this analogy presently.

For the time being let us consider the behavior of the rat. When first introduced to the new situation the animal runs

[1] *Op. cit.*, pp. 206–219.　　　　[2] Page 142.

hither and thither, doubling on its tracks repeatedly, going in and out of blind alleys until chance directs it into the final runway that leads to the food box. The entire time required to secure the food is almost half an hour. In the process every part of the maze is traversed, and the total

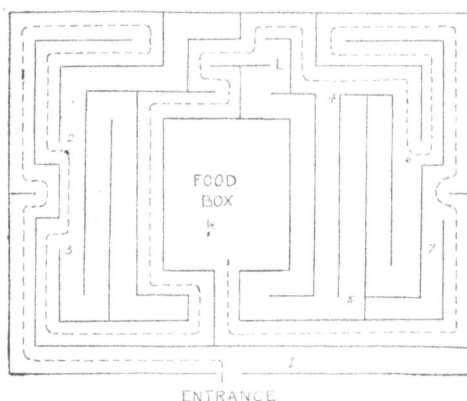

FIG. 16.— Diagram of the Hampton Court Maze. (After Watson.)
The true path to the food box is shown by the dotted line. Blind alleys are indicated by numbers. The letter L indicates an alley that leads to the food by a longer route. As designed for Watson's experiment with rats, the alleys were 4 inches wide and 4 inches high. All parts were made of wood 7/8 of an inch thick. The top of the maze was covered with wire netting. The maze as employed in this experiment was 5 feet wide and 7 feet long. This makes the distance from the entrance to the food box, indicated by the broken line, 40 feet long. For more detailed account see Watson (35).

distance covered by the rat may have been about 3600 feet, when the minimum distance from the entrance to the maze to the food compartment is but 40 feet. This enormous excess of movements together with the evidently accidental nature of the final entrance into the successful path indicates that the rat cannot be said to have *solved* the problem, if that term is intended to connote reasoned analysis. To ascertain whether the animal can profit at all from this experience, it is placed back into the beginning part of the maze on repeated occasions. If on these subsequent trials the time required to reach the food box and the distance traversed is reduced, the possibility of such profiting is demonstrated. As indicated in Figure 17, it has been found that

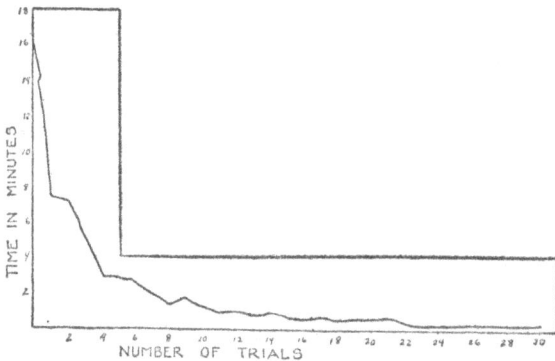

FIG. 17.— Learning curve showing the average time per trial for 19 normal rats. (After Watson.)

Note the slope of the curve indicating the gradual, as opposed to sudden, mastery of the maze. The flat stretch of the curve for the last five or six trials may be regarded as illustrating the approach to the physiological limit. In this case the physiological limit would be approximately 20 seconds for the 40 feet of the true path to the food box. For discussion of the physiological limit see section on *The Influence of Practice on Learning*.

after thirty such trials the rat will scamper along the appropriate alleys in approximately half a minute. That is, it will confine its movements to just those paths that will get it to the food as quickly as possible. It will limit itself to the 40 feet representing the shortest distance from the entrance to the feeding place. This reduction in time required and the distance covered came gradually in the course of the thirty trials. There was no precipitate reduction such as we find when we suddenly see into the principle of a problem in mathematics. In the sense that the rat finally responded to the problem-situation in an expeditious, efficient manner, it may be said to have learned the situation.

But how did it learn? That rational analysis on the part of the rat will not account for it has already been pointed out. Furthermore, the law of parsimony would render such an explanation odious to the scientist if a simpler mode of explanation were available. Before we can proceed with the latter, it is essential that we have a clear understanding of the details of the question. We want to know, in the first place, what particular sense organs or receptors were used by the rat in finding its way about. Did it see its way, smell its way, hear its way, or feel its way? Possibly several or all of these receptor mechanisms coöperated in the process. In the second place, we want to know by what means the incorrect responses — running into culs-de-sac, taking the longer of two alternative paths — were eliminated.

Watson undertook the task of first determining whether vision was essential to the learning by finding out whether rats could thread their way in the maze in darkness as well as in the light. The results of this test showed that absence of light did not interfere with the successful execution of the performance, the animals negotiating the maze as quickly in the dark as in the light. This did not prove that vision was unessential in *learning* the maze. To demonstrate the latter it is necessary to place untrained rats in an unilluminated maze and record the resulting behavior. If they succeed in mastering the pathways as quickly and effectively as those trained in the light, the case for the dispensability of vision will be strengthened. Actual tests showed that such untrained rats succeeded in learning the maze in normal time, despite the fact that they were deprived of visual clues. However, the criticism might be made that the darkness was not absolute and that faint visual stimulation may have guided the rats. To forestall this objection Watson went one step further and repeated his experiment with two groups of rats whose eyes had been excised by means of a surgical operation. One of these groups had been trained in the maze and the other group had never been subjected to the maze situation. According to the experimenter (36), "the trained group of blind rats ran the maze with only a slight loss in efficiency which might have been predicted when we recall the fact that after the animals had been operated on, they were not again tested in the maze until 40 days had elapsed; consequently there was a slight loss of retention."[3] He found further that the wholly untrained but blinded rat learned to run the maze in the standard time. In this way he demonstrated that the eyes are not needed at all, either in the establishment of the learned performance or in regulating its execution after it is learned.

By dissecting out the olfactory bulb Watson found that the resulting loss of olfactory impulses did not militate against the learning, the behavior being in every way like that of the normal rats. They too succeeded in the dark maze as well as in the light. With two receptor mechanisms disposed of the matter was not yet settled. It might be that the animals learned as a result of auditory stimulations reproduced by the faint sounds made when their feet came into contact with the floor of the maze — that they learned to locate different parts of the enclosure by slight differences in sound, just as we can tell whether a man is walking on a boardwalk or a stone pavement. This possibility was dismissed when it was found that animals whose hearing mech-

[3] *Op. cit.*, pp. 213-214.

anism had been surgically interfered with accomplished the task of mastering the maze in normal time.

As is well known, the rat possesses rather prominent " feelers " or vibrissae, as they are called. Among other things it remained to determine the part played by these vibrissae in learning. Cutting them off failed to make any difference in the performance of those rats which had previously been trained (provided they were given a few days in which to recover from the effects of the operation), nor did it prevent untrained rats from responding to the training in the standard way. To ascertain whether the animals were aided either by temperature variations or by air currents within the maze, Watson deliberately modified the temperature and shifted the air circulation without producing any change in the rats' ability to run the course. He also ruled out the possibility of direct contact by anaesthetizing the snout and bottom of the feet. Such disturbances of contact sensitivity failed to produce a retardation, diminution of time, or other observable interference of maze learning ability.

The only relevant remaining system of receptors is that of the proprioceptive system, in particular, the kinaesthetic receptors of the kinaesthetic system. These receptors, it will be recalled, are found embedded in the muscle tissue and in the tendons as well as on the joint surfaces. Whenever movement takes place they are automatically stimulated. Movement is controlled and perceived (apart from vision) largely through such stimulation. Having failed to account for the rat's maze learning on the basis of vision, smell, hearing, the various forms of contact and so forth, Watson concluded that the learning proceeded by means of this one remaining receptor system.

To conclude that the rat learns to run a maze by means of its kinaesthetic apparatus is a legitimate inference reached by the logical process of elimination. But it is not wholly conclusive. It is in the nature of negative proof. An ingenious modification of his apparatus enabled Watson to render the requisite positive proof of the essentially kinaesthetic nature of the maze behavior. He constructed a maze that could be adjusted in such a way that the length of the different parts could be altered without changing the general relation of the parts to each other. In this way he could train one group of rats in a maze that had short pathways and another group in a similar maze that had long pathways. If the animal depends primarily on its kinaesthetic system for guidance through the maze, then any alteration in the dimensions of the maze should interfere with the execution of habits established in a maze of different size. Reasoning in this way, Watson trained one group of animals in the shortened form and after the learning was completed he placed them in the maze for whose dimensions they presumably had no kinaesthetic clues developed. His expectations were realized: those rats which had been trained in the shortened form tried to make the turns too soon when placed in the lengthened form, while those which had been trained in the lengthened form, over-ran the alleys when placed in the shortened type of maze. The kinaesthetic impulses or proprioceptive stimuli were thus demonstrated to function as the principle guides in this particular experiment.

In connection with this phase of his conclusion Watson states that " one objection has been raised to the resolving of the maze habit process into the functioning of a serially chained kinaesthetic system. It may be stated as follows: in man and in animals kinaesthetic arcs function in perfect habits until some disturbance occurs, *i.e.*, until rival impulses coming in over other receptors become sufficiently strong to produce inhibition of the customary movements.

It is held that a similar situation exists in the case of the rat in the maze. The animal may be automatically traversing the maze at a high rate of speed when suddenly a loud noise, a strange odor, or an intense itching occurs. The chain of movements is broken. How does the automaticity become reëstablished? The human being under similar circumstances — when momentarily lost while executing a purely automatic habit — remains unoriented until supplementary distance sense data are at hand; e.g., he glances at the score if playing a piece of music. These reactions at hand, the reign of kinaesthetic arcs is reëstablished and the automatic character of the acts again becomes apparent. But in the case of the rat do distance sense data function in this way? We conclude, on the basis of a large amount of experimental work, that automaticity is reëstablished for the rat solely from the distinctive kinaesthetic impulses which function exactly as do the visual impulses in the case just stated for man. If the trained rat is put down in a part of the maze other than the entrance, he runs at first randomly. He may wander about, turn round and round in the alleys, but suddenly he darts off and traverses the remainder of the maze in the usual automatic way. We hold that during the period of random activity the animal passed over what we may call a 'kinaesthetic unit,' thereby arousing a certain sequence of kinaesthetic impulses which could not be aroused in any other part of the maze. This distinctive group of impulses is sufficient to reëstablish automaticity." [4]

Some Further Considerations of the Maze Problems. In the rather extended description of the experimental procedure resorted to by Watson we have a good illustration of the way in which the psychologist attacks his problems. On the basis of the results obtained it is clear that maze learn-

[4] *Op. cit.,* pp. 217–218.

ing in the rat is largely a matter of kinaesthetic integration. The question of the function of the other receptors might be raised. Of what use are eyes, ears, vibrissae, if the animal can learn as effectively without them? Or does the finding of Watson apply exclusively to the maze situation? It is interesting to note that both Vincent (32, 33) and Carr (3) have shown that Watson's results are not to be regarded as having universal application. The former investigator demonstrated by means of appropriate modifications of the maze conditions that contact, olfactory, and visual receptors can be made to play an effective part in the learning. Carr has verified and amplified Vincent's results to the extent of showing that there are numerous individual differences in the degree to which rats are affected by the loss of given receptors. He also showed maze learning to be dependent upon a variety of factors that at first sight might appear to be unrelated to such learning. For example, the position of the experimenter during the trials, rotating the maze itself, changing the position of the cage in which the rats were kept between trials were all shown to influence maze mastery. His data also indicate that with respect to some of these factors loss of vision is advantageous in the learning, while it is a handicap in other respects.

Such findings do not necessarily imply a flat contradiction of Watson's results. They indicate rather that care should be exercised in the interpretation of the work of Watson as referring to the conditions prevalent during his experiment and to the particular animals he employed. Carr's investigation and Vincent's results are not a refutation of the earlier findings that the fundamental receptor system involved in maze learning is the kinaesthetic. As Carr points out: " The work of Watson, Bogardus and Henke, Vincent, *et al.* has shown that the white rat learns the standard type of maze primarily in tactual and kinaesthetic terms, that during the learning the control is gradually transferred from contact to kinaesthetic, and that after the problem is thoroughly mastered the act is to be regarded as a kinaesthetic-motor coördination with an occasional reliance upon contact in time of emergency." [5]

While we have no radical refutation of Watson's essential findings, we must understand his work to mean that under his experimental conditions, loss of exteroceptive cues made for no measurable handicap in the rat's maze learning ability. This is not the same thing as saying that the rat does not use them when they are present. It would be rash to conclude even on the basis of Watson's experiment considered separately that eyes, ears, vibrissae, and other exteroceptors are of no functional significance to the rat when confronted with the maze problem. All we are justified in concluding is that so far as maze learning under his experimental situation was concerned, their *loss* was not a serious handicap. An illustration may possibly be of service in clarifying this point. Let us assume that we have a shelf of books containing volumes of different types of bindings. This shelf represents our working library — we have been using these books for years and are thoroughly familiar with their location. We then have a friend measure the speed with which we can take out any book he names. In this way we take out ten books, always replacing the one we have removed after the time has been taken. This will give us the average time of location and removal of a book. Now if this test should be conducted in daylight, then repeated when the room is pitch black and the average time in both instances is found to be the same, the conclusion that vision plays no part in the test conducted in daylight would be unjustified. Such a test merely demonstrates that when confronted with the necessity of dispensing with vision

[5] *Op. cit.,* p. 259.

we can get along by means of the tactual and kinaesthetic receptors without demonstrable handicap.

The Problem Box Experiment. While much information concerning the learning ability of animals has been accumulated by the use of various types of maze with different species of animals (including man), much additional and supplementary information has been obtained by means of other experimental devices. One of these that has been particularly fertile in its results is known as the problem box experiment (Fig. 18). This experimental method, introduced into animal psychology by Thorndike, has also been tried out on a diversity of animals, including such species as birds, rats, cats, dogs, raccoons, and monkeys. While the technique differs, depending on the animal species, its essential principle is that of placing the animal in a problem-situation that can be solved by means of manipulating some mechanical locking device. A hungry animal is locked inside a cage-like box and food is placed on the outside in sight of the animal, or else the food is placed inside and the animal outside. In order to get the food it is necessary for the animal to " solve " the locking device. The solution may involve pulling a string attached to a latch, opening a spring door by tearing off strips of paper holding it in place, turning a button, locating an opening at a given part of the box by removing a pile of sawdust concealing it, and so forth. Having secured the food, the animal is put back on repeated occasions to see what effect the previous experience will have on its later behavior. Like the maze experiment it is intended to reveal the extent to which the animal can profit by experience. In terms of our previous analogy of the starving man lost in a department store, the situation is similar to the experience that would be his, if upon reaching the restaurant, he should find the door bolted with a combination lock. Or else we might compare it to the behavior of a person engaged in trying to solve a mechanical puzzle.

When confined in the problem box the animal, such as a cat, reacts to that situation by attacking the different features of the enclosure in an impulsive, unsystematic, try-try-again manner. It scratches, claws, bites, pushes, tugs now at this slat and now at that, shifting from one wall to the next until eventually as a result of this *trial and error* behavior the correct reaction is made and the food secured. Upon successive trials the animal gradually dispenses with the useless movements until, finally, its reaction is limited to the part of the box regulating the locking device and its movements are limited to those necessary for securing release. The number of trials required for the animal to attain this degree of competence gives a measure of its learning ability. The behavior manifested in the process might be compared to that of the man trying to get into the restaurant when he bangs and pulls at its door, kicks it, turns the knob to the right and left, pushes and pulls it, until in the course of these random reactions he accidentally hits upon the precise combination of movements that results in the door swinging open.

The Three Basic Problems of Learning. Careful consideration of the behavior changes brought about by repeated maze or problem box experiences reveals three fundamental problems which have already been anticipated in our question concerning the mechanism of learning. It should be borne in mind that these problems are not limited to animal learning, but apply to human learning as well. However, their nature and their proposed solution can be more easily explained in terms of animal experimentation.

The first problem is to explain the nature of the driving force impelling the organism to indulge in learning activity. What is the mechanism of food seeking in the case of ani-

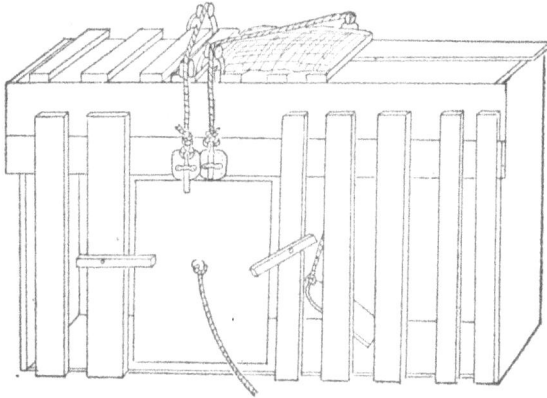

A

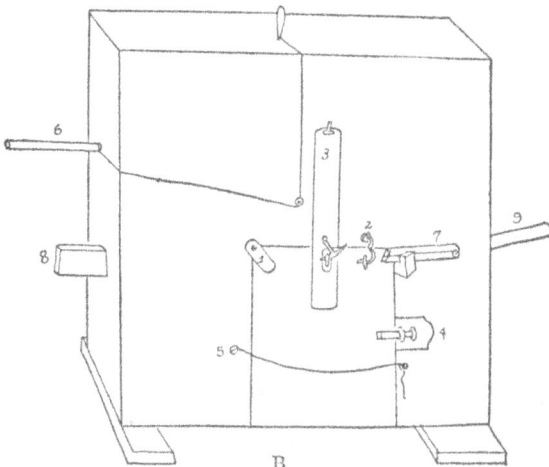

B

FIG. 18. — Two problem boxes employed in experiments on animal learning. The upper box has been used in experiments on rats and the lower one in experiments on monkeys. The sequence of operations required to open the latter box is indicated by the numbers.

mals confined in a maze? The second problem is to show how movements which bring the animal to the food are eventually combined into a definite, appropriate series of " correct " movements. The third problem, in some respects the obverse of the second, is to demonstrate how " incorrect," maladaptive, useless movements indulged in at first are finally eliminated.

A rather large body of controversial literature has accumulated in the endeavor to solve these problems. It will prove instructive to examine briefly some of the main points raised in this discussion. The problem involved is really far-reaching in its significance as will be seen in the subsequent consideration of the pleasure-pain theory. Since the purport of this and other theories is to explain the fundamental mechanisms of learning — both human and animal — they are usually referred to as theories of learning.[6]

THEORIES OF LEARNING

(1) **The Pleasure-Pain Theory.** One of the oldest and perhaps most frequently invoked explanations is the pleasure-pain theory. According to the proponents of this view, the pleasure or satisfaction that accompanies the attainment of a goal the organism is striving to reach causes all the acts that contribute to this attainment to be retained; while, on the contrary, all the acts that interfere with, retard, or inhibit such attainment are eliminated because of the pain or dissatisfaction they engender. In terms of our threefold view of the general problem of learning, the adherents of this theory would maintain that the desire for pleasure or satisfaction furnishes the motivation and that any act con-

[6] The writers are much indebted to the article by Kuo (15) for suggestions in the treatment of theories of learning. They are particularly grateful for his excellent summary of the principal theories and his bibliography.

tributing to this satisfaction will be retained, while any act frustrating this end will be eliminated. Such a theory has a superficial plausibility that possibly accounts for its rather widespread implicit popular acceptance. Ask a mother why she slaps little George for stealing a cookie and she will reply that the sting produced by the slap is unpleasant; and consequently, if on a subsequent occasion George is tempted to repeat his disobedience, the memory of the unpleasantness will cause him to refrain. In a similar fashion she will defend her course of action in whipping the family dog for snapping at the baby. In fact, our current penal philosophy is most often justified by an appeal to the deterrent influence exercised by the punitive measures sanctioned and executed by law.

Such a theory is essentially sound as a *description* of the facts, but a careful analysis will show that it is not an *explanation*. It does not tell us *how* pleasure as such and pain as such bring about their alleged effects. We want to know how the rat, for example, ceased to frequent blind alleys as the maze experience recurred. To say the rat came to perceive the blind alleys as responsible for the unpleasant delay in securing the food is an inadequate explanatory account. It fails to demonstrate how a state of consciousness such as unpleasantness comes to modify the series of neuromuscular mechanisms functioning in learning.

Such an explanation is comparable to the contention of the small boy who insisted that a locomotive moves because it " chugs." As a description of the phenomenon, the boy's statement is irreproachable. The locomotive does not go unless it is chugging, but this does not mean that the chugging causes it to go. Before we can accept this description as an explanation the manner in which the chugging produces the movement must be made clear. In the same way, although it is very true that a whipping is unpleasant to the dog, this does not mean that it is the unpleasantness which is effective in breaking him of his tendency to snap at the baby. Furthermore, this theory places too great a strain on our credulity when applied to animal learning. If the rat comes to eliminate a cul-de-sac because of its unpleasant consequences, we are forced to grant by implication that the animal not only sees the connection between the feeling and the blind alley which causes it, but actually remembers it. We have no evidence to support such inferences. To introduce material that so far as we know is applicable only to the mental life of man in order to account for the mental life of a rat is to be guilty of the crassest type of anthropomorphic reasoning. It is far safer to endeavor to reverse the process and explain the mental life of man in terms of established principles governing animal behavior, provided, of course, that such principles suffice to cover all of the known facts. This procedure is safer because it tends to diminish the number of unnecessary assumptions.

In addition to the designated objections to the pleasure-pain theory there is one other significant objection to it that merits attention. If, as a theory, it is intended to account for *all* the aspects of the learning process, then every separate phase of that process must be governed by it. This means that practically every retained act is retained because the organism is aware of the manner in which that act contributes to the resulting pleasure, and that practically every act is eliminated because it is either directly unpleasant, or indirectly so in that it conflicts with the final satisfaction. Now it is not difficult to demonstrate that innumerable acts are retained and eliminated under circumstances that fail to square with these requirements. In acts of skill, such as sewing, boxing, and operating a phonograph, we exhibit movements which at the time they were learned were not consciously appraised in terms of the relative satisfaction and dissatisfaction they contributed. In learning to play the violin, the learner is unable to state which position of the little finger of the hand that holds the bow is most desirable, so far as it influences the finished performance. Most of us are unable to describe the detailed movements that are made by the fingers in tying a bow-knot. The isolated movements are made automatically. Consciousness may accompany the process, but not in the sense that it directs each and every movement, deciding which shall be conserved and which shall be dispensed with.

Yet it is precisely this aspect of the phenomenon of learning that we are endeavoring to explain: how are certain responses retained and certain others eliminated? In the sense that we are not conscious of making some of them, we cannot be aware of any alleged feeling they may arouse, at least not to the extent of linking up the feeling with the reaction that is supposed to cause it. We cannot associate a thing we know with a thing of whose existence we are totally oblivious. From this point of view the theory is faulty even as a *description* of the facts of learning.

(2) **Thorndike's Modification of the Pleasure-Pain Theory.** In the light of the preceding discussion of the pleasure-pain theory it will not be difficult to grasp the theory of learning sponsored by Thorndike. His theory represents, from some points of view, an application of the pleasure-pain philosophy to the problems raised by the psychology of learning. In his treatment of learning Thorndike does not occupy himself with the problem of " drive," but centers his attention on the problems of fixation and elimination. It will be remembered that the two latter problems have to do with these two questions: (a) Why and how are certain acts retained? and (b) Why and how are certain acts eliminated?

Thorndike (28) answers these questions by formulating

three laws or principles. These are the *law of use*, the *law of disuse*, and the *law of effect*.[7] The first two laws are intended to describe what takes place *after* a given response has been made to a specific part of the learning situation. According to the law of use, if such a response should be repeated the mechanism responsible for it would be strengthened; while according to the law of disuse, if no repetition takes place, it will be weakened. On the analogy of the physiology of muscles these two laws are frequently combined into one, the *law of exercise*. Use or exercise a muscle and it becomes stronger; neglect it and it becomes weaker or atrophies. Thorndike simply extends this conception to the sphere of mental reactions. But what determines whether the exercise shall take place or not and, consequently, whether a given act shall be retained or eliminated? The law of effect is intended to answer these questions. Briefly stated, the latter law says that the *consequences* of the act determine whether it will be repeated or not. That is, in Thorndike's terminology, if the act is accompanied or followed by a satisfying state of affairs, it will be stamped-in or retained; if it is accompanied or followed by an annoying state of affairs, it will be stamped-out or eliminated. By substituting the words " satisfying " and " annoying " for pleasure and pain, Thorndike endeavors to escape some of the objectionable connotations of the older terms. But the underlying concept is the same, except that it may be more readily thought of in physiological terms.

It is obvious that this modification of the older pleasure-pain theory does not suffice to dissipate all of the difficulties inherent in its acceptance. Both Holmes (9)[8] and Cason (4), among others, have by means of trenchant criticisms brought out the existence of these difficulties so far as they

[7] *Op. cit.*, pp. 70–71.					[8] *Op. cit.*, Chapter VII.

apply specifically to Thorndike's theory. We have space to consider but one of these criticisms by way of illustration. Referring to the terms satisfying and annoying as employed by Thorndike, Cason states: [9]

" *Satisfyingness and Annoyingness* are defined by Professor Thorndike as follows: ' By a satisfying state of affairs is meant roughly one which the animal does nothing to avoid, often doing such things as attain and preserve it. By an annoying state of affairs is meant roughly one which the animal avoids or changes.' A good many reactions of the organism would come under this category, but some of them would not be in the least ' satisfying,' as the term is used in popular speech. We are not at all aware of many of our physical activities. If Professor Thorndike means that the satisfying reaction is simply one which the animal makes, then the application of the law of effect would be a circular argument; for the animal would then be said to make the reaction because it is satisfying, and a satisfying reaction in turn would be said to be the one which the animal makes."

It is clear then that Thorndike's reformulation of the pleasure-pain theory by no means disposes of the objections to that theory. The law of effect does undoubtedly represent an improvement over the older view to the extent that it calls attention to the underlying bodily conditions responsible for conscious states of pleasure and pain, or satisfyingness and annoyingness. In this way it tends to avoid the troublesome problem of the mechanism by means of which a state of consciousness can bring about the movement of a bodily part This way of viewing the problem, while a step in the right direction, is not much more helpful than the previous view. It amounts to saying that those acts which tend to produce a bodily condition that is subjectively pleasurable or satisfying are retained, while those that

[9] *Op. cit.*, p. 406.

tend to produce a contrary effect are eliminated. Again we find description substituted for explanation.

(3) **The Confirmation and Inhibition Theory.** To offset the difficulties in the pleasure-pain type of theory, the English student of animal behavior, Hobhouse (7), has proposed a different theory to account for selection and elimination of responses in learning. This theory is called the confirmation and inhibition theory.[10] It possesses the merit of " not involving any general theory of the physiology of pleasure and pain," as Holmes points out. To understand its meaning we might endeavor to apply it first to maze learning and then to problem box solution. In the maze the animal enters a particular cul-de-sac, let us say. The obstruction causes its entrance to be followed by withdrawal. We thus have two mutually inconsistent, or antagonistic, responses of approach and avoidance associated and as a result of this inconsistency they *inhibit* each other. The principle involved is illustrated by the case of the pedestrian in the middle of the street who manifests the counter impulses to hasten forward and to retrace his steps when an automobile threatens him. As the result of the antagonistic impulses, he comes to a dead stop. His walking movements are inhibited. Hobhouse would find it unnecessary to explain such inhibition on the basis of resulting pain or annoyance. In a similar manner we might say that the cat in the problem box clawing at an unyielding slat inhibits the approaching response to that slat as a result of the neutralizing effect of the contradictory responses of extending and withdrawing the paw. The objectivity of this view, apart from other considerations, renders it scientifically preferable to the subjectivistic pleasure-pain theory.

Hobhouse illustrates his theory by reference to an experiment performed by Lloyd Morgan (18) on young chickens.

[10] *Op. cit.,* Chapter V.

According to Morgan's observations the young chick's feeding reactions are at first directed to " *anything* of suitable size: grain, small stones, bread-crumbs, . . . beads, cigarette-ash and ends, their own toes and those of their companions, maggots, bits of thread, specks on the floor, their neighbors' eyes — anything and everything, not too large, that can or cannot be seized is pecked at and, if possible, tested in the bill." That is, in the absence of previous experience or the guidance of older birds the newly hatched chick fails to discriminate edible from inedible substances. But this discrimination is soon acquired and the *sight* of an object suffices to determine whether it is to be pecked at or not.

Morgan studied the development of this discriminatory behavior by the following experiment: " To some . . . chicks I threw cinnabar larvae, distasteful caterpillars, conspicuous by alternate rings of black and golden-yellow. They were seized at once, but dropped uninjured; the chicks wiped their bills — a sign of distaste — and seldom touched the caterpillars a second time. The cinnabar larvae were then removed, and thrown in again towards the close of the day. Some of the chicks tried them once, but they were soon left. The next day the young birds were given brown loopers and green cabbage-moth caterpillars. These were approached with some suspicion, but presently one chick ran off with a looper, and was followed by others, one of which stole and ate it. In a few minutes all the caterpillars were cleared off. Later in the day they were given some more of these edible caterpillars, which were eaten freely; and then some cinnabar larvae. One chick ran, but checked himself, and, without touching the caterpillar, wiped his bill — a memory of the nasty taste being apparently suggested by association at sight of the yellow-and-black caterpillar. Another seized one, and dropped it at once. A third subsequently approached a cinnabar as it crawled along, gave the danger note and ran off. Then I threw in more edible caterpillars, which again were eaten freely. The chicks had thus learnt to discriminate by sight between the nice and nasty caterpillars." [11]

In the terminology of Hobhouse the tendency of the chick to peck at certain things was confirmed, while its tendency to peck at certain others was inhibited. By confirmation Hobhouse means that the tendency in question is in a sense justified by its consequences and so " stamped-in," to use Thorndike's term. In fact, there is very little difference between this aspect of Hobhouse's theory and that of Thorndike's; for he too postulates something akin to pleasure and pain in human experience as the agency that determines whether a given reaction shall be confirmed or inhibited. It is only with respect to his analysis of the mechanism of inhibition that we can detect an advance over the law of effect. The nature of this mechanism has already been described. With respect to its application to the avoiding reaction built up in the chick, Hobhouse states that " a movement of rejection, a movement adapted to getting rid of a nasty taste, is evoked by sight of the caterpillar just as it was in the original experience by its presence in the chick's mouth." This view is a striking anticipation of the conditioned reflex type of explanation discussed below.

(4) The Congruity Theory. Closely allied to the theory of Hobhouse is that of the American zoölogist, Holmes (8). His theory is called the congruity theory because it endeavors to reduce the mechanism of learning to the elimination of " incongruous " movements and retention of those that are " congruous." So far as the mechanism of elimination is concerned, his view is precisely that of Hobhouse. In fact Holmes admits his indebtedness to Hobhouse and employs the same illustration of Morgan's experiment with

[11] *Op. cit.*, pp. 40–42.

the chick and the caterpillar to drive home his conception. The difference between the two theories is to be found in the endeavor Holmes makes to get away from the "stamping-in" or "*confirming*" effect of pleasure as an explanation of the retention of learned reactions. Since it is in connection with this aspect of the learning problem that Holmes tries to overcome the shortcomings of the previously enumerated theories, it is advisable to give a verbatim account of his interpretation:

"Let us consider . . . the case in which the chick pecks at a caterpillar which has a good taste. The presence of the caterpillar in the mouth excites the swallowing reflexes; in the presence of a similar caterpillar the pecking response is made more readily than before, and whatever hesitation there may have been at first disappears. Is not the difference from the pain-response due to the fact that there is an organic incompatibility between the first and second responses in the pain response, while there is an organic congruity or mutual reinforcement of these responses in the other? Pecking and swallowing form the normal elements of a chain reflex; when one part of the system is excited it tends to excite the rest, to increase the general tonus of all parts concerned in the reaction.

"According to the view here presented, whether a particular response to a stimulus tends to be repeated more readily or discontinued, depends not upon the peculiar physiological state which may be produced in the brain,[12] but upon the kind of responses which the stimuli brought by the act call forth. If an outreaching reaction becomes coupled with a withdrawing response the result is inhibition. If the reaction, on the other hand, brings stimuli which produce con-

[12] Holmes refers to the view which regards the brain processes accompanying pleasure, rather than pleasure as a distinct conscious entity, as responsible for selective action.

gruent reactions the association formed with these latter reinforces the first reaction. The pleasure-pain response then resolves itself into the formation of associations. Withdrawing and defensive responses are usually initiated by pain-giving stimuli, and the instinctive or random movement which brings a painful stimulus is inhibited under similar conditions in the future, not because of the pain or its physiological correlate, but because it comes to be associated with a withdrawing or defensive, and hence an incongruous or inhibitory reaction. Pleasure and pain thus interpreted have no mysterious power of stamping in or stamping out certain associations. Whether the result is reinforcement or inhibition depends on the way in which a reaction and secondary responses resulting from the situation in which the organism is thereby brought, happen to harmonize." [13]

This view of Holmes represents an excellent attempt to reduce learning to an objectively verifiable process. Briefly stated, it amounts to saying that all acts that are not inhibited, are retained; or conversely, acts are retained because they are not inhibited. His utilization of the Hobhouse conditioned reflex view of inhibition is more satisfactory and illuminating than his explanation of retention of successful acts. To say that an act will be retained provided it is not inhibited is at best but a partial account of learning phenomena. It fails to emphasize the problem of motivation in learning; that is, it fails to make clear the persisting, repetitive character of learning as revealed for example by an animal in a maze, or in a problem box. Of course by implication Holmes attributes the matter in question to the energy changes brought about by an aroused chain reflex. However, the relationship between *new* acts prompted by these energy changes and their fixation is only negatively accounted for by the view of Holmes. A group of psycholo-

[13] *Op. cit.*, pp. 177–178.

gists have occupied themselves with the problem of incorporating the persisting phase of the learning behavior into an adequate theory, and it might be profitable to summarize their view at this point.

(5) **The Drive or Motor-Set Theory.** The central problem of learning for the sponsors of the drive or motor-set theory is what in popular language we should describe as its " purposive " character. The animal or human when confronted with a problem keeps at it, persists in attacking it now this way and now that until the problem is either solved or abandoned. Ordinarily we say the animal " is seeking food " or " is trying to escape from the box." The psychologist wants to understand the mechanism of " trying " or " seeking." If possible, he wants to account for such " purposive " activity in terms of stimulus and response.

From the adult human point of view the behavior of a rat in a maze seems to be directed to an end, to be teleological. Now the law of parsimony renders untenable the naïve explanation that the rat " sees " its difficulty, and being " aware " of the end it is striving to attain, adjusts its movements to satisfy that end. In fact, to guard against such scientifically unwarranted, anthropomorphic explanations of animal behavior, Lloyd Morgan long ago formulated a principle to guide students of animal behavior. This principle, known as *Lloyd Morgan's Canon,* is really a specialized application of the law of parsimony to the interpretation of animal life. According to Morgan (17), " in no case may we interpret an action as the outcome of the exercise of a higher psychical faculty if it can be interpreted as the outcome of the exercise of one which stands lower in the psychological scale." [14]

Consequently, any explanation of the rat's behavior in

[14] *Op. cit.*, p. 53.

Q

terms of teleology would be ruled out of scientific court by Lloyd Morgan's Canon. In order to meet the needs of a serviceable working hypothesis to explain the facts of behavior apparently " purposive," several psychologists such as Woodworth (39), Perry (21), Tolman (31), and Kuo (14) have endeavored to present a strictly stimulus-response, non-metaphysical conception of purpose. It would lead us too far afield to take up the varying details of the views of these different writers. At bottom the essential aspects of their views are pretty much the same, even though they differ somewhat in terminology. We shall content ourselves in the main with the general idea and terminology as given by Woodworth. As has already been mentioned in the previous chapter, Woodworth employs the term *drive* to refer to the persisting or motivating character of behavior. The nature of the drive mechanism was there explained. What interests us here is the application of this drive theory to the problem of selection and elimination. The drive is looked upon as the selective agency. In the case of the rat in the maze it is the hunger drive that is dominating and regulating its activity. Securing the food is spoken of as the *end-reaction* or the *consummatory response*. The latter represents the goal toward which the activity is directed. Any act which plays a part in the attainment of this goal is said to facilitate it, whereas any act which retards or hinders such attainment is said to inhibit it.

The term *motor-set* refers to a certain adjustment or set of the musculature. A cat about to pounce on a mouse is a good example of such a motor-set. This motor-set or drive theory stresses the dynamic aspects of the learning process. This push or dynamism is furnished by the aroused *reaction tendency* of the drive. An aroused reaction tendency of this sort means that the organism is, during the duration of the drive, predisposed by virtue of the bodily adjustment that goes with it to react to those things that facilitate the achievement of the end-goal. The rat in the maze, being under the influence of the hunger drive, is consequently predisposed to react to those features of the maze that lead to food. It is also predisposed to disregard features that fail to lead in that direction.

It will be recalled that hunger is an organic state resulting from abstention from food, and characterized by rhythmic contractions of the stomach and pronounced activity of the striped musculature. Ordinarily this activity continues until the hunger is appeased. But under the maze conditions it cannot be appeased until the animal has worked its way to the food compartment. According to the drive theory, the rat emerges from a blind alley because such a pathway fails to contribute to the end-result called for by the particular drive. On subsequent occasions it will not even enter the cul-de-sac, the original entering response having been *inhibited* since it was not in line with the aroused reaction tendency. Similarly, those responses that lead to food will tend to be retained because they *facilitate* the attainment of this goal. It should be clearly understood that such retention and elimination does not imply anything in the nature of insight into the causal relations between the satisfaction of hunger and the pursuit of the appropriate alleys. The theory rather directs attention to the fact that the hunger drive makes for unsystematic, random, but *persisting* movements until food is obtained. That these movements become systematic and directed is due to the functioning of the mechanisms responsible for inhibition and facilitation.

This view of learning, when taken in conjunction with the detailed view of the mechanism of inhibition as first propounded by Hobhouse plus a satisfactory explanation of the precise mechanism of facilitation, would represent a real step forward. The drive theory certainly helps us to get a better understanding of the process of learning viewed as persisting activity. In calling attention to the need of viewing learning as an integrating activity, it performs a service that is indeed worth while. This is particularly well exemplified in the work of Peterson, whose explanation, while essentially similar to the drive theory, nevertheless brings into greater prominence the influence of the unitary character of the process of learning.

(6) **The Completeness of Response Theory.** Peterson (22) recognizes that problem solving — whether maze, problem box, or solution of mechanical puzzles — calls for an intricate interaction of a multitude of stimulus-response mechanisms, some inhibitory and some reinforcing. This interaction makes it necessary to account for the mutual influence of these mechanisms on the total problem situation. He illustrates his conception of the way in which these inhibiting and facilitating mechanisms influence the general response of getting to the food by means of an analogy. This general response — or drive — he likens to "a stream of water making its way initially over an uneven and loose soil. Now the water plunges mainly into this little hollow place drawing noticeably upon neighboring portions of the stream; now, this place being filled (cul de sac), the principal part of the current passes on to fill some other depression into which a small overflow had already begun but was impeded by the main plunge of the stream into the preceding hollow."[15] That is, we have an overlapping of many reactions, not isolated, separate, more or less insulated movements. Whether they are selected or rejected depends on the *completion* of the major or dominating response, the getting of the food or whatever the consummatory reaction may be. Let us note how Peterson applies his theory to maze learning:

[15] *Op. cit.*, pp. 156–157.

" In the case of the maze problem the animal on entering a cul de sac — or any other path, in fact — responds at first more or less *incompletely, because all the subordinate activities involved cannot take place at once.* If the animal's progress is soon checked in a blind alley the animal is not seriously nonplussed. Certain elements of the general response are tending to drain into other alleys that may recently have been passed, thus partially dividing the animal's activity. These elements now prevail when the others are checked. Let us suppose that the correct path, A, has just been passed when the animal suddenly comes to the end of the cul-de-sac, B. The tendencies to respond to A are still surviving and now direct the impeded activity into this, the successful, path. If, on the other hand, the correct path had been chosen the first time the distracting impulses toward B would have become fainter and fainter as the animal proceeded into A, and would finally have faded away. . . . When the food is finally reached all the remaining delayed reactions, the tendencies, still persisting, to go into other alleys recently passed, are relaxed — the act as a whole is complete." [16]

As Peterson has noted, his theory stresses the fitness or congruity of the overlapping acts in a manner similar to the theory of Holmes. In fact the motor-set theory, the congruity theory and the theory of Peterson have much in common. They all stress the integrative nature of learning, its non-vitalistic character and the importance of accounting for elimination of wrong responses, as well as the fixation of correct responses. In thus incorporating more or less successfully several phases of the complex phenomena that characterize learning, they avoid the danger of formulating a theory so simple as to cover but a small portion of the facts. In this connection one is reminded of the theory

[16] *Ibid.,* pp. 155-156.

sponsored by Watson, which has the merit of simplicity, but is inadequate to account for some of the important and indisputable facts of learning.

(7) **The Frequency-Recency Theory.** Watson's explanation of learning phenomena stresses the two factors of *recency* and *frequency* of response (36). As a consequence his theory is usually referred to as the frequency-recency theory. It represents an application to problems of animal learning of two laws of association that have already been explained.[17] These are the laws of frequency and recency. It will be recalled that according to the former law " if two or more events have been experienced together with a third one, and if on a subsequent occasion the latter is re-experienced, then, all other factors being constant, of all the associates with that experience, the one that has occurred most *frequently* will more likely be reinstated than any other." It will also be recalled that the law of recency states that " if two or more events have been experienced together with a third one, and if on a subsequent occasion the latter is re-experienced, then, all other factors being constant, of all the associates with that experience, the one that has occurred most *recently* will more likely be reinstated than any other."

With these two laws in mind it will not be difficult to understand the theory of learning favored by Watson. In fairness to him it should be pointed out that he does not regard his theory as a *complete* explanation. While laying principal stress on the factors of *frequency* and *recency* as accounting for the main facts of learning, he also grants that other factors, such as inhibition, reinforcement, and summation of stimuli have a part to play in the process.[18] However, inasmuch as he neglects to use these other factors in

[17] Review the discussion of The Laws of Association, pages 82–88.
[18] *Op. cit.*, Chapter VII.

his tentative theory of learning, it seems clear that he re-gards the factors of recency and frequency as pivotal in his theory, and it is on the basis of these factors that it has been severely criticized. The nature of these criticisms will be-come clear as soon as Watson's conception is described.

While many of the students of learning conceive of the underlying physiological changes as being the establishment of new " pathways " in the nervous system, Watson (37) denies the need for such a conception and questions the evi-dence for it.[19] He maintains that there are more than enough original movements to account for the entire gamut of *learned* movements. All that learning represents is the selection and organization of appropriate original move-ments. Such selection makes for the automatic rejection of other movements. There is no necessity for postulating new nervous connections. It is solely a matter of selecting and fixing the useful movements, and the crux of the problem, therefore, is to account for this selecting and fixing. Ac-cording to Watson's view, all of the animal's repertoire of acts are equally likely to take place at the start of learning; but the law of chance or probability favors those that lead to the goal, provided the animal is kept in the problem situa-tion until it reaches the goal. As a consequence, the move-ments leading to success will occur more *frequently* than those that lead to failure. For example, let us assume that the animal is placed in a simple T-maze of the following sort (Fig. 19) : The animal is introduced into the maze at A. Since there is but one path from A to B the animal must fol-low that; but arriving at B it can go either to the left and get the food at D, or go to the right along the blind alley to C and then double on its tracks and go to D. As soon as it gets to D the trial terminates. The question that con-fronts us is to explain why after the maze is mastered the

19 *Op.cit.*, p. 293.

animal always goes directly from B to D and not from B to C to D. Watson maintains that the law of probability would give the advantage to the left turn in this case. At the start either the right or the left turn is equally probable,

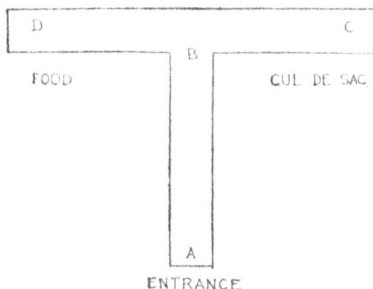

FIG. 19. — A simple T maze.

but since each trial ends with the attainment of the goal D, the final left turn *always* takes place, while the right turn need not take place each time. This can be shown by means of a hypothetical series of ten trials made by the animal.

First trial: A to B; B to D.
Second trial: A to B, B to C, C to B, and B to D.
Third trial: A to B, B to C, C to B, and B to D.
Fourth trial: A to B, B to D.
Fifth trial: A to B, B to D.
Sixth trial: A to B, B to C, C to B, and B to D.
Seventh trial: A to B, B to D.
Eighth trial: A to B, B to C, C to B, and B to D.
Ninth trial: A to B, B to C, C to B, and B to D.
Tenth trial: A to B, B to D.

It will be recalled that Watson demonstrated that maze learning proceeds in kinaesthetic units. In other words, the right and left turns we have spoken of represent the functioning of kinaesthetic units. Inspection of our series of ten trials will show that each trial terminated by a left turn and therefore the *left turn* kinaesthetic unit would have the advantage over the right in terms of *frequency* alone. Another characteristic of the situation is to be noted in the fact that since each trial ended with a left turn, such a kinaesthetic unit would be the most *recent* one when the animal is returned to the maze for the succeeding trial. *Recency of response* would then coöperate with *frequency of response* to make for the strengthening and fixing of the successful acts.

Criticisms of Watson's Theory. The weakness of Watson's view has been brought out by Thorndike (29). Thorndike points out that Watson's theory is inadequate in that it is based on an utterly untenable assumption; namely, that the animal in any given trial will perform each act once only and will then indulge in a different act. We know that a rat will repeatedly double on its tracks in a given blind alley, or that a cat will claw at a particular slat of the problem box many times before relinquishing the unsuccessful attempt. In cases such as these *frequency* should be on the side of the movement that is useless and that is actually eliminated. According to Watson's principle useless acts would have to be retained along with useful ones. If frequency is a determining factor it might account for the successful attainment of the goal, but it does not account for elimination. In terms of our T-maze illustration, the factor of frequency might account for the animal getting from A to D, but not for the elimination of the movement from B to C. So far as frequency is concerned the animal might just as likely go to D by way of C as by the more direct route. We have endeavored to illustrate this in our hypothetical series of ten trials by showing that five times the animal traverses the short route and five times the longer, the short route being from A to B and B to D, while the longer route is from A to B, from B to C and then from C to D. In a word, frequency *might* account for fixation of responses, but not for elimination.

It might be objected, however, that the factor of *recency* that Watson also recognizes might be sufficient to compensate for any shortcomings of frequency, considered as the sole explanatory factor. In this connection Woodworth (40) has pointed out that recency cannot be a very potent factor.[20] While he grants that the successful response always completes each trial period and in that sense is the most recent, such recency can only be influential if the succeeding trial takes place immediately. Actually a day often intervenes between successive trials. Very often the response immediately preceding the last one is incorrect. In terms of our illustration the animal might go from B to C and then from C back to B before making the correct move from B to D. Here the advantage of recency is represented by a difference of a few seconds. If the next trial followed at once, this difference might be an important one; but if a whole day elapses before commencing the next trial, the final successful and most recent response is twenty-four hours old, while the immediately preceding unsuccessful response may be twenty-four hours and a sixth of a minute old. Such a relatively insignificant temporal difference cannot be very important.

These a priori criticisms of Watson's theory have received experimental confirmation by both Peterson (23) and Kuo (15). The latter, by means of an ingenious arrangement of a maze, demonstrated that " many rats learned to select a correct path not only *not* because of recency or frequency, or both, but in spite of them." [21] The maze employed by

[20] *Op. cit.*, p. 393.　　　　　[21] *Op. cit.*, p. 17.

Kuo was so arranged that the rats could get to the food box by traversing either a long or a short route. Out of thirteen animals all but two selected the short route finally. In totalling the number of entrances to these longer and shorter compartments, Kuo found that the shift from the longer to the shorter in many instances came about *suddenly* and with the advantage of frequency on the side of the longer path. If frequency and recency alone are responsible for selection and elimination in learning, such shifts ought to occur gradually and not suddenly.

It is not unlikely that, given a correct response, frequency will fix it, but frequency alone will not establish it in the first place. Neither will frequency plus recency explain this. The most vulnerable side of Watson's theory is thus its utter failure to account for the elimination of wrong responses. His theory is applicable only to the learning that ensues after the faulty, maladaptive, useless responses have been shunted off. Only if we view the learning problem as demanding that the animal go from the entrance to the goal can the factor of frequency be regarded as effective in determining the solution. But Watson does not refer to the frequency of this *total* series of responses, but to the frequency of any one *partial* response that is correct. If he were to refer to the former, his theory would, to a certain extent, be similar to Peterson's. Under such conditions his view would have more to commend it, but it would be a very different type of explanation. In fact, as Peterson (23) has suggested, frequency and recency would not explain the learning, but the learning would explain the frequency and recency.[22] What is meant by this is that since learning is characterized by a *modification* of original behavior, we have not explained it until we have accounted for the modification. Frequency and recency account for

[22] *Op. cit.*, p. 364.

what occurs *after* the modifications have been introduced, and hence leave the problem still the same old
problem.

(8) **The Intensity Theory of Carr.** Before dismissing
the frequency-recency theory it might be well to call attention to the fact that Carr, while accepting these facts, has
added another, that of *intensity,* in order to account for the
selection of appropriate movements. We have already described what the factor of intensity is in terms of the law
of association. Carr (2) applies this to maze learning by
pointing out that movements along the true path become
more vigorous or *intense* than those along blind alleys. The
latter make for " hesitation, caution, investigation, or disastrous sensory consequences. The true path presents fewer
obstacles; it offers greater encouragement to freedom, con-
tinuity, rapidity, and vigor of motor expression. The difference is merely one of degree. The blinds check, thwart, and
suppress activity more than does the true path, while the
latter encourages and facilitates activity more than does a
blind alley. The principle of relative intensity is here effective; acts are selected or eliminated according to whether
the *sensory* [23] consequences tend to facilitate and intensify
them on the one hand, or to disrupt and suppress them on
the other." [24] This view of the part played by the factor of
intensity is excellently illustrated in terms of the drive concept as elaborated by Woodworth. The energy of the drive
is like steam in a boiler. A cul-de-sac prevents this energy
from finding an outlet. In fact the thwarting of the drive
intensifies the energy. It becomes dammed up. As a result,
the accumulated energy makes for a much more intense reaction when the stimulus leading to the consummatory response is attained. Although such a view may not be adequate to render the mechanisms of elimination particularly

[23] Italics ours.   [24] *Op. cit.,* p. 162.

intelligible, it does tend to shed light on the mechanism of fixation.

(9) **Smith and Guthrie's Conditioned Reflex Theory.** The problem of elimination has been excellently handled by Smith and Guthrie (26). They account for the inhibition of wrong responses by means of the conditioned reflex type of mechanism. It will be recalled that Hobhouse endeavored to make a mechanism of this sort an integral part of his theory, although he formulated his view before the time of the general prevalence of the conditioned reflex idea. Smith and Guthrie have recast this earlier explanation of Hobhouse into the language of the conditioned reflex. Their exposition of the matter is so lucid that it will bear repetition. They point out that " the situations the cat faces in the problem box are composed, for the most part, of visual stimuli that attract him, followed by stimuli to his proprioceptors and sense organs of touch that repel him, and these two classes of stimuli are given *by the same object*. He is instinctively attracted by the sight of the bars, but on reaching them, especially if they are rigid, he is instinctively impelled to turn away. This turning away is due to the resistance of the bars to his attempted manipulation and to his efforts to force his way between them. Approach and retreat are here original tendencies called forth by a single object.

" With repetition the sight of the bars becomes the conditioning stimulus for retreat, so that the conditioned response inhibits the original response. One by one the movements of approach to the various confining surfaces of the box are inhibited by the conditioned responses of retreating, until at last the animal is attracted by the door-opening device. The reason that this last movement is not inhibited is that that device itself never serves as the source of a stimulus that is instinctively avoided. Although the cat turns away from the button in response to the open door, he does so not because the button repels him but because the open door attracts him. Approaching the button and approaching the open door are the only approach responses that are uninhibited by conditioned avoidance responses, and while the door is closed the button alone calls forth an uninhibited response." [25]

This conception can very readily be applied to the elimination of blind alley responses in maze learning. The entrance to a particular cul-de-sac becomes the conditioned stimulus for avoidance. In the case of the rat with intact receptor systems the conditioned stimulus may be a visual one — the *sight* of the entrance. Blind rats may well have kinaesthetic stimuli acting as the conditioning factors, the learning of the maze proceeding in terms of kinaesthetic units, as Watson demonstrated. The significant aspect of Smith and Guthrie's theory is that it gives us at least an intelligible notion of the way in which the inhibitory phases of learning may be accounted for.

Concluding Considerations of the Theories of Learning. The foregoing sketch of the outstanding theories of learning renders one matter clear; namely, that the phenomena of learning are decidedly complex and that no single existing theory is entirely adequate to account for all of them. As was stated at the beginning of this section, there are three fundamental problems that must be solved by any theory that is intended to be comprehensive. These are: (1) The problem of perseveration or persistence or keeping at the task until it is mastered; (2) the problem of fixation of appropriate responses; and (3) the problem of elimination of maladaptive responses.

Reviewing the theories we have presented in the light of these problems, it is evident that in some of them emphasis

[25] *Op. cit.*, pp. 124–125.

is placed on one of these problems to the partial or complete neglect of the others, while in others stress is laid on a different problem. It is clear, for example, that the drive theory centers on the first problem and that the frequency-recency theory is more occupied with the second.

Although our knowledge of the intimate physiological processes involved in learning is still too limited to justify the formulation of a *complete* theory of learning, nevertheless the tenable parts of existing theories may be used in constructing a comprehensive, if tentative, theory. Such a tentative theory would give us a serviceable working conception, until the accumulation of new experimental facts brings about an improvement or modification of our conception. In this tentative working conception we should incorporate the drive or motor-set mechanism to account for the phenomenon of persisting behavior that is characteristic of maze and other learning. In addition, we should feel constrained to include the principles of frequency, recency, and intensity to account for the various phenomena of fixation. This does not necessarily mean that every case of learning involves all of these fixating principles. It is altogether likely that one intense response may be the equivalent of many weak responses. Intensity may thus be regarded as having the same influence as frequency except that the summational effect of the latter is achieved in one fell swoop, so to speak, by the former. Finally, to account for the third problem, that of elimination, we should feel obliged to complete our working conception by interpreting the inhibition of wrong or maladaptive responses in terms of conditioned reflex mechanisms as explained by Smith and Guthrie.

Human Learning

The use of language gives humans a tremendous advantage over animals in the mastery of problems that beset living beings. Part of this advantage comes from the fact that written records and oral tradition enable each succeeding generation to use the solutions of previous generations. The new generation can start where the old left off. To the extent that animals are unable to employ language data in the way man employs them when he reasons out a problem, animals lack the use of man's chief instrument of thought. But is there not an analogous or substitute mechanism by means of which some of the higher animals, at least, can deal with their environmental difficulties in a way that involves something of the nature of reasoning? Another way of putting the same question is to ask whether humans attack their problems in a way similar to the method employed by animals. Is there a peculiarly and exclusively human way of solving problems? Do humans learn by trial and error or is this uniquely characteristic of animals? As usual, to answer these questions psychologists, rather than endeavor to dispose of them by recourse to anecdotal literature and philosophical speculation, have put the problems to experimental test.

The Maze Experiment with Humans. In studying maze learning in humans psychologists usually employ what is known as a pencil maze. This consists of a miniature animal maze whose pathways are traversed by a pencil or stylus held in the subject's hand. The pathways are made by cutting grooves through a sheet of metal or a piece of board. During the entire course of the learning the subject is not permitted to see the maze, being either blindfolded or compelled to " feel " his way through a maze that is concealed from view by a canopy of dark cloth. By thus limiting his direct sensory experience to tactual-kinaesthetic cues the situation is rendered more comparable to that which such an animal as a rat undergoes in the maze.

Of course it may be argued that guiding the hand through

a maze is not analogous to guiding the body through one. However, to construct a large enough maze for an adult to use involves too much expense and would consume too much laboratory space to render experimentation of that sort readily feasible. Furthermore, it has been shown that the pencil maze is sufficiently like a genuine " life-sized " maze to render the results comparable. Some years ago Perrin (20) in a study of human maze learning obtained the use of a maze located in one of the Chicago amusement parks. This maze, called the " Mouse-trap," was admirably suited to the purpose, being close to 150 feet in circumference and so arranged that from an elevated platform the experimenter was able to observe and note down each significant move made by the subject. Comparative studies of the results secured from such a maze and from pencil mazes of several different patterns indicated that the human learning process in the maze was not a different process in the two types of mazes. There were certain differences in the results, but these were shown to be due to differences in the *patterns* of the mazes employed, rather than to the different physical reaction called for. Accordingly, we are fully justified in resorting to the pencil maze technique in investigating the process of human maze learning for purposes of comparison with similar learning in animals.

The pattern of one of the pencil mazes employed by Perrin in his study was practically a replica of the one used by Watson in his investigation. To that extent the findings are more comparable than would be the case if the patterns were different. Since Perrin's subjects were adults with intensive training in psychology the verbal description of their learning experience is particularly suggestive and furnishes us with an instructive and relatively reliable picture of the " inner " side of such learning. This does not mean, however, that we may legitimately infer that such a picture is also representative of what the rat probably experiences in learning a maze. The observable behavior is all that lends itself to reliable comparison.

As is to be expected, there was neither an absolute uniformity of verbal report nor of behavior in the case of these human subjects just as there is not absolute uniformity in the behavior of animals. Men as well as rats show individual differences. However, just as there was sufficient identity in the general behavior of Watson's rats to permit the formulation of a composite conclusion regarding their learning, so in the case of humans learning a pencil maze a general account of the process is possible. On the side of behavior it was found that the early trials of the subjects "consisted in a seemingly aimless trying-out of paths that offered themselves, a performance that strongly suggested the efforts of a newly-caught animal to escape from a pen."[26] This initial exploratory behavior was followed in the succeeding trials by more activity along the true pathway. Accompanying this, of course, was a reduction in the frequency of entering blind alleys as the learning progressed. The blind alley was not recognized as one until the subject was obstructed in his progress by coming into contact with the blind end. Another general tendency that the experiment revealed was the inability of the subjects to profit by a single cul-de-sac experience. The same cul-de-sac would be repeatedly entered for several successive trials. It might then be avoided for a few trials, only to be reentered in one of the later trials. Such trial and error behavior was manifested not only in the culs-de-sac, but whenever the subject became confused, even in the true path.

The introspections or verbal reports of the subjects showed that they attacked the maze problem with the intention "to develop an ideational control over the maze," to

[26] *Op. cit.*, p. 7.

get an " image " of it. The various parts of the maze gradually become familiar in the course of the trials as a result of three chief elements:

a. Associating different positions of the arm with different parts of the maze. The arm might be extended in one part and flexed in another.

b. Differences in kinaesthetic experiences as the arm was moved along different lengths and in different directions.

c. " The image scheme of the maze, as checked up by these various sense factors."

The last statement indicates that it was the sensory experiences coming from actual active investigation of the maze that was fundamentally operative in bringing about mastery. As in Watson's work the cutaneous and kinaesthetic cues were of basic importance. While the subjects approached the maze problem with the advance information that it was a maze (information that in the nature of the case rats could not be presumed to possess), and while, further, they tried to handle the problem rationally, their general handling of the situation was not outstandingly different from that of the animals. The reasoning indulged in was neither systematic nor effective. " Adequate interpretations were suggested to the learner as the result of prolonged exploration, rather than reasoned out. Cues which logically should be utilized for correct inferences were disregarded, and ideas were acted upon in an uncritical manner until they were proven by trial to be incorrect. The explanation of the meagre attempts at reasoning is to be found in the fact that the learner had no past experience to apply to the situations, and in the fact that he was unable to select his data — maze paths must be traversed in order." [27]

Since on the basis of the introspections the subjects utilized such devices as memorizing the sequence of pathways

[27] *Ibid.*, pp. 94–95.

in the simpler maze situations, and studying the situations in more complex cases, it cannot be maintained that pure " trial and error " characterized the learning method. It is even more certain that " pure reason " or " ideational learning " is totally inadequate to describe the method. If we were to ignore the introspections and limit the interpretation to the observed behavior during the progress of the learning, then whatever interpretation we have to offer for animal maze learning would serve to account for the manifest aspects of similar learning in humans. Neither the observed behavior nor the learning curves showed any radical difference in the manner of mastering this kind of situation, under the given conditions. To the extent that the term trial and error learning describes the behavior of animals in a maze, it also describes human behavior. In the sense that such a term is more descriptive than explanatory it cannot be said to furnish a satisfactory picture of the underlying method. This point has already been emphasized in our preceding discussion of animal learning.

Ruger's Experiment with Mechanical Puzzles. The learning procedure of an animal in a puzzle box or problem box was regarded by Thorndike to be completely of the trial and error variety. This kind of procedure is opposed to learning by " insight " or by reasoning, usually regarded as limited to human learning. By *insight* is meant that the organism sees into the principle of the problem. It perceives the relation between existing difficulties and the means that must be employed in order to overcome those difficulties. If a monkey confined in a cage, the door of which is fastened by means of a string tied in a bow-knot, should upon its first experience with such a situation immediately attack the knot and after undoing it, glance at the hinges and pull the door in or out, depending upon the location of the hinges, it might be said to possess " insight." It would react as though it perceived the connection between just those features of the situation that were responsible for its confinement and the appropriate measures that must be taken to escape from confinement. In his work with animals in problem boxes Thorndike was unable to find evidence for the existence of such insight. There was no direct perception of relationships. As a natural outgrowth of this finding, the question arose as to whether humans when confronted with analogous problems would manifest insight or would have to resort to trial and error procedure, or possibly would combine the two.

This was the question that Ruger (25) endeavored to answer. Instead of confining his subjects in problem boxes, he gave them mechanical wire puzzles to solve. The well-known Chinese ring puzzle is an example of the kind he used. He not only observed the behavior of his subjects, but also took the time required for solution and asked for their introspections. In addition, he gave the subjects puzzles based upon essentially the same principle, but differing somewhat in construction in order to ascertain whether the learning of one puzzle would suffice to enable the solution of another by means of an application of the just mastered principle. In general, he found that trial and error characterized the learning. Simple manipulations that were obviously ineffective in bringing about a change of the parts of the puzzle were repeated again and again. Such " stupid " behavior is not at all unlike that of a cat pawing at the same unyielding slat, or of a rat repeatedly scurrying into the same cul-de-sac. In a few cases the solution was mediated by reasoning, but in the main it was the result of chance. That is, movements which resulted in success were more frequently due to accidental, unpremeditated manipulation than to systematic, intentional manipulation.

It is of interest to note that once such chance success was

achieved the subject on subsequent trials with the same puzzle would endeavor to bring the puzzle around to the same position or place that gave rise to success previously. The place or position became the pivot around which the later efforts swung. Such " place analysis " has also been noted in animal learning. Once having been released from a problem box by manipulating a latch, an animal is likely to focus its subsequent attempts on the latch. It will be recalled that Watson found that a rat dropped into the middle of a maze which it has already learned, scampers around for a short distance and then veers off into the correct direction. Reaction to location or position is thus characteristic of animal as well as human learning. In some puzzles, where the subject had mastered the " principles " as well as the puzzles themselves, he was able to carry these over to related ones. However, when there was not mastery of principle, then the new, but related, puzzle had to be solved in the trial and error fashion just as though there had been no previous experience with that type of difficulty.

Ruger's learning curves for solution of the puzzles often reveal rather precipitate drops. According to Ruger, these sudden decreases in time indicate the presence of insight. They show that the subject has suddenly grasped the principle of the puzzle. In this interpretation he is supported by Thorndike, who argues that a gradual drop in the learning curve is characteristic of learning of the trial and error variety, while a sudden drop is indicative of learning with insight. Whether such an abrupt descent in a learning curve can be regarded as a criterion of insight, or its absence diagnostic of no insight is open to serious question. To argue one way or the other without additional corroborative evidence is apt to be very misleading. The first part of the learning curve for rats in a maze shows a sudden drop. Does this mean insight? On the other hand many curves for human learning of such acts of skill as typewriting or telegraphing are more gradual than many of Thorndike's curves for animal learning. In these cases, the absence of sudden shifts in the direction of the curve cannot be explained on the grounds of insufficient insight. Factors having to do with the relative slowness of the building up of new habit systems are adequate to account for the lack of sharp descents (or ascents). In fact, in some cases it is well-nigh impossible to invoke such an argument.

Furthermore, as Koffka (13) has pointed out, even some of Thorndike's animal curves reveal such precipitate breaks and therefore might be taken to show insight on the part of the animal. Koffka has little patience with Thorndike's defense that these apparent exceptions to the principle of trial and error learning are to be found where the learned act required is " very simple, very obvious, and very clearly defined." An act which appears simple and obvious to the experimenter is not necessarily simple for the animal.[28] This is the essence of Koffka's contention, and it is a difficult one to meet. Of course, it does not necessarily invalidate Thorndike's fundamental thesis regarding the trial and error nature of animal learning, but it does weaken whatever support Thorndike tries to give his thesis by appealing to alleged differences in human and animal learning curves. In fairness to Ruger it must be said that his inference concerning the meaning of the sudden, sharp drops in his curves was supported by the introspections of his subjects. In the light of the criticisms just made, however, it must be clear that any attempt to apply such influences to *all* learning curves is likely to be a treacherous proceeding. We might clinch this criticism by means of a partially hypothetical illustration. If we were to plot a learning curve of the serving of a novice at tennis, whose " slowness " at mastering the tech-

[28] *Op. cit.*, p. 165.

nique of serving causes him to serve many doubles and many " easy " balls for the first two years of his playing, we would get a gradual, trial and error type of curve in Thorndike's sense. Would such a curve mean that the individual concerned did not possess sufficient " insight " into the principles of the game to realize that the kind of service to have is one that is speedy, accurate, and devoid of doubles? To establish the presence or absence of insight we must resort to some means other than a study of the character of the learning curves.

Gestalt Psychology and Learning. To secure a clearer understanding of Koffka's criticisms a knowledge of his psychological viewpoint may be helpful. Koffka adheres to what is known as *Gestalt* psychology.[29] It will be recalled that this term, as defined in Chapter II, refers to the configuration or pattern characteristic of a given experience. According to the *Gestalt* psychologists, learning should be explained on the basis of such configurations. They maintain that attempts to account for learning in terms of the integration of reflexes, the influence of specific stimuli, or sensations are necessarily futile; for as they view it the learning activity is a total experience, and not a fragmentary, partial experience. On the basis of this reasoning they deny the validity of conclusions regarding animal learning and thinking unless the experimental conditions render it physically possible for the animal to grasp the total problem situation. A problem box with the exit concealed from view by sawdust or with the door bolted from the outside cannot be expected to test the animal's possession of insight. Of neces-

[29] A full description of Gestalt psychology cannot be presented here. For a comprehensive account in English see the series of articles by H. Helson on " The Psychology of Gestalt." The first article appears in *The American Journal of Psychology*, 1925, *36*, 494–526. The others are to be found in subsequent issues of the same journal.

sity it must resort to trial and error manipulations. If the psychologist is interested in discovering the animal's ability to think or reason, he must arrange conditions which make it possible for the problem to be solved by such means.

The *Gestalt* psychologists further contend that the conception of a response to a specific stimulus is an artificial abstraction not found in concrete experience. The response is always elicited by a configuration or a *Gestalt*. A *Gestalt* is more than the sum of its parts or its component stimuli: it possesses unique properties of its own that its separate parts do not possess, just as water possesses characteristics not found in either hydrogen or oxygen. The perception of a square is not to be explained as the result of four separate lines stimulating the eye. On the contrary, such a perception is a *unitary* affair or a *Gestalt*. This, in brief, represents the fundamental thesis of *Gestalt* psychology.

As applied to learning, this thesis is readily illustrated by a series of experiments performed by Köhler and summarized by Koffka.[30] Köhler performed his experiments on chimpanzees and hens, and on a child not quite three years old. His problem was to determine whether such organisms react to specific stimuli, as opposed to stimulating situations or configurations. His method varied to suit the particular animal being tested, but the general plan was the same for all. We may briefly consider the experiment with the child to indicate the plan. Two boxes were presented to the youngster and he was told to choose one. One of these boxes had a bright cover and the other a dark. The former contained candy, but the latter was empty. After 45 trials made over a period of two days, the child always chose the bright box and neglected the darker. The critical test was then made by substituting in place of the darker box one that was still brighter than the bright box; the child

[30] *Ibid.*, pp. 138-142,

was thus forced to choose between the box for which it had presumably established a fixed habit of selection and another that was even brighter. In the words of Koffka, " the child invariably and without hesitation chose the new and the brighter box." Similar results were obtained by using grey papers in feeding the hens. The reaction was evoked not by an absolutely fixed, specific stimulus but by the relatively darker or lighter stimulus in the configuration.

Whether it is necessary to interpret results of the kind just cited in terms of *Gestalt* psychology may be questioned. Certainly it is possible to explain the findings on the basis of current psychological concepts. It has long been recognized that our reactions are to situations rather than to discrete stimuli, except under artificial laboratory conditions. In stressing the importance of the complete pattern of stimuli and the organism as a whole, the *Gestalt* psychologists merely reflect the trend of modern psychology. This does not mean that an analysis of stimuli and part reactions is a futile method of study. Even granting that in psychology the whole is more than the sum of its parts, we should never be able to establish such a fact unless we first determined the parts.

Consciousness and Learning. Studies such as Ruger's, in which introspective as well as objective data are secured, raise the problem of the function of consciousness in learning. Unfortunately, the existence of this problem has been ignored in many scientific as well as popular accounts of the learning process. It is frequently taken for granted that when confronted with a problem to be solved, the learner *consciously* analyzes the steps to be taken and then proceeds to execute these steps. It is further assumed that once the problem is solved, the consciousness of the learner is free to attend to other things. This theory of learning assigns a definite function to consciousness in the initial phases of the learning process. In other words, it regards consciousness as a *directing agent* during these phases.

As an example of this kind of explanation we might consider the following quotation from Angell (1): " While one is *learning* to write, consciousness is involved in the most alert and intense manner. . . . The position of the hand, the mode of grasping the pen, the model to be copied, the movement necessary to form each part of the letter — all these things, one after the other, are the objects of vivid attention." [31]

Two additional illustrations will serve to explain further this alleged rôle of consciousness in learning. In typewriting, the beginner is aware of every stroke made, but as he progresses, his attention is more and more free to wander in other directions. When the stage of expert competence is attained, the whole process of typewriting is reeled off automatically while the individual's " mind " is occupied with such more difficult problems as planning the wording of succeeding sentences. In learning to dance, it is maintained that at the start we must give our whole attention to each step; we can " think " of nothing else, and only as we succeed in rendering the series of steps automatic are we free to turn our attention or " consciousness " to such activities as carrying on a conversation with our partner. In case we stumble, we are again aware of the dancing movements and consequently we are forced to give our attention to them long enough to permit consciousness to extricate us from the difficulty. Of course, since such analyses are based on introspective, or rather retrospective, observations, they are usually limited to the part played by consciousness in human learning. Only by inference and analogy are they extended to animal learning.

If we are to trust everyday experience, consciousness does

[31] *Op. cit.,* pp. 50–51.

seem to direct affairs at the beginning of learning. But it is one thing to assert that consciousness is present, and another thing to assume that it *effects* the learning. In our earlier discussion of the pleasure-pain theory we noted the difficulties involved in ascribing to consciousness any directing influence upon behavior. But over and above this theoretical criticism, certain factual difficulties argue against an acceptance of this view. It is difficult to see how conscious analysis can direct such a process as learning to walk on a tight wire, when only the gross movements involved can be described introspectively. The fact that children obviously incapable of analyzing their coördinations nevertheless succeed in acquiring difficult coördinations also militates against the theory. Likewise, the explanation fails to account for the acquisition of habits by animals. The achievements of a trained seal represent a case in point. In practically all cases of difficult motor learning we fail to discover a conscious process which adequately explains the learning.

There are two respects in which we are " more conscious " during the initial stages of learning than at the end. (1) In the case of learning to dance, the newness of the act, the awkwardness of the learner, and nature of the social situation all conspire to produce a pronounced emotional disturbance. Assuredly, the novice is conscious of this disturbance; but it is doubtful if his progress is facilitated by this consciousness. In so far as the emotion takes the form of self-consciousness, it is a liability rather than an asset.

(2) The beginner in dancing is likely to employ verbal aids. He is furnished with such directions as " step, slide, one, two, right, step, slide." These are verbal formulae or clues which " touch-off " the appropriate movements. They cease to function as progress is made, hence to the extent that they can be regarded as conscious processes, conscious-

ness subsides during the course of the learning. After a creditable degree of efficiency is attained, the learner may stumble or perhaps tread on his partner's toe; and in this event the original consciousness comes back, together with a renewed necessity for employing verbal aids.

But verbal functions cannot be defined in terms of conscious states. Psychologists classify words in the general category of stimulus-response mechanisms. In our illustration the word "step" is a stimulus conditioned upon the response involved in moving the leg in a definite way. So far as the psychological principle is concerned, the human learns to respond to this word in just the same way that the colt learns to respond to the crack of a whip.

Other stimuli may be equally effective in producing the dance steps. In fact, so far as we know, verbal clues may be entirely dispensed with in acquiring coördinations of this sort. An individual can learn to dance by responding to the cutaneous, kinaesthetic, and visual clues furnished by his actual learning performance on the dance floor. On seeing or "feeling" his partner's leg move forward, his natural response is to move with his partner. This act produces a proprioceptive stimulation, which tends to elicit the ensuing response, and this movement in turn is effective in making a third response. In this way the dancing movements are made in proper sequence, each act tending to result in the appropriate subsequent act. Additional aid is rendered by the mechanism of rhythm, controlled by the auditory stimuli. This serves to regulate the tempo of the movements. An integrated series of movements such as we have just described is often called a *habit hierarchy,* since it represents an organization of unit responses.

If our analysis is correct, the alleged function of consciousness in learning must be questioned. Liberally interpreted, the principles of stimulus-response psychology not only describe but explain the learning process. We cannot assume that consciousness, as such, at first exercises some unanalyzed and mysterious power of control and regulation in the initial stages of learning and then relegates this power to a habit mechanism. The same nervous system responsible for the final execution of an act is responsible for its development.

We can illustrate the difference between the functional view of consciousness and the explanation of learning which we have submitted for it by the following diagram, in which X represents consciousness, Sit. the dancing situation made up of music, the dance-floor, the partners, and the other dancers, and S and R respectively the stimulus and the response.

According to the functional view of consciousness:

The sequence at the beginning of the learning is

Sit. $\longrightarrow$ X $\longrightarrow$ R $\longrightarrow$ X $\longrightarrow$ R, etc.

The sequence at the completion of learning is

Sit. $\longrightarrow$ R

According to the view which explains learning as an integration of stimulus-response mechanisms:

The sequence of events at the beginning is

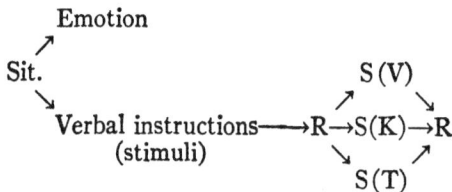

$$
\begin{array}{c}
\text{Emotion} \\
\nearrow \\
\text{Sit.} \qquad\qquad\qquad\qquad \text{S (V)} \\
\searrow \qquad\qquad\qquad\qquad \nearrow \quad \searrow \\
\text{Verbal instructions} \longrightarrow \text{R} \rightarrow \text{S(K)} \rightarrow \text{R} \\
\text{(stimuli)} \qquad\qquad\quad \searrow \quad \nearrow \\
\text{S(T)}
\end{array}
$$

This last R, supplemented by the stimulus of the verbal formula, reinstates the first R; this is followed by the visual, kinaesthetic, and tactual stimuli which produces another R;

and thus the process continues in circular fashion. When the act is practically mastered the sequence of events is

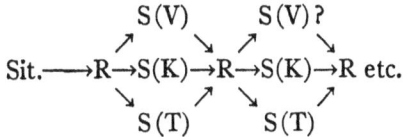

$$
\text{Sit.} \longrightarrow R \rightarrow S(K) \rightarrow R \rightarrow S(K) \rightarrow R \text{ etc.}
$$

with $S(V)$ and $S(V)?$ above, and $S(T)$ and $S(T)$ below.

(The visual stimulus is questioned since it is not essential except to guide the body in avoiding obstacles and other dancers on the floor.)

This last diagram also serves to indicate the order of events in the case of individuals who learn to dance without verbal aids. Their learning is more directly trial and error in character. Evidently, to the extent that the verbal stimuli provoke responses which are inadequate to the situation, they may be either a detriment or hindrance in the learning. This, it will be recalled, was the case with those individuals who attacked the maze problem " rationally." Sometimes we find that the connection between the verbal (conscious) stimulus and the movement called for fails to be made. This is true of a pitcher, who having thrown three " wild " balls, indulges in the inner formula, " I've got to pitch the next one over the plate," and then actually throws another wild one. Under such circumstances we cannot say that he failed to find the plate because he lacked enough consciousness. This is a *reductio ad absurdum*, but it will serve the purpose of throwing into bold relief the nature of the fundamental objection to the current, popular notion of the function of consciousness in initiating and controlling our behavior.

Verbal reactions are frequently useful if not indispensable in learning. In some situations, as the one just referred to, where the individual's " pitching form " is below his usual standard, no amount of verbalizing may be effective. In other situations, however, the use of verbal reactions may make the difference between a poor performance and an excellent one. For example, Warden (34) tested the influence of various methods of approach in learning a stylus maze. Some of the subjects attacked the problem in the straight trial and error way; others used what they described as visual imagery in conjunction with their direct motor experience of the maze; while a third group resorted to a verbal technique. That is, this last group employed language to facilitate the learning. As the subjects reacted to various parts of the maze they endeavored to build up a verbal description of the result. In traversing the correct pathway, for instance, one of the subjects verbalized the experience by saying, " Well, I made a U-shaped turn at the entrance, then three turns away out to the right, then I found I had to drop back a couple of places," and so on. As a result of measuring the influence of these various methods, Warden found that the word reaction or verbalizing method of learning was the most economical, " requiring on the average less than $\frac{1}{4}$ as many trials for complete mastery as the motor reaction method, and approximately $\frac{1}{2}$ as many trials as the so-called visual imagery method." [32] But this is vastly different from saying that the group that was most *conscious* was most efficient.

The Influence of Practice on Learning. The practice factor in learning has been subjected to extensive experimental attack. Laboratory evidence as well as everyday experience confirms the popular statement that " practice makes perfect."

This proverb is often taken to mean that practicing a given act makes that act perfect as the learning of it progresses; but as a description of what takes place such an interpretation is faulty. Consider the familiar case of a child learning

[32] *Op. cit.*, p. 273.

to write. In the beginning it indulges in a multitude of superfluous movements. It twists its legs around the chair, squirms about, wrinkles its forehead, grasps the pencil with excessive force and with the whole hand; in short, its whole body is active. With continued practice these unnecessary, extraneous movements are eliminated and the writing movements more limited to those essential to that act. In other words, the practice did not improve the act that took place at the beginning, but brought a different act into being. In the same way the service of a novice at tennis becomes a different act when the novice becomes a champion. Only in terms of attaining the objective of learning does practice tend to make perfect.

Actually, nobody ever achieves perfection in any absolute sense of the word. So far as motor performances are concerned the most that we can hope to do is to attain our physiological limit for the given performance. Such attainment represents the nearest we can come to perfection. By physiological limit is meant the utmost that our bodily equipment will enable us to do. A track coach, for example, can teach a sprinter to negotiate the hundred yard dash in a style which, so far as form is concerned, is that of the world's champion sprinters. But despite the fact that he can teach them the requisite style, he cannot make all of the track candidates ten-second men. It may be that a given candidate on his first attempt sprints the distance in 14 seconds. As a result of practice and following the coach's suggestions, he eventually cuts his best time down to 12 seconds. Then, despite the utmost diligence and effort, he fails to better his 12-second performance. His physiological limit for the hundred yard dash would be 12 seconds. For human beings in general the limit is a fraction less than 10 seconds. In all seriousness we might ask why it is that nobody has ever succeeded in lowering the record to 8 seconds, or even less than that. The answer, of course, is that a definite minimum time must elapse for the bodily machinery involved to function. Nothing takes place in no time. In the case of running a certain amount of time must be allowed for the transmission to the brain mechanism for hearing of the afferent impulse set up by the starter's pistol. An additional amount is consumed in the passage of the neural disturbance from the latter mechanism to the muscles used in sprinting. Even after the efferent impulse reaches the muscle a measurable interval elapses before the muscle responds to that impulse. It will be recalled in this connection that the speed of transmission along a motor nerve is about 125 meters per second. The time required for the functioning of the physiological mechanisms operative in a given activity sets a limit to the speed with which that activity can be executed. It is this limit which is referred to by the term physiological limit. It will differ for different persons, but to the extent that they succeed in performing the given activity in the minimum time that their particular physiological equipment permits, they may be said to have reached perfection so far as speed of performance is concerned. In this *relative* sense the performance of our trained 12-second sprinter is as " perfect " as that of a 10-second man, despite the absolute difference of 2 seconds in their records.

The physiological limit for any given activity can be approximately determined only by experimentation. One of the important psychological questions connected with such experimentation has to do with the rate of improvement by means of which this limit is approached. Assuming that it required ten weeks of training, one trial per week, for the sprinter to reduce his time from 14 to 12 seconds, did this reduction come at a uniform rate of $\frac{1}{5}$ of a second per trial, or did some other irregular type of rate characterize the learning? It may be stated quite dogmatically that so far as existing experiments are considered, the improvement is never of a constant, uniform character from the beginning of the learning until the physiological limit for that activity is reached.

One difficulty involved in the study of this question is that of deciding when the learning *begins*. This is known as the problem of *zero preparation*. A subject may have had no previous experience with the precise activity he is setting out to learn, but to the extent that he is capable of going through the elementary movements required in the initial stages of the learning, he is not starting from "scratch." For example, Thurstone (30) reports that in learning to typewrite a subject who has never touched a typewriter before may succeed in writing as many as 27 words in four minutes.[33] In the same way it may be demonstrated that the student just beginning piano lessons does not start from zero ability. In the very first lesson he succeeds not only in striking the keys, but also to some extent in striking the correct ones. The best that psychologists can do under the circumstances is to start their experimental work as far back in the learned performance as circumstances will permit and to regard this start as a sort of arbitrary zero.

Learning Curves. In the endeavor to get a picture of the influence of practice on the rate of improvement the customary method is to draw a practice curve. It is obvious that the curves of learning presented on the previous pages are also practice curves inasmuch as they give a graphic picture of the improvement wrought in an activity by repetition. Whether a given curve is to be called a learning curve or a practice curve is largely a matter of emphasis since it depends on the particular purpose for which the experiment was undertaken. As indicated on the accompany-

[33] *Op. cit.*, p. 26.

ing practice curves, it is customary to use the abscissa or x-axis to represent the lapse of time and the ordinate or y-axis to represent the improvement as measured by increase of speed or increase of amount of work done. Sometimes it represents a decrease of the number of errors, or possibly a decrease in the time required to complete a unit of work.[34]

Inspection of the learning curves shown in Figures 20, 21, and 25 shows that their general tendency is to approximate the type of curve represented in Figure 22, the so-called "typical" learning curve. The student of physics will recognize this curve as one that shows *negative acceleration*. The term means that as the learning continues, less and less is accomplished in each succeeding practice period compared with the previous one. If the distance per unit of time traversed by a long outfield fly were measured and plotted we would get a curve showing negative acceleration. In other words, the speed of the ball grows less as it recedes from the home-plate; that is, the ball covers less distance each succeeding interval of time. Such a learning curve indicates that improvement is relatively more rapid in the beginning than in the later stages of practice. It will be noted that the final stretch of the curve tends to be parallel with the base line. This final stretch is the graphic indication of the physiological limit. It represents *zero acceleration*.

It will be noticed that actually none of the curves are perfectly smooth. Such deviations from an ideal form are due in part to factors other than practice. Subjects vary from day to day in interest, incentive, fatigue, and physiological condition. Even weather conditions and the nature of the room temperature tend to influence human performances. Disappointment and elation have been known to influence

[34] See Figure 17, the curve for maze learning in the case of rats.

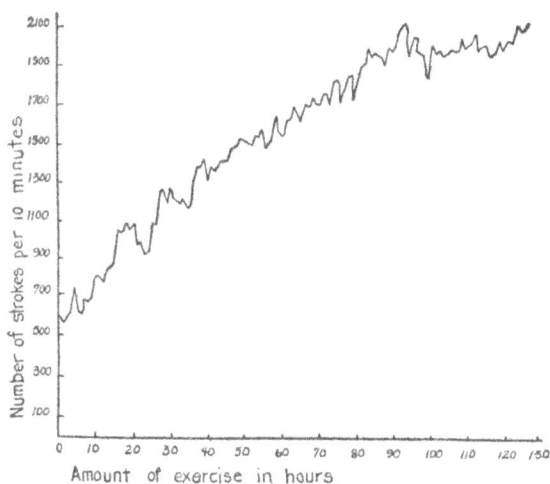

FIG. 20. — Learning curve showing influence of practice in learning to typewrite by the touch method in the case of one individual. (From Book, W. F., *The Psychology of Skill.* Gregg Publishing Company, New York, 1925.)

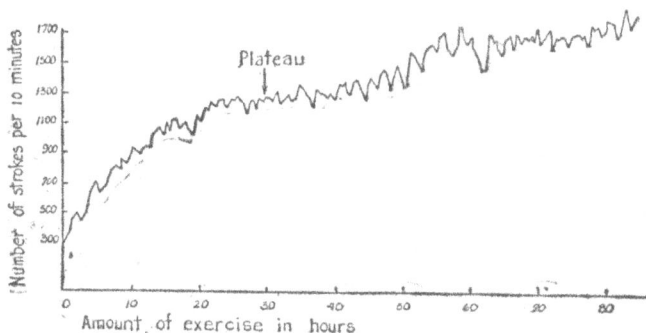

FIG. 21. — Learning curve showing influence of practice in learning to typewrite by the sight method in the case of one individual. (After Book.)

learning experiments, just as they have been known to inter-fere with school examinations. With such a multitude of uncontrolled factors playing a part in the experiment, it is not astonishing that the curves show so many fluctuations and deviations from a theoretically " smooth " form.

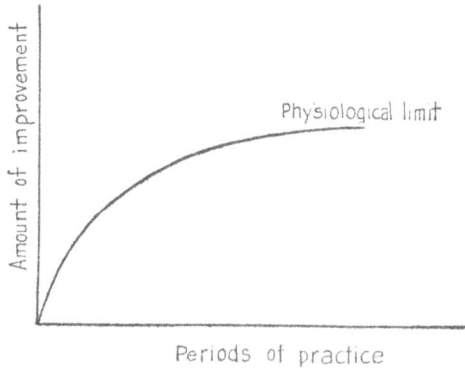

FIG. 22. — The so-called typical learning curve.

As explained in the text, this curve is often regarded as typical of learn-ing. Reference to Figs. 20, 21, and 25 will show that they tend to ap-proximate a curve of this shape. It may be doubted, however, whether one is justified in regarding any particular kind of curve as *typical* of learning. The kind of curve obtained in learning experiments varies with the measure of progress employed, the number and duration of the practice periods, the physical condition of the subjects, and a number of other factors. Even if it is assumed that a curve such as this one is ap-proximately typical, it deviates from actual, as opposed to theoretical, curves in two respects: (1) it starts from zero (zero preparation) and (2) it is too smooth or continuous. Actual learning curves are charac-terized by many fluctuations. At best, this curve typifies a theoretical ideal.

Ladd and Woodworth (16) designate a curve like the above as " a typical curve of learning." (*Op. cit.*, p. 575.) Thurstone (30) has shown that the character of a learning curve varies with the way it is graphed. He takes the " speed-amount " form as basic and " usually hyperbolic."

Considerable controversy has arisen concerning one aspect of these fluctuations. Reference to Figure 21, the practice curve of typewriting by the sight method, will show a level portion in the middle of the curve. A level of this kind is called a *plateau*. It is interpolated behind the initial spurt in the acquisition of ability and a second increase of achievement. Since plateaus are generally absent in curves of animal learning, they are regarded by some psychologists as uniquely characteristic of human learning. Other psychologists regard them as artifacts, produced artificially by crude measurements of learning. Apparently the plateau indicates that for a relatively prolonged period the learner is not profiting by his experience. In other words, his improvement is at a standstill. In the opinion of some psychologists, the plateau represents actual improvement of a kind which is not indicated by the objective results. Evidence for this view is found in the spurt of improvement which follows the plateau. All psychologists agree that plateaus do not universally characterize human learning curves. They are absent, for example, in Figures 20 and 25.

The Curve of Forgetting. In addition to the curves so far described, psychologists have often plotted *curves of forgetting*. Such curves give graphic pictures of the speed with which we forget material once committed to memory. The technique used in such experimentation varies, depending on the kind of material that is memorized. In general, it calls for learning the material to a definite standard of efficiency and noting how much of it is retained after the lapse of a stated time interval. As in other kinds of memory work, the subject is often required to memorize *nonsense syllables*. By this is meant a syllable made by combining a vowel and two consonants into a meaningless combination of letters, such as ZIK, POG, RAJ, NUR. The consonants always flank the vowel. This material is superior to common words, prose, or poetry because it enables the experimenter to control the factor of familiarity.

Ebbinghaus (6), who introduced the nonsense-syllable technique into experimental psychology, studied the question of the rate of forgetting by this means. One of his curves is shown in Figure 23. It will be noted that forgetting is very rapid immediately after the learning and becomes less and less rapid as time goes on. Such a curve indicates negative acceleration. A similar curve is shown in Figure 24. This curve, as indicated by its accompanying description, shows the amount of lecture material retained by students after varying intervals of time. In this study students of elementary psychology were tested to find out how much of a college lecture is retained. Jones (10), who conducted the investigation, reports among other results that at the close of an ordinary 40-minute college lecture students retain on the average but 62% of the contents of the lecture.[35] As he states it, " only about 2/3 of a lecture ' gets across.'" After 3–4 days but 45% is retained and at the end of 8 weeks only 24% of the lecture can be recalled.[36] These results, it should be said, apply to *new* and insufficiently learned material.

Individual Differences and Practice. Another unsettled problem is concerned with the influence of practice on the variability of individuals. Does practicing a given act make individuals more alike, less alike, or the same with respect to that act? Consider the following example:

Ten boys of the same age with no previous training in pole vaulting are given systematic practice in that performance. Before the practice, which extends over a period of years, their relative abilities are measured. At that time X is best, Y is poorest, A is fifth, and the others rank in between. Now while it is agreed that practice will improve

[35] *Op. cit.*, p. 23.   [36] *Op. cit.*, p. 62.

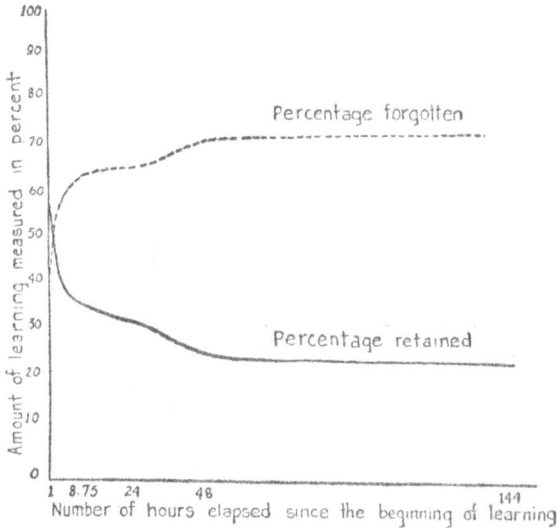

FIG. 23. — Curves showing the rate of forgetting a series of nonsense syllables learned to the point of one correct reproduction.

The solid curve indicates the percentage of time saved in re-learning the lists of nonsense syllables after they had been forgotten. The broken curve shows the percentage forgotten after the lapse of varying intervals of time. Curiously enough the former curve is usually designated a *curve of forgetting*. Actually it is a *curve of retention*. Compare the broken curve with the curves of learning shown in the preceding figures.

The following data from Ebbinghaus (6) were used in constructing these curves: [1]

Time Interval	No. of Trials	Percentage Saved In Relearning (Av.)	Percentage Forgotten (Av.)
19 min.	12	58.2%	41.8%
63 min.	16	44.2%	55.8%
525 min.	12	35.8%	64.2%
1 day	26	33.7%	66.3%
2 days	26	27.8%	72.2%
6 days	26	25.4%	74.6%

[1] *Op. cit.*, pp. 93–103.

Percentage retained

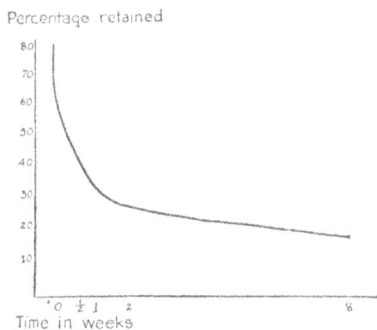

FIG. 24. — Curve of forgetting for content of a college lecture.
(From Jones.)

This curve illustrates graphically the speed with which the material presented in a college lecture, 40 minutes long, is forgotten. Although the amount retained at the end of the lecture is given as 80%, the actual average percent obtained was 62%. The former figure represents a statistical correction introduced into the data to allow for the fact that the memory test given at the end of the first lecture, designed to measure immediate recall, as opposed to delayed recall, does not perform this function in an absolute sense of the word *immediate*. As Jones (10) puts it: "From what we know of the curve of forgetting for just learned material, it is probable that the content of a lecture is forgotten more rapidly during the lecture itself than at any time afterward. This implies that our forgetting graph, as shown above, should not begin at 62%, the mean for the first test, but at some higher point, just how much higher we cannot say. If every item presented and discussed is at some time . . . apprehended by every member of the class, the curve would begin at 100%. But this ideal is probably never realized in any classroom, and for convenience we have designated the starting point of the curve at the midpoint between 62 and 100, which is at least as probable a position as any other." [1]

The above curve is based on the following data.[2]

Delay Interval	No. of Lectures	No. of Cases	Mean Immediate	Mean Delayed	Med. Dev.
Immediate	30	782	62.0	. . . .	4.0
3–4 days	15	422	56.8	45.3	7.9
1 week	4	111	58.6	34.6	14.3
2 weeks	5	101	63.3	30.6	15.4
8 weeks	3	69	64.4	24.1	12.2

[1] *Op. cit.*, p. 32. [2] *Ibid.*, p. 30.

the performance of each one, the question is whether the improvement will be the same in amount for all of them. At the end of two years of practice will X still be first, Y last, and A fifth? Or will Y be first and X last and the others similarly finish in inverse order? In technical language, how does practice affect the relative and absolute variability of individuals?

As has already been stated, no absolutely certain answer can be given to this problem. Kincaid (11), however, has gone over 24 publications dealing with a diversity of performances, including mental multiplication, addition, reading, ball tossing, javelin throwing and so forth, and has treated the results obtained by refined statistical methods. The results of her study show that the level of ability manifested in the early stages of practice is prognostic of later relative ability. The brunt of the evidence also indicates " that differences generally decrease with practice." According to these statements, the relative standing of individuals tends to remain approximately the same, while the amounts by which they excel one-another tend to become less.

Spaced Versus Unspaced Learning. Among the important problems of learning is the determination of the most efficient way to distribute practice periods. Is it more economical of time and energy to concentrate our learning into a single long practice session, or should the practice be spread out over a period of days, weeks, or months? If we have 100 new French words to learn, or if we want to learn to ride a bicycle, or drive an automobile, shall we keep practicing these tasks at one sitting until we master them or become exhausted, or shall we put in half an hour a day for a sufficient number of days until success is attained? The question is which method, that of concentrated or *unspaced practice,* or of distributed or *spaced* practice, will make for greater retentivenes and less energy expenditure?

It is obvious that where the act to be perfected calls for actual changes in the bodily tissues the practice must be spaced. The benefits to be derived from the " daily dozen " will not accrue if the exercise is postponed until every twelfth day and then one concentrated " gross " substituted for the days that were skipped. If in the course of spring practice a batsman finds he must hit about a thousand balls before his " batting eye " returns, clearly he will not achieve the same end by devoting a single day to an orgy of batting. While the superiority of spaced practice is thus obvious when extreme cases are selected, its superiority is neither obvious nor to be taken for granted in less extreme cases.

Even in extreme cases the question of the exact amount of practice to be indulged in at any one practice period cannot be settled out of hand. Neither can the related question of the optimum interval between one practice period and the next be decided by guesswork. From one point of view, even experimentation cannot settle such matters in any *absolute* way. The number of combinations and permutations for any single activity is infinite. Let us assume that the activity to be mastered is that of memorizing fifty lines of poetry requiring five minutes for one reading. What is the best way of accomplishing the task? Consider some of the possibilities. The poem may be read once a day for as many days as are necessary to memorize it. It may be read 12 times in one hour, then an interval of an hour may be permitted to elapse, followed by another hour of study and so on. Or else the interval may be reduced to half an hour or ten minutes or two days. Or shall the poem be read three times every third hour? So far as such infinite possibilities are concerned no one method is to be regarded as the most efficient, except in the *relative* sense that of all the combinations that have been tested with the given kind of material, one is demonstrated to be superior to the others.

The following simple experiment performed by Starch and quoted by Strong (27) may be considered in this connection. Four groups of people were drilled for 120 minutes in a substitution test in which digits were used to replace letters. The mental processes involved are comparable to code writing. While the total time expended by each group

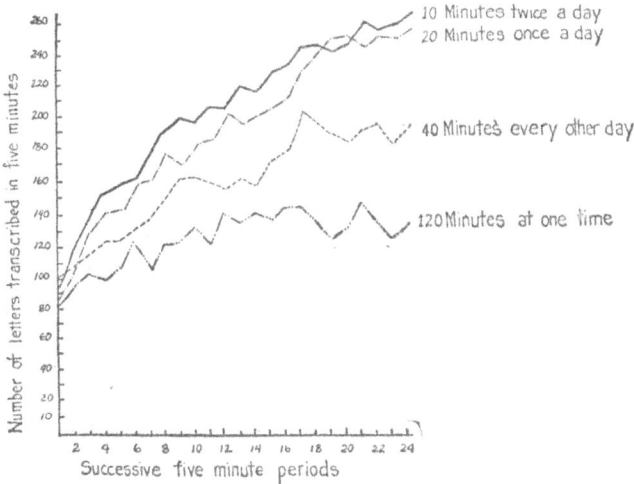

Fig. 25. — Curves showing influence of spaced versus unspaced learning in a substitution test. (After Starch, D., *Educational Psychology*, 1920.)

was the same, the distribution of the time differed for each group. Group number one spent two 10-minute periods per day for six days on the task; group number two worked 20 minutes at a time each day for six successive days; group number three put in one 40-minute period every other day for three days, while group number four concentrated the work into a single 120-minute period. The results are indicated in Figure 25. It will be noticed that the first group accomplished the most, with group number two a close second, the 40-minute group third, and the fourth group last. The first two groups achieved very much more than the last two, practically twice as much, and this despite the fact that they devoted no more actual time to the learning. However, so far as extent of time intervening between the beginning and the end of learning is concerned, the six-day interval tells in favor of the concentrated group, assuming that by devoting about 300 minutes to the work they could have equalled the performance of the first group. In general, it may be said that spaced study is superior to unspaced so far as time spent in work is concerned, while unspaced is superior so far as extent of time is concerned.

Part Learning and Whole Learning. Closely related to the problem of spaced and unspaced learning is the problem of the relative advantages of learning a thing part by part, or sectionally, as opposed to learning it as a whole. This is usually referred to as the problem of part versus whole learning. To illustrate by a few concrete cases, is it more efficient in learning a poem by heart to memorize it stanza by stanza than to read it over from beginning to end until it is mastered? In learning to play golf should one first practice gripping the driver, then devote one's attention to the correct stance, follow that with practicing the swing, and then complete the learning by practicing the whole act of teeing off? Or should the act as a whole be practiced from the start? Should the swimming instructor have his pupils first practice the leg movements until those are perfected, then the arm movements until they are correctly executed, and finally have them practice the simultaneous combination, or would his teaching be more effective if he required the pupils to practice the arm and leg movements together right from the start of the learning? In teaching reading is it more efficient to have the pupils first become familiar with the letters of the alphabet and then learn to perceive them as combined into words, or is it more economical to teach them to perceive the words as units directly without instruction in the individual letters?

It will be noticed that four illustrative examples have been chosen. These represent four types of situations in which the advantage of either method may vary with the problem to be mastered. We have first, verbal learning of a serial nature as in memorizing a poem or speech; second, motor learning of a serial nature as in driving a golf ball or learning to write; third, motor learning of a simultaneous nature as in swimming or piano playing; and fourth, perceptual learning as in reading or listening to a conversation.

(1) Unfortunately no definite answer can be given to the question of which method is superior. It is certain though that " common sense " and " experience " cannot be trusted to furnish a reliable answer; for in some cases which " common sense " ordinarily handles by the part method, experimental investigation has made the indisputably greater economy of the whole method evident. The entire question is complicated not only because of the fact that in some situations one method is better, while in another it is worse, but also by the difficulty of deciding what to use as a measure of relative superiority.

Let us consider the question of learning a poem by heart. One investigator [37] reports the results of an adult's work in memorizing three stanzas of a poem by the part method and three by the whole method. It required about 24 minutes to learn by the part method and about 36 minutes by the whole. Using *time* as a measure of economy it would seem that in this case the part method was superior. But we also find that in learning by the part method the total number of times the stanzas had to be repeated was about 33, while

---

[37] Pentschew, quoted by Reed (24), p. 109.

only about 17 repetitions were required for the whole method. As a consequence, if we were to utilize *number of repetitions* as our criterion of superiority, we should be forced to decide in favor of the unmistakable superiority of the whole method.

Aside from this factor of deciding on a common measure, the problem is further complicated by the fact that established habits of memorizing may militate against one or the other method. A subject who has been accustomed to memorize by the part method may find the whole method unsatisfactory both subjectively and with respect to actual measurement, because of the necessity of memorizing in an unaccustomed way. The reverse, of course, would be the case if he had been trained from earliest childhood to use the whole method and was subsequently forced to memorize by the part method. It is difficult to equate these factors of previous habituation, when older children and adults are used as subjects. Possibly when young children with no pronounced habits of memorizing are tested some of the conflict in existing experimental reports will disappear.

Although many psychologists are presumably persuaded that whole learning is superior to part so far as rote memory is concerned, it must be admitted that the matter is not yet conclusively established one way or the other. On the one hand, we find such a result as the following cited by Woodworth (40) in support of the whole method:

" If you had to memorize 240 lines of a poem, you would certainly be inclined to learn a part at a time; but notice the following experiment. A young man took two passages of this length, both from the same poem, and studied one by the whole method, the other by the part method, in sittings of about thirty-five minutes each day. His results appear in the table.

LEARNING PASSAGES OF 240 LINES, BY WHOLE AND
PART METHODS

(Pyle and Snyder)

Method of Study	Number of days required	Total number of minutes required
30 lines memorized per day, then the whole reviewed till it could be recited ... 12		431
3 readings of whole per day till it could be recited ... 10		348

" Here was an economy of eighty-three minutes, or nearly twenty per cent., by using the whole method as against the part method." [38]

On the other hand, we find Reed (24) getting results that are quite irreconcilable with the foregoing. He tested out the efficiency not only of the whole and part methods, but of an intermediate method, termed the *part progressive method*, or what might be called the *cumulative method*. The latter consists of memorizing the first stanza, then the second, then the first and second together, then the third, then the first, second, and third together, and so forth. He used a total of 113 subjects. The problem was to memorize 12 stanzas of poetry. The results showed that on the average the cumulative method was the best, the part method next best, and the whole method poorest, although the actual differences were not very great, the best method being 13 per cent shorter than the poorest. By tabulating his results in terms of individuals he found that of the 113 sub-

[38] *Op. cit.*, pp. 343–344.

T

jects, 31 did best when they used the part method, 26 when they used the whole method, while 56 secured best results by using the part progressive method.

With the available results in such a contradictory state it is premature to generalize one way or the other. Until the matter is more definitely settled, possibly the soundest practical procedure in the light of existing evidence is to read over the material to be memorized from beginning to end first, in order to get its general meaning, and then in committing to memory, to use the part progressive method.

(2) So far as motor learning of a *serial* nature is concerned, the work of Pechstein (19) is suggestive. This investigator was interested in determining the relative influence exerted by whole and part learning, in the case of mastering a pencil maze, in four different ways: (a) whole learning with spaced trials, (b) whole learning with unspaced trials, (c) part learning with spaced trials, and (d) part learning with unspaced trials. He found that with respect to spacing the whole method yielded the better results, while with respect to the unspaced technique the part method was superior. Of all the combinations, the best results were obtained by the unspaced part method. To the extent that his findings are applicable to the problem of learning to drive a golf ball, we might say that if economy of time with reference to number of days spent is desirable, then the whole method might be more advantageous, while if economy of actual playing time is the objective, the part method is to be chosen.

(3) The problem of the relative economy of the two methods of learning in the case of motor learning of the *simultaneous* type had been experimentally investigated by Koch (12). This psychologist had her subjects learn to manipulate two typewriters simultaneously in a way comparable to that of the finger movements employed by a pian-

ist when playing with both hands. The completed performance showed the fingers of the right hand of the subject pressing the first five keys of the middle row of a typewriter in the sequence 2 4 3 2 1 5 4 5 2; while at the same time the fingers of the left hand were pressing the adjacent first five keys of the middle row of the other typewriter in the sequence 3 2 1 5 4 2 1 4 5. The numbers indicate the particular finger employed, 1 referring to the thumb, 2 to the index finger, 3 the middle finger, 4 the ring finger and 5 the little finger. In addition to learning to execute the movements simultaneously in the prescribed sequence, the subjects had to press the keys at the rate of " one for each beat of a metronome set at 140." One group of subjects tackled this task by the whole method, while the other employed the part method. In this experiment, of course, the whole method consisted in learning to react to both typewriters simultaneously from the very beginning of the learning, while the part method called for first learning to manipulate each typewriter separately and then simultaneously. The general results showed a manifest superiority of the part as opposed to the whole method, both in the case of individuals with previous experience in piano playing and in the case of those with no such experience. None of the subjects " had had any contact with typewriting."

The following table is illustrative of the nature of the results. It shows the average total time, the number of trials, and the number of errors *per individual* in the case of the group with training in piano playing.[39]

Measure	Whole Method	Part Method	Diff.	P.E. Diff.
Av. total time	53.74 ± 3.30	47.04 ± 3.78	6.70	5.01
Av. total errors	391.66 ± 24.35	384.12 ± 21.04	7.45	32.18
Av. total trials	536.46 ± 31.37	431.76 ± 29.60	104.70	41.13

[39] *Op. cit.*, p. 372.

(4) So far as *perceptual learning* is concerned the results, in the case of learning to read, are decidedly against the part method. As is well known, the modern teacher of reading no longer utilizes the part method of a generation ago, but has the youngster react at once to word and phrase wholes. To require the pupil to master the letters of the alphabet first and then gradually by means of phonetic instruction come to recognize syllables, and then attempt simple words, is a slower and more tedious method than the other. To what degree this finding applies to other forms of perceptual learning must be determined separately for each form. One must proceed cautiously in so complex a realm as that of the psychology of learning.

Transfer of Training. The necessity for caution and careful experimentation is also clear in the case of another learning problem that has been somewhat more successfully coped with than the part-whole problem. This is usually referred to as the question of *transfer of training*. It is the problem of determining to what extent learning one thing carries over to more or less related performances. Does learning to drive an automobile of a given make help or hinder (and to what degree) when we try to learn to drive one of a different make? Will a child who is trained to be neat in his dress carry over this particular habit of neatness to his penmanship, his note-taking, or his care of animal pets? Does training in algebraic reasoning improve one's ability to reason out legal, ethical, and literary problems? Does training our memory for telephone numbers automatically improve our memory for names, dates, faces, titles of books, daily appointments, and chemical formulae? Students of pedagogy will recognize this as the familiar educational problem of *formal discipline*. The rigid supporter of formal discipline is in reality an adherent of the antiquated faculty psychology. Like the phrenologist he conceives of the mind as being made up of fixed forms or faculties. Accordingly, if one of these " faculties " like that of memory is trained or disciplined with one kind of exercise such as memorizing poems, then the beneficial results of this training will be evident in the markedly improved retention of everything else. Since the study of grammar calls for the analysis of sentences, the discipline it gives the " analytic faculty " will fortify the student's ability to analyze business problems, chemical compounds, murder mysteries — in short, any affair that involves analysis.

While no psychologist today lends credence to this extreme application of the principle of transfer of training, it is unfortunately true that many educated, non-psychologically trained individuals do. Concrete laboratory experiments have shown that the amount of transfer is not only limited, but that often it is either completely absent or even negatively present. As Webb (38) has pointed out, we may have *positive* transfer when learning in one situation aids in a subsequent situation and *negative* transfer if the former hinders the latter. When the first learning exerts no effect on the second we may speak of *absence* of transfer. It is also well to recognize that the acquisition of new material may influence the retention of old material. A baseball player who takes up football may find, upon resuming the former game, that his football experience aids, hinders, or has no effect upon his baseball playing. The term *retroaction* is used to refer to the possible influence of a new act on an old, established act. Theoretically, there are also three retroactive possibilities: positive, negative, and absence of retroaction. If mastery of a new situation strengthens the retention of an old habit, we have *positive* retroaction. In terms of our example, if the ball-player is helped by his football training, it is a case of positive retroaction. Should there be an actual loss in his baseball proficiency due to his playing football, the process would be called *negative* retroaction, or *retroactive inhibition*. Finally, if the new habits exercise no influence on the old, we speak of *absence* of retroaction.[40]

Owing to the relatively small amount of transfer revealed in many experimental investigations, a misinterpretation to the effect that there is absolutely no transfer of training has been introduced into semi-popular debates on the formal discipline question. Such an assertion is as unwarranted as that of the extreme adherent of formal discipline who maintains that there is a tremendous amount of transfer. It is all a question of degree. Coover (5) has studied this question very intensively and critically. In the course of this study he presents a summary of 18 investigations covering a wide diversity of mental functions.[41] In all of these there was *some* improvement carried over.

According to prevalent interpretations of such improvement, however, it is not due to the training of any general mental " powers " or " faculties," but rather to the training of specific functions or attitudes that are common to the two performances. In this sense an individual who has found that his memory for names is improved if he writes the names down soon after hearing them, may be able to transfer this mnemonic device to other memory material such as dates and titles of books. To the extent that such increased success in remembering names gives him confidence in his " memory," the general attitude of confidence may be transferred to other memory situations. A person who has difficulty in perfecting his technique of piano playing because of inability to control the movements of the fingers of the left hand may find that after practicing typewriting for several months his piano work has improved. This would be a transfer of the specific movements of the fingers in the

[40] *Op. cit.*, pp. 1–2.   [41] *Op. cit.*, pp. 31–32.

direction of increased control due in part to mere strengthening of the muscle groups involved. To argue from such a finding that the would-be pianist should practice typewriting would be absurd. Yet such an argument is no more absurd than that of the pedagogue who asserts that all would-be lawyers should study chemistry or mathematics, because such subjects call for close reasoning and the good lawyer must be able to reason closely.

The practical implications of experimental studies of transfer of training should be fairly clear; namely, that training should always be of the process or processes that the individual intends to use. If an individual desires to become competent as a pianist or lawyer, he ought to occupy his time with piano practice or legal problems. If he wants to be a chemist he requires training in chemical reasoning and not legal reasoning. That is to say, it would be inefficient for him to study law solely because such study would *in part* train mental functions brought into play by chemistry when those same functions would be exercised directly in the course of his chemical studies. On the other hand, we must not overlook the fact that since there is *some* transfer of training from one activity to the next we may be profiting more than we realize from much of our activity. The exact nature of this transfer can only be determined by actual experiment, for what superficially appear to be identical functions may really be antagonistic. Actual measurement of presumed transfer effects should replace a priori guesswork.

It is also well to remember, as Thorndike (28) has pointed out, "that a very small spread of training may be of very great educational value if it extends over a wide enough field. If a hundred hours of training in being scientific about chemistry produced only one hundredth as much improvement in being scientific about all sorts of facts, it would yet be a very remunerative educational force. If a gain of fifty per cent in justice toward classmates in school affairs increased the general equitableness of a boy's behavior only one-tenth of one per cent, this disciplinary effect would still perhaps be worth more than the specific habits." [42]

Concluding Remarks. In the course of our discussion of learning behavior we have outlined the major problems of learning. The methods developed by the psychologist for studying these problems both in human and in animal learning have been sketched. Where circumstances permitted we have called attention to some of the practical applications of the results that the experimental investigations brought to light. Study of the previous pages should render it clear that progress of a genuine sort has been made by the psychologist in his study of learning phenomena. Apart from any definite conclusions attained, the mere realization and formulation of a specific problem is in itself a sign of progress. In addition, the development of appropriate experimental methods, the introduction of stimulating theories and their revision in the light of accumulating new evidence all serve to mark the approach of more comprehensive answers to these problems. To have grasped the import of these problems means that we have deepened our insight into psychological facts — that we have broadened our psychological horizon.

References

1. ANGELL, J. R. An Introduction to Psychology, Second Edition, 1920.
2. CARR, H. Principles of Selection in Animal Learning. Psychological Review, 1914, 21, 157–165.
3. —— Maze Studies with the White Rat. 1. Normal Animals. Journal of Animal Behavior, 1917, 7, 259–275.

[42] *Op. cit.*, p. 282.

4. CASON, H. Criticisms of the Laws of Exercise and Effect. Psychological Review, 1924, 31, 397–417.

5. COOVER, J. E. Formal Discipline from the Standpoint of Experimental Psychology. Psychological Monographs, No. 87, 1912.

6. EBBINGHAUS, H. Über das Gedächtnis, 1885.

7. HOBHOUSE, L. T. Mind in Evolution, 1901.

8. HOLMES, S. J. The Evolution of Animal Intelligence, 1911.

9. —— Studies in Animal Behavior, 1916.

10. JONES, H. E. Experimental Studies of College Teaching. Archives of Psychology, No. 68, 1923.

11. KINCAID, M. A Study of Individual Differences in Learning. Psychological Review, 1925, 32, 34–53.

12. KOCH, H. L. A Neglected Phase of the Part-Whole Problem. Journal of Experimental Psychology, 1923, 6, 366–376.

13. KOFFKA, K. The Growth of the Mind, 1924.

14. KUO, Z. Y. Giving Up Instincts in Psychology. The Journal of Philosophy, 1921, 18, 645–664.

15. —— The Nature of Unsuccessful Acts and their Order of Elimination in Animal Learning. Journal of Comparative Psychology, 1922, 2, 1–27.

16. LADD, G. T., AND WOODWORTH, R. S. Elements of Physiological Psychology, 1911.

17. MORGAN, C. L. Introduction to Comparative Psychology, 1894.

18. —— Habit and Instinct, 1896.

19. PECHSTEIN, L. A. Whole vs. Part Methods in Motor Learning. Psychological Monographs, No. 99, 1917.

20. PERRIN, F. A. C. An Experimental and Introspective Study of the Human Learning Process in the Maze. Psychological Monographs, No. 70, 1914.

21. PERRY, R. B. Docility and Purposiveness. Psychological Review, 1918, 25, 1–20.

22. PETERSON, J. Completeness of Response as an Explanation Principle in Learning. Psychological Review, 1916, 23, 153–162.

23. —— Frequency and Recency Factors in Maze Learning by White Rats. Journal of Animal Behavior, 1917, 7, 338–364.

24. REED, H. B. Part and Whole Methods of Learning. Journal of Educational Psychology, 1924, 15, 107–115.

25. RUGER, H. A.   The Psychology of Efficiency.   Archives of Psychology, No. 15, 1910.

26. SMITH, S., AND GUTHRIE, E. R.   General Psychology in Terms of Behavior, 1923.

27. STRONG, E. K.   The Learning Process.   Psychological Bulletin, 1918, 13, 339–343.

28. THORNDIKE, E. L.   Educational Psychology, Briefer Course, 1914.

29. ——   Watson's "Behavior."   Journal of Animal Behavior, 1915, 5, 452–467.

30. THURSTONE, L. L.   The Learning Curve Equation.   Psychological Monographs, No. 114, 1919.

31. TOLMAN, E. C.   Instinct and Purpose.   Psychological Review, 1920, 27, 217–234.

32. VINCENT, S. B.   The White Rat and the Maze Problem.   Journal of Animal Behavior, 5, 1–24, 140–157, 175–184, 367–374.

33. ——   The Function of the Vibrissae in the Behavior of the White Rat.   Behavior Monographs Series, No. 5, 1912.

34. WARDEN, C. J.   The Relative Economy of Various Modes of Attack in the Mastery of a Stylus Maze.   Journal of Experimental Psychology, 1924, 7, 243–275.

35. WATSON, J. B.   Kinæsthetic and Organic Sensations: Their Rôle in the Reactions of the White Rat to the Maze.   Psychological Monographs, No. 33, 1907.

36. ——   Behavior: An Introduction to Comparative Psychology, 1914.

37. ——   Psychology from the Standpoint of a Behaviorist, Second Edition, 1924.

38. WEBB, L. W.   Transfer of Training and Retroaction.   Psychological Monographs, No. 104, 1917.

39. WOODWORTH, R. S.   Dynamic Psychology, 1918.

40. ——   Psychology: A Study of Mental Life, 1921.

CHAPTER VI

INTELLIGENT BEHAVIOR

Intimately related to the problem of learning behavior is the question of the organism's use of that which it has learned. This question is concerned with the appropriateness or fitness of learned responses to given situations. Ordinarily this is referred to as the problem of intelligence. It is a study of the manner and extent to which humans and animals succeed in adapting means to ends in coping with their difficulties. Although from this point of view the question of intelligent behavior is closely allied to many of the specific problems considered in the last chapter, it is, nevertheless, sufficiently different from the general problem of learmng to merit separate analysis and discussion.

MENTAL DEVELOPMENT

On the previous pages we have often referred to *mental* reactions without ever saying precisely what the phrase means. In general the context served to suggest a temporarily adequate meaning. It is now time to try to define the term. To formulate a brief and readily understandable definition is by no means easy. As will soon be evident, before such a definition can be formulated certain preliminary information is necessary. The situation is comparable to the problem of explaining the binomial theorem to a person ignorant of arithmetic and algebra. That this statement is not too extreme will be seen as we build up our definition.

Mental and Non-mental Reactions. Let us first endeavor to clear the field by considering some reactions that
obviously are not mental. All will agree that the rebound
of a rubber ball is not a mental, but a *physical* reaction.
Similarly, it is a *chemical* reaction that causes iron to rust,
just as it is a series of *physiological* reactions that cause our
food to be digested. On the other hand we refer to such activities as adding a column of figures, reading a book, con-
versing with friends, or memorizing a poem by a different
term. We call them *mental* reactions.

Without entering into too much debate we might raise a
legitimate question and ask why a conversation, for example, should be called something mental and digestion be
called something physiological. Obviously the former activity brings physiological mechanisms into play: the auditory receptor and its neurons, the cerebrum, motor nerves
to the speech organs and so on. Nevertheless we should refuse to regard the activity as the same in kind as digestion
or respiration. Although we may not be able to indicate the
difference immediately, we feel that in some way it must be
different.

Consciousness and Mental Reactions. Frequently it is
said that the essential characteristic of a mental reaction, as
opposed to any other kind, is the participation of consciousness. According to this view any activity involving
consciousness is mental. The more conscious it is, the more
mental it is said to be. An explanation of this sort is helpful to the extent that an intelligible definition of consciousness is given along with the word mental. This is not often
done. For example, Dunlap (13) states first that "*consciousness* . . . means merely *awareness* of something, and
wherever we find the word consciousness we can substitute
perfectly the word *awareness.*" He then proceeds to point
out that "*mental* is the adjective corresponding to con-

sciousness: anything directly connected with, or relating to, awareness, is *mental*." It should be obvious that the fruitfulness of such a definition hinges upon the way in which the word *awareness* is defined. And yet a little further on in his text Dunlap declares that " we cannot describe or define awareness." [1] In justice to Dunlap it must be stated that he recognizes the limitations of his definitions. To him they refer to something ultimate and " nothing which is really ultimate can ever be defined or described, but can merely be ' pointed out,' by describing complex situations in which it occurs." [2]

As a consequence, it is conceivable that the criterion of consciousness may be employed to separate mental from non-mental reactions, even though no intimate explanation of consciousness is made. We might say that everybody knows what we mean by the term and to insist on a formal definition is but irritating pedantry. A person taking this stand would be holding a rather strong position were it not for the fact that difficulties arise as soon as we begin to use our criterion. It fails to do its work when applied to concrete cases. On the basis of consciousness, for instance, we find it impossible to find a sharp line of separation between unmistakably mental and avowedly physiological reactions. Sneezing is accompanied by consciousness, yet we should hesitate to regard it as a mental activity. On the contrary, an habitual act, such as lighting a cigarette, may take place " unconsciously," but we should not therefore call it a physiological process. This difficulty is not lost sight of by many psychologists who, nevertheless, feel constrained to continue invoking the test of consciousness in determining whether a given reaction is to be regarded as a mental one. For them it represents the best we can do at present. They are content to let the problem rest after showing that the

[1] *Op. cit.*, pp. 22–25.　　[2] *Ibid.*, footnote bottom of page 29.

test is not to be too rigorously applied. An excellent ex-ample of this group of psychologists is to be found in Wood-worth (50) for whom "a mental activity is typically, though not universally, conscious." He maintains that " we can roughly designate as mental those activities of a living creature that are either conscious themselves or closely akin to those that are conscious." [3]

Because of these difficulties in the use of the criterion of consciousness, it is evident that we have not progressed very far in our attempt to ascertain the essential characteristics of a *mental* activity. This does not mean that we deny the facts of consciousness, but that we cannot make efficient use of these facts in our endeavor to define the nature of mental reactions, as distinguished from physical, chemical, or physi-ological reactions.

The Genesis of Mental Acts. If we reject the proposi-tion that mental acts are to be defined in terms of conscious-ness, what are we to offer in place of it? The simplest ap-proach to an understanding of our proposed substitute is to study the genesis and development of such acts. In other words, let us first secure a clear, if elementary, idea of the way in which mental reactions originate. To facilitate mat-ters we shall present a single, detailed example by way of illustrating our conception.

It is well known that a new-born baby will immediately grip any object placed in its hand. This is called the *grasp-ing reflex*. A stick or rod brought into contact with the in-fant's palm will be automatically clasped even if the child is asleep. Nobody would call this a mental act. It is a physiological reaction of the " pure " reflex type. In fact, Watson (45), who has made a close study of this reflex, re-ports the case of one baby born without a cerebrum in whom " the reflex was practically perfect up to the day of

[3] *Op. cit.*, p. 17.

its death at 18 days." [4]   There can be no doubt about the reflex nature of this infantile response. Any painless tactual stimulus applied to the palm of the hand will evoke it.

Not to complicate matters unduly we shall consider certain changes that might be introduced in this reflex, disregarding for the time being the influence of vision. Let us assume that we are experimenting with an infant that was born blind, but otherwise perfectly healthy. We note that for several hours each day the infant lies in its crib cooing and moving its arms about in random fashion. It is apparently indulging in play, after being well fed and after a long nap. Now what is the stimulus that results in the arm movements? In the interests of simplicity we may say that it is *metabolic*. By this term we mean that the complex processes of digestion and assimilation of food have activated various interoceptors and that the neural impulses from these interoceptors eventually reach the efferent neurones going to the arm muscles. The resulting arm movements automatically stimulate the proprioceptive receptors of the moving limbs and the consequent kinaesthetic impulses serve to keep up the movements, with the circular reflexes involved. In the course of these random movements the hands come into contact with each other and many other objects. Such contact results in flexion of the fingers — the grasping reflex. In this way the baby comes to take hold of many objects and manipulate them. Suppose we suspend a slender stick over the crib near the youngster's head low enough for him to touch it when his arm is extended. He will come to take hold of this in the course of his chance movements just as he comes to take hold of the blankets, his toes, the nursing bottle or any other sufficiently small object. There is no means of predicting precisely what ob-

[4] *Op. cit.*, p. 262.

ject he will grasp at this stage of his development. It is all quite aimless.

Among other things we observe that if we stand a few feet away from the crib and talk or make a slight noise by tapping on the floor with our foot he turns his head in the direction of the sound. When the auditory stimulus ceases he resumes his random movements. Irrespective of what we say or what kind of a light noise we make there is always this momentary turning of the head in the direction of the sound, accompanied by a cessation of the play activity which is resumed soon after the sound stops. We may say that he was giving his attention to the sound. *Attention* thus means an adjustment or orientation of the body or some part of the body with respect to the source of stimulation. This head movement in response to the sound may be regarded as the unconditioned reaction to a moderate auditory stimulus.

We now watch the youngster during his waking hours and each time he touches the suspended stick we speak the phrase, " Grab the stick." From our knowledge of the conditioned reflex we know that in a short time the youngster will take hold of the stick when the phrase is uttered. Instead of the original response of turning the head we get a response of reaching for the stick. It is a case of substitution of one response for another. A stranger witnessing the behavior of the baby would say that the baby *understands* the meaning of the words " grab the stick."

Although this particular illustration is hypothetical, it is in keeping with the facts of concrete observation of infant behavior. For example, one of the writers, by employing this method of auditory conditioning, succeeded in getting a 14-months-old infant to clap its hands at the words " loud applause."

Our simple and somewhat artificial illustration of the

blind baby reaching for the stick in obedience to a spoken command gives us a clue to the origin of " mental " acts. It seems that in part they are closely related to the acquisition of language. In fact people judge the " intelligence " or " mentality " of an infant by the way in which it responds to words. The parents are elated each time the baby manifests a new conditioned response of this sort. They regard it as additional evidence of its developing " mind." When the infant begins to articulate words they feel that another stage of mental development has appeared. It should be clear then that an analysis of language acquisition may

LANGUAGE ACQUISITION

Before discussing the subject of language acquisition the scope of the problem involved should be briefly outlined. As a matter of convenience the subject of language may be considered with respect, first, to its sensory phases and, second, to its motor phases. The former includes the understanding of words that are heard or written, and printed material that is seen, as well as the ability to understand the significance of gesture and facial expression. It may also include lip reading and the reading of raised type by means of the finger tips as is called for by the Braille system. Among the receptors brought into play in connection with the sensory phase are those of audition, vision, contact, and, as will be explained shortly, the receptors of the kinaesthetic system.

In connection with the motor phase we have to include speech and writing, making gestures, drawing, sculpturing, painting — in short, any device employed that will arouse meaning. The striped musculature is primarily involved in this phase of language acquisition, particularly the muscles

U

of the fingers, tongue, lips, and those of articulate speech in the throat region. To the extent that the glandular apparatus and the smooth musculature participate in emotional expression they may also be classified with the motor side of language.

A survey of the activities embraced by the term *language* indicates the fact that it is a much broader term than *speech*. Taken strictly, the latter term should be limited to vocal utterance while the term *language* itself may be extended to *any* means of *symbolization* or representation, including speech. In this sense the gesture of pointing out an object, curling the lip in contempt, writing a letter, drawing a picture, playing a tune on a musical instrument, noting that x (a + b) = ax + bx and so on — all these represent language activities.

Careful consideration of the bodily structures used in language reactions will show that our division of these reactions into sensory and motor phases is merely for the purpose of simplifying the presentation. There is no question of the sensory phase being more important than the motor or effector phase, or of one appearing before the other, or even of an exact line of separation between them. They arise concurrently and they are mutually so interdependent

This futility is readily demonstrated by means of the example of auditory conditioning to the phrase " grab the stick." It will be recalled that the grasping movement was already present when the auditory stimulus was introduced. However, this does not argue that the motor side of language activities must appear *before* the sensory side; for the initial act of grasping was induced by stimulating the tactual receptors. Furthermore, the fact that the grasping movement after being initiated is regulated by kinaesthetic impulses from the moving limb lends additional support to the view that receptor-effector relationships are so intimately coöperative that their separate consideration is justified only on the grounds of descriptive convenience. Accordingly, with this understanding, we shall proceed to sketch first the receptor phase of language acquisition and then the effector phase.

The Receptor Phase of Language Acquisition. Reverting to our earlier example of auditory conditioning, we may note that the grasping response may be brought about not only by the words " grab the stick," but by any sound or sequence of sounds, just as a salivary secretion may be conditioned to any sound. Practically this means that the infant may learn to execute the same movement when the phrase employed during the training period is " take hold of the stick," or " prends le bâton," or " nimm den Stock," or " cape baculum," or " prendi il bastone," or " nà dráttese tô bastuni," depending on whether the conditioning takes place in English, French, German, Latin, Italian, or Greek. Even a nonsense syllable such as " kaj " may be made to serve as an effective conditioning stimulus. From this point of view a person who understands several languages has merely increased his range of effective substitute stimuli. In so far as we regard language attainment as one index of mentality this way of viewing such attainment is psychologically significant.

Along with the establishment of auditory language stimuli other forms of conditioning such as the visual and tactual merit brief description. In the case of a baby with vision intact it is not a difficult matter to get him to react to the stick when someone points to it. He is so conditioned that he responds to the visual stimulus of the instructor's moving arm and pointing finger. Moving the head or eyes in the direction of the stick may likewise be used as conditioning devices. In any event, irrespective of the exact nature of the visual stimulus employed, we ordinarily regard the ease with which such reactions are built up and their number as indications of the child's increasing *mental* powers. We say that he is beginning to understand the meaning of gestures. A further step in advance is registered when he can point to pictures of a stick and later when he can recognize the written or printed word "stick." As in the case of audition, the greater the number of visual stimuli (different languages) that are linked up with the stick as a physical object the higher is our estimate of the individual's mentality. How these visual language stimuli are presented is immaterial so far as the possibility of conditioning is concerned. They may take the form of gestures, pictures, words printed with the letters in left to right sequence as in English, or the reverse as in Hebrew, or vertically as in Chinese, or diagonally, or any other way.

Although the cutaneous receptors do not ordinarily play an extensive part in language development, they do come to serve as important language mechanisms in the case of the blind who learn to read with their finger tips. Certain patterns of tactual stimuli come to stand for words; that is, the substitute stimuli are presented in the form of cutaneous impressions. In this connection it may be of interest to recall that in learning to typewrite by the touch method the tactual and kinaesthetic receptors become spatially conditioned with respect to the distribution of the letters on the keyboard.

The Effector Phase of Language Acquisition. Just as the receptor side of language acquisition has to do with the interpretation or understanding of the words or language signs made by others, so the effector side is concerned with the speaking of words or the execution of language signs. As has already been mentioned, the effector phase includes such language activities as gesticulating, articulate speech, writing, and the various plastic arts as well as drawing, painting, and music. For our purposes it will suffice to study the acquisition of the gesture and speech forms with some care and to give but passing mention to the others.

Allport (1) points out that the genesis of gesture language in infancy is readily explained on the conditioned reflex principle. By way of illustration he traces the origin of the common gesture of shaking the head to indicate dissent or negation. " At the beginning the baby turns his head away so as to prevent undesired substances which touch his lips from entering his mouth. This is the stage of simple *avoidance* or *withdrawing*. By conditioning response the sight of the undesirable object later calls forth the same reaction, and the effect is now avoidance in advance, or *refusal*. The movement serves as a sign which is readily understood and reacted to by the person offering the rejected substance. . . . It is now *used as a sign;* in other words, it has become a gesture." [5] By means of the same principle we can account for the rise of such gestures as waving the arm aside in indication of dismissal, thrusting the arm outward as a sign of opposition, keeping the arms extended as a token of welcome, pointing at desired objects beyond one's reach, and many others. Of course many gestures of a stereotyped sort are acquired by the individual as a result of social tradition rather than the conditioning of infantile movements in the manner described. Shaking hands, the military salute, the traffic officer's signals, bowing the head in submission, placing the finger over the lips to call for silence or secrecy, the criss-cross movement of the index fingers to register " shame on you," and numerous other gestures are cases in point. They are acquired by a conditioning process, it is true, but the acquisition is more the result of deliberate teaching on the part of others than is the case with

[5] *Op. cit.*, pp. 178–179.

the former group of gestures. Throwing a kiss as a gesture of affection or appreciation is conditioned differently from throwing up the arms as a gesture of self-defense.

The development of *articulate speech* is also readily described in terms of the conditioned reflex principle. On a previous page the influence of metabolic stimuli in provoking random movements of the infant was mentioned. Among these movements are those of the vocal apparatus. The baby exercises the complex speech mechanisms in the same idle fashion in which it exercises its arms and legs. These pre-linguistic exercises are conventionally described as babbling, cooing, or chattering. Articulate speech arises out of this infantile, reflex vocalization.

Phonetically considered this random vocalization is the same in all babies, just as their early random movements may be regarded as the same. This does not mean that infants' voices are identical in pitch, timbre, or intensity, but that the identity is to be found in the fact that they make the same kind of vowel and consonantal sounds. The mechanics of the vocal apparatus renders this possible. Accordingly, the same elementary sounds that are finally combined into speech are to be found in all babies with normal speech organs, irrespective of their nationality. Stated differently, the German, Chinese, Eskimo, American, or Polish infants of, say 6 weeks, all make the same sounds. Yet by the time they are 6 years old they all speak different languages. This is brought about *by differences in the conditioning processes.*

For an adequate understanding of these differences we must briefly study the nature of the conditioning processes themselves. Following Allport we may divide the problem of learning to speak into the three following stages: [6]

(1) Random articulation with fixation of responses

[6] *Op. cit.,* pp. 181–188.

(2) Influence of the speech of others on the fixed responses

(3) Influence of objects and situations on the fixed responses

The first stage may be presumed to be the same for all infants. It refers to the period of random, vocal play during which the elements of articulation become strengthened and susceptible of control through the ear. It is essentially a process of self-conditioning. As the baby utters a particular sound, such as " dee," its own auditory receptor is automatically stimulated. Due to the common infantile tendency to prolong the vowel sound, the ear is stimulated while the response that produced the stimulus is still in progress. A circular relationship is thus established which finally results in the *production* of the sound " dee " whenever it is heard. An auditory stimulus may be said to have been substituted for the original metabolic stimulus responsible for the chance vocalization. As a result of this self-conditioning the baby in the course of time comes to repeat any simple sound he hears.

With the appearance of the ability to reproduce these simple phonetic elements, the second stage of development is reached. During this stage the child responds to words that it hears by uttering the nearest approximations that its previously acquired auditory-vocal reflexes will permit. It is a stage of social stimulation and consequently it marks the period when the vocalization of infants becomes diversified. German infants begin to make " German " sounds and Chinese infants " Chinese " sounds. In connection with this stage, it is well to note that, as Allport says, we are dealing with a parrot-like performance that is ordinarily described as " learning by imitation." This term " is however both inexact and misleading, for it suggests that the process is one of learning the speech reactions of others by voluntarily copying them; whereas it is really the touching off of *previously acquired* speech habits by their conditioning auditory stimuli." [7] Strictly interpreted, this stage of the development of word habits is not to be regarded as one of genuine language functioning. The words uttered are not used as a means of social control, for they have no *meaning* for the baby.

In the third stage the words begin to achieve a true language function. Actually, of course, there is no separation in time between stages two and three. It is only in the interests of analysis that such a separation is justified. This becomes evident when we consider what takes place during this third stage. It is a period when a given word becomes attached to a given object. For example, while feeding the child the parent pauses every now and then and says in a questioning voice, " More? " The child repeats this at first in parrot-like fashion, but later the situation of food being withheld provokes this same verbal response even in the absence of a question from the parent. The child's cry for " more " results in a response on the part of the parent. Language as a form of social control is beginning to assert itself at this stage. This development is also achieved by means of the conditioned reflex mechanism. To illustrate this, one additional instance may be considered; namely, learning to call objects by name. The child in the course of its vocal play utters the syllable " ba." To the parent it sounds like " box." By holding a box in front of the child and saying " box " at the same time, the parent causes the visual appearance of the object to be connected with the name of the object. Later the sight of the box suffices to evoke the response " ba." A visual stimulus has been substituted for an auditory one. By means of similar conditioning the child comes to " recognize " a box by manipulating

[7] *Ibid.*, pp. 184–185.

resentative assortment of examples in which the term *think-ing* occurs, we should find that it can be divided with approximate accuracy into the following four classes:

(1) Mere opinions of a simple descriptive nature expressed in a casual, unreflective, effortless manner. Examples of this group are to be found in such statements as " I think golf is a wonderful game," " I think it is bedtime," or " I think I'll wear my new shoes today." The word *believe* is often substituted for *think* when employed in this sense.

(2) Any consideration of events or things not present in concrete reality. In this sense of the term we can *think* of last month's issue of a magazine, of our next birthday, of our departed friends, of the sound of a violin, of the arrangement of the rooms in our childhood home, or of what we are going to have for lunch tomorrow. Our playful fancies and daydreams represent thinking of this sort. Synonyms for this usage of the word are *imagine* or *picture*.

(3) Cases that involve an element of doubt or uncertainty as illustrated by such expressions as " I think it must have been close to 9 o'clock when he arrived " or " I think I may become a lawyer." Thinking of this sort demands a certain amount of reflection. To a limited extent the pros and cons bound up with the issue under consideration are hastily reviewed. In this type of usage we find the word *think* synonymous with *judge, estimate,* or *consider*.

(4) Thinking of the problem-solving type. A convict planning his escape, a physician trying to diagnose a puzzling illness, an engineer designing a new kind of engine, or a business man deciding on momentous investments — all are indulging in this type of thinking. It is also described by such verbs as *ponder, cogitate, reflect,* and *reason*.

Of course such a four-fold classification has no hard and fast lines of distinction. It is easy to find examples that

a sign or signal that stands for that overt activity. In the same way such words as " upon," " near," or " under " symbolize relations of position as when the child is told to " grab the stick near the end." Words like " now," " yesterday," " after," " before," similarly symbolize relations of time.

The way in which verbal cues serve to modify our behavior has already been mentioned in connection with certain aspects of learning.[8] It is now necessary to indicate in a less restricted manner the wider significance not only of verbal material, but of language in general. That language, psychologically considered, represents a system of vicarious or substitutive stimulus-response mechanisms should be plain even on the basis of our superficial analysis. Our immediate task is to demonstrate the significance of such a system.

In terms of the problem we set out to solve — the problem of defining the term, " mental reaction " — we might note that one significant feature of language, when viewed as a stimulus-response system, is that it furnishes us with our needed definition. If language is regarded as involving more than verbal reactions (as we have conceived the term) then it should be obvious that mental reactions are closely allied to language reactions. In fact, all language reactions are mental, but not all mental reactions are language. The meaning of this statement will be clarified presently. For the time being, we may content ourselves with defining *mental activities as substitute or symbolic responses.* They are reactions that *stand for or are a sign of other reactions.* The accuracy of this definition should be judged by the manner in which it works when applied to concrete and genuine cases of behavior that all agree in designating as mental. In other words, the definition should be judged in the

[8] See section dealing with *Consciousness and Learning.*

light of its usefulness as a means of describing such activities as writing a poem or planning a meal, activities that everybody would regard as *mental* in some degree. People designate them as mental because, as they say, " one must *think* in order to write poetry or to plan something and *thinking* is something *mental*." Let us proceed to find out what thinking is and in the process we shall not only put our definition to the test, but shall also find out a little more concerning the psychological significance of language.

The Nature of Thinking

The close connection between language and thought is well known. Titchener (43) summarizes this excellently in these sentences: " It has often been said that thought would be impossible without words; and it is true that we can hardly conceive of human thought save as formed and embodied and expressed in language. Thought and articulate speech grew up, so to say, side by side; each implies the other; they are two sides of the same phase of mental development." [9] Whether all language behavior is to be classified as thinking, will depend on how rigidly we define the term *thought*.

Different Uses of the Term "Thinking." Ordinarily the words *thought* and *thinking* are employed in a wide variety of senses. Dewey (10) has pointed out that any kind of reaction from an idle fancy to a piece of complicated reasoning is indiscriminately labeled " thinking " in our daily speech.[10] We find people saying that they " think it must be time for lunch " or that they " think the maid is dishonest." Sometimes they " think heredity is more important than environment," just as they " think the price of coal is exorbitant," or that the doctor " thinks the patient's illness might be pneumonia." If we were to collect a rep-

[9] *Op. cit.*, p. 267.   [10] *Op. cit.*. Chapter I.

resentative assortment of examples in which the term *think-ing* occurs, we should find that it can be divided with approximate accuracy into the following four classes:

(1) Mere opinions of a simple descriptive nature expressed in a casual, unreflective, effortless manner. Examples of this group are to be found in such statements as " I think golf is a wonderful game," " I think it is bedtime," or " I think I'll wear my new shoes today." The word *believe* is often substituted for *think* when employed in this sense.

(2) Any consideration of events or things not present in concrete reality. In this sense of the term we can *think* of last month's issue of a magazine, of our next birthday, of our departed friends, of the sound of a violin, of the arrangement of the rooms in our childhood home, or of what we are going to have for lunch tomorrow. Our playful fancies and daydreams represent thinking of this sort. Synonyms for this usage of the word are *imagine* or *picture*.

(3) Cases that involve an element of doubt or uncertainty as illustrated by such expressions as " I think it must have been close to 9 o'clock when he arrived " or " I think I may become a lawyer." Thinking of this sort demands a certain amount of reflection. To a limited extent the pros and cons bound up with the issue under consideration are hastily reviewed. In this type of usage we find the word *think* synonymous with *judge, estimate,* or *consider*.

(4) Thinking of the problem-solving type. A convict planning his escape, a physician trying to diagnose a puzzling illness, an engineer designing a new kind of engine, or a business man deciding on momentous investments — all are indulging in this type of thinking. It is also described by such verbs as *ponder, cogitate, reflect,* and *reason*.

Of course such a four-fold classification has no hard and fast lines of distinction. It is easy to find examples that belong partly in one class and partly in another; but for purposes of convenient reference this classification may prove helpful. It certainly emphasizes the variety of meanings attached to the term *thinking*. For some of these varieties we have special names depending on the dominant characteristic of the particular case of thinking. If the thinking is concerned with an object immediately perceived, the thinking is said to be *perceptual*. An automobile mechanic trying to think of the reason for a peculiar sound he is listening to as the engine is running is indulging in perceptual thinking. Another example is that of a chemist who, while looking at a particular solution, remarks, " I think this acid is not chemically pure."

Often thinking is predominantly occupied with objects or events that are not present to sense. Such thinking is described as *imaginative*. A novelist is thinking imaginatively when, in the privacy of his study, he constructs the plot and decides on the characters of his next story. In case he thinks of including some event of his school days just as he experienced it, the event is said to be *reproductively* imagined. Thinking of it is a matter of *memory*. If he modifies the event to fit the plot of the story more dramatically, the event will then be *productively* or *creatively* imagined. In the latter instance he reconstructs the details of the event to suit his plans. However, both in reproductive and productive imagining the experience of the individual is utilized. All elements of imagination are rooted in experience. For this reason we cannot even in imagination conceive of the taste of magnetism or the sound of light. What we can do is to re-arrange the items of our experience into a pattern or *construct* which we have never experienced. In this way we can imagine a herd of sheep reading Latin, or a world composed exclusively of altruistic people.

Frequently aesthetic attitudes represent the focus of

thinking, as when we admire the beauty of a landscape or the majesty of a tree. As in other cases of thinking presently to be discussed, the striped musculature is often noticeably involved in *aesthetic* thinking. For example, in gazing at the Leaning Tower of Pisa the observer may involuntarily set his body at an angle opposite to that of the tower. His aesthetic judgment regarding the poor balance of the tower may be a projection of his own unstable equilibrium. The technical name for this tendency to " feel oneself into a situation " is *empathy*. Empathic reactions are responsible for many aesthetic opinions. A familiar instance of this kind of thinking is found in our dislike of a small, light picture suspended from the molding by a thick, heavy cord.

There are still other kinds of thinking that might be listed, but those enumerated serve to show their extreme variety. Actually, of course, thinking as such differs not in *kind,* but in its *product.* Whether a given specimen of thinking is to be described as perceptual, abstract, reasoned, imagined, creative or stereotyped depends on the result of the thought. As will soon be indicated, there is no unique process characteristic either of thinking in general, or of any so-called particular type of thinking.

It should be clear that the term " thinking " possesses many meanings. Is there any one factor common to all of these meanings? As psychologists we are curious to learn why such apparently diverse forms of reaction should all be called by the same name. In everyday language we should not hesitate to describe any of these reactions as *mental* ones. It may well be that the common factor is to be found in the essentially mental nature of the thinking reactions.

Thinking Described as a Mental Reaction. If thinking is to be explained as a mental reaction, it is necessary to demonstrate its vicarious or substitutive character;

otherwise, in the light of our definition of mental reactions, it does not belong to that class of responses. It should be noted that we speak of thinking as a way of reacting; in other words, it is our purpose to show that thinking is a form of *behavior*. To accomplish this purpose more readily let us first consider a simple case of behavior that may be presumed to call for no thought. While dressing, a man drops his collar button. He is in a hurry to catch a train. With swift movements he surveys the floor, but the button is not in sight. Accordingly he gets down on his knees and peers underneath the bed, the chairs, the bureau, and other bedroom furniture. The button is not to be seen. Muttering imprecations he jumps up, glances at his watch and perceives that his time is limited. He begins to ransack the room for another button, but to no avail. Finding this a futile endeavor, he renews his search for the button he dropped. Again he looks all over the floor and underneath the furniture. In baffled fury he begins to move the dresser away from the wall in order to make sure the button is not tucked away in a remote corner. Suddenly he decides that he might have a shirt with a collar attached. A hurried examination of his wardrobe shows that this too is a fruitless clue. He returns to the job of moving the dresser when he chances to glance in the direction of the partly opened closet and spies the button just barely inside of it. His search is over and his problem solved. However, the solution of his problem was in no sense of the term due to thinking. His behavior was like that of an animal in a maze. The solution was brought about by *trial and error* exploration.

Let us assume that his search ended by discovering that he had a shirt with a collar attached. In this case we might say that an element of thinking entered into his solution. In fact, in telling of his experience the man would say, " As

I was about to move the dresser, the *thought* came to me that I might have a shirt that didn't require a collar button." When we consider what takes place when such *thoughts* come to us, under the simple conditions of our assumed problem, we may succeed in securing an understanding of the nature of thought. It will be to our advantage, therefore, to continue using the given illustration of searching for the lost button by way of indicating what takes place when we are *thinking*.

After the first preliminary survey of the floor the man pauses in the midst of his active search, let us say, and remains standing still for a few minutes. His eyes are seemingly focussed on some distant point; his brows are knit and the muscles of his face obviously tense. An outside witness would unhesitatingly say that the man was *thinking*. Yet so far as his overt movements are concerned, he seems to be doing nothing. Nevertheless, according to our view, the man is really active while thinking. He is carrying on the search for the lost button, but instead of moving the furniture about he is moving *symbols* such as " bed," " dresser," " chair," about. He is also conducting the search by means of abbreviated gestures that the casual observer does not notice. These gestures are also *symbols*.. In other words the man is struggling with his problem by means of language mechanisms. He is talking to himself: " I've got to hurry. Train leaves in thirty minutes. Sure that button is on the floor. Heard it fall. Rolled some distance. Guess I'll look under the bed. No, it couldn't have gone that far. Now let's see, I was standing right there " (eyes move in direction of corner and slight increase in tension of arm and finger muscles takes place as *if* he were about to point) " when I dropped it. Seemed that I heard it roll to left. Guess I'll move that desk aside. Couldn't have rolled that far though." In this fashion we can continue writing out the possible sequence of his talking or *thinking*. An astute observer would note the slight finger movements, changes in head positions, shifts in the position of the eyes, and other movements of the bodily parts. These we take to be abbreviated gestures, as when a slight finger movement *represents* " moving the desk." All this time the man has said nothing out loud, nor has he moved from his original spot in the room. His talking has been of the sort we indulge in when talking to ourselves: mere incipient movements and delicate adjustments of the organs of speech without actual utterance. His gestures may have been of the same incipient sort. Yet the man was reacting. The reactions consisted in *language* (words and gestures) reactions, even though they were going on beneath the surface and in incomplete fashion. It has already been pointed out that language is a vast system of *substitution*, that a language reaction is a *mental* reaction. Now the actual trend of the man's language reactions showed considerable lack of orderly progress. He mentally (by word or gesture or both) tried to hunt for the button underneath the bed, move the desk, go to the other end of the room, and so on; that is, he was still attacking his problem in trial and error fashion, except that he was doing it by means of his language mechanisms. Thinking may thus be regarded as *mental trial and error behavior*. Bain (4) has described it most effectively as " restrained speaking or acting." [11]

Bain's striking definition should be understood as referring to those cases where the individual is not *explicitly* talking or acting, the so-called silent thinker. Thinking may take the form of overt speech as when we are " thinking out loud," or it may take the form of pronounced acting or gesticulating or other overt movements, as when we " write out our thoughts," or draw diagrams. The impor-

[11] *Op. cit.*, p. 358.

v

tant psychological characteristic is that, irrespective of the degree of overtness present, thinking is always a form of substitute *behavior*. Instead of manipulating the objects in our environment, we *manipulate* symbols that stand for these objects. This symbolic manipulation is not exclusively limited to the use of words or gestures, in the sense of language symbols. A variety of either explicit or implicit movements can be employed as symbolizations of the same object or activity. In thinking of a carpet-sweeper, for example, we may use the *words* " carpet-sweeper," or the movements in pantomime of pushing one, the gesture itself. These would be language symbols; that is, if they were rendered articulate or overt, another person with sufficient experience with carpet-sweepers would know what object our symbols represented. On the other hand, we might move any part of the body such as the tongue, head, trunk, finger, leg in a to-and-fro manner and such a movement would suffice to symbolize carpet-sweepers to *us*, but not to anybody else. In this sense it would not be a language reaction, but it would be a *mental* reaction none the less, since it *symbolizes* either the object carpet-sweeper or the activity of sweeping a carpet. Our earlier statement to the effect that *all* mental reactions are not language reactions should now be clear. Indirectly, of course, even these mental reactions are connected with language reactions, since they are derived from them. They may be regarded as symbolizations of symbols.

The degree of symbolization of this kind that may prevail is exceedingly great. It indicates that thinking may involve very many stimulus-response mechanisms. Certainly there is no scientific justification for limiting thought to some kind of cerebral activity to the exclusion of co-acting receptors and effectors. As Heidbreder (19) points out in her experimental investigation of thinking, there is no " unitary process " that we can isolate and label *thinking*.[12] In fact, she found that the most striking characteristics of those mental operations we ordinarily regard as reasoning or thinking were to be found in their " great flexibility " and " their *lack* of uniformity." [13]

The Experimental Study of Thinking. Because of this absence of uniformity, along with the marked flexibility of substitution that characterizes thinking, it has been impossible to work out a conclusive experimental proof of the theory presented here. Several investigators have tried to obtain experimental verification of the view that thinking is largely " suppressed articulation " or sub-vocal speech. To do this they employed various methods. Some of them placed a sensitive rubber membrane, or tambour, connected with an automatic recording device on the larynx of the subject. Others placed a rubber bulb, similarly connected, in the subject's mouth. Clark (8) employed both methods simultaneously. When the apparatus was in place the subject was given various problems to solve, and the presence or absence of incipient articulatory movements noted. The results secured in investigations of this sort are neither uniform nor convincing. Some experimenters found that there is always some movement of the speech organs in thinking, while others found it in some subjects but by no means in all.

The main difficulty with this kind of experimental attack is the failure to control the functioning of other mechanisms that may serve as substitutes for the speech movements. Various attempts to effect such control have been made. Thorson (42), for example, immobilized the head of the subject by placing it in a fixed framework. Furthermore, to rule out vocal and gestural movements, the subject was required to tap with his fingers and sing " ah " while merely

[12] *Op. cit.*, p. 174.   [13] *Ibid.*, p. 164.

thinking of a phrase like " experimental psychology." [14]   It should be obvious that such devices are unsatisfactory as methods of control, for they leave the rest of the muscu-lature still free to serve as possible substitutes. In addition, in this particular case there was no certain means of finding out to what extent the subject's " thinking " of the phrase was successfully accomplished. Years ago William James (22) called attention to the way in which our thinking of such a word as " bubble " may be modified when we try to think of it while keeping the mouth partly open.[15] Accord-ingly, neither the results favorable to the conception of thinking we have sponsored, nor those opposed to it can be regarded as very weighty. The experimental technique em-ployed in this type of investigation is inadequate to settle the problem one way or the other.

Much of our insight into the nature of thinking has come from experimental studies of a sort that we have already discussed in connection with our analysis of learning be-havior. The ways in which people solve mechanical puzzles or maze problems may furnish data on the psychology of thinking as well as learning. It will be recalled that both in Ruger's study of the solution of mechanical puzzles and Warden's study of maze learning, trial and error manipula-tions characterized the behavior of the subjects. It will also be recalled that those of Warden's subjects who em-ployed verbal devices did better than the others. In the light of our analysis of thinking, we can now say that those who used mental trial and error along with the explicit form of that behavior made better records than the others.

Such mental trial and error behavior has been investi-gated in a variety of ways. Ruger, in addition to observing the behavior of his subjects while trying to solve the puz-zles, had them describe the methods of solution they were using. In some experiments on thinking the latter method of introspection was used exclusively. The subject was given a problem to solve, such as a riddle or a problem in mental arithmetic, and requested to describe the process of thinking either after he had completed the solution, or while it was in progress. In Heidbreder's experiment, previously mentioned, ingenious geometrical combinations constituted the problem material. Kuo (25) has studied certain aspects of thinking by confronting the subjects with lists of Chinese writing. The method he employed, while too intricate to be summarized here, is of particular interest in that his technique did not involve obtaining introspective reports. It was entirely objective. The important thing to note is that, irrespective of the methods used in these different studies, they all tend to verify the view that when we solve problems by means of " thought " we are indulging in mental trial and error. Our behavior may be implicit instead of explicit, symbolic instead of actual, but it is *behavior* none the less.[16]

INTELLIGENCE AND ABILITY

As we have just seen, a human being is essentially an acting or a behaving creature who, even when he is thinking, is by no means physically passive. Both his thinking and the more overt forms of his behavior yield products which are capable of measurement and evaluation. Literary and artistic compositions and mechanical inventions are thus the products of human behavior. Creative behavior is also manifested by animals. The nest built by a bird is truly an accomplishment, the product of a certain form of behavior.

---

[16] In this elementary sketch of *thinking* many problems of importance have been slurred over or altogether neglected. For more complete discussions of many of these problems consult the books and articles listed at the end of the chapter.

Even the lowly amoeba shows behavior which represents the accomplishment of some end. Behavior which results in *accomplishment* is known as ability.

In using terms to designate the various forms of ability we must avoid the fallacies of the antiquated faculty psychology. As we pointed out in Chapter II, psychological functions are not faculties. Man does not remember his experiences by virtue of a faculty called " memory " nor does the bird build a nest because it possesses an " instinct " for so doing. The act of remembering and the act of nest-building both involve the entire psychological equipment of the organisms concerned. Unfortunately, psychologists have tended to isolate one particular form or manifestation of ability, called " intelligence," and to regard it as an entity or a faculty. As a matter of fact, different aspects of the actual psychological phenomena ordinarily labeled " instinct " or " intelligence " have been discussed in all the chapters of this book.

Broadly speaking, all behavior is intelligent in so far as it results in successful adjustment to the environment. The white rat, in learning the shortest pathway to food in the maze, displays an activity which can be so designated. Moreover, of two rats confronted with the maze situation (other things being equal) the one that masters it in the shorter time and with fewer errors is the more intelligent. Likewise, the university student is intelligent to the extent that he adjusts himself to the social life of the campus as well as to his studies. The respective abilities manifested by the lawyer in conducting cases, by the physician in diagnosing and treating ailments, and by the business man in managing his affairs are all specific manifestations of intelligence. This usage of the term even includes skill in playing baseball and tennis, since aptitude in such activities literally includes adjustment to environmental stimuli. Indeed, such a conception does not appear extravagant when we reflect that the skill required in these and similar games is far beyond people of low-grade intelligence. Since the environment of higher organisms, man in particular, is social as well as physical, intelligence is shown in an extremely wide variety of responses. Without doubt, human intelligence is expressed in such traits as tact, emotional poise and control, the ability to understand human motives, motor dexterity, and facility in the use of language. From this standpoint intelligence and ability are synonymous terms.

The Concepts of Intelligence. Although the majority of psychologists accept in substance the view of intelligent behavior just indicated, a number of them restrict the term intelligence to mental activity which results in adaptive behavior. According to their position, intelligence is the cause and intelligent behavior is the effect. In reality, so they argue, the two factors are so distinguishable that the mental process may not result in overt behavior of any kind. Thinking does not always result in overt acting. One advocate of this view, Roback (34), goes so far as to state that, " To see a problem sometimes denotes a higher degree of intelligence than to solve one." In general, this view holds that superior mental ability, and ultimately nothing else, differentiates human beings from animals, and intelligent men from morons and idiots.

Even psychologists who thus restrict intelligence to mental processes concede and frequently stress its function in making adjustments. For example, Angell (3) defines reasoning as purposive thinking and as problem-solving imagination. Thinking with a purpose in mind means thinking directed toward the solution of some problem. It is regarded as good thinking to the extent that it is successful in solving the problem. Many insane patients *think*, sometimes with amazingly sound logic, and they are occasionally quite skillful in verbal arguments, but they are insane, nevertheless, because their thinking does not result in a successful adjustment to their environment. Of course in any act of thinking the problem concerned may be highly specialized, and only indirectly related to the biological or even the social welfare of the organism. No one questions the intelligence of Poe, notwithstanding his unpractical nature. But on the other hand, few people regard fruitless daydreaming or fantasy building as manifestations of intelligence. Mental activities of this sort do not result in mental accomplishment. Intelligence is limited to demonstrations of real ability.

In a similar way, all views concerning the nature of mental processes assign to intelligence the function of making effective adjustments. In other words, all views regard intelligence as functional. This also applies to views of animal intelligence. According to Köhler (24), higher apes are capable of analyzing what they see only when the important items in the situation are plainly visible. They will use a rope to pull a suspended basket of fruit toward them provided that both basket and rope are in the direct field of vision. Although Köhler explains animal mental processes in terms of the configuration hypothesis, he obviously accepts adaptive behavior as the ultimate criterion of intelligence. In the sense that all stimulus-response activities are adjusting reactions, there can be no other criterion.

Definitions of Intelligence. There are evidently two ways of viewing intelligence: it is either (1) overt adaptive behavior, or (2) mental activity responsible for overt adaptive behavior. The theoretical distinction between the two views of intelligence becomes fairly definite when we note how various psychologists define the term. Perhaps Stern's definition is the best known of those which express the second view (37). According to this psychologist, "Intelligence is a general capacity of an individual consciously to adjust his thinking to new requirements. It is general mental adaptability to new problems and conditions of life." Other definitions are given in a symposium on the subject published in one of the psychological journals (9). In this symposium Colvin takes exception to Stern's definition on the ground that it is too narrow and offers as a substitute the following: "An individual possesses intelligence in so far as he has learned, or can learn to adjust himself to his environment." Colvin argues that his definition "does not unduly emphasize the problem aspect of intelligence and rightfully attributes intelligence to those animals whose sole ability to learn is confined to the hit-and-miss try-out of experience ('trial and error')." In a somewhat similar vein Woodrow states that intelligence is an "acquiring-capacity," and Dearborn states that intelligence is "the capacity to learn or to profit by experience." He defines experience in terms of objective or behavioristic psychology. Thorndike defines intellect as the power of good responses from the point of view of truth or fact, but qualifies his definition by stating that "it is probably unwise to spend much time in attempts to separate off sharply certain qualities of man, as his intelligence from such emotional and vocational qualities as his interest in mental activity, carefulness, determination to respond effectively, persistence in his efforts to do so; or from his account of his efforts to do so, or from his moral or aesthetic taste."

Several contributors to the symposium point out groups of factors which constitute intelligence. For instance, Freeman mentions such factors as mental balance, coördination of the mental processes, judicious management of the processes of learning or reflection, mental control, and a due degree of non-suggestibility. Thurstone lists three components of intelligence: (1) the capacity to inhibit an instinctive adjustment, (2) the capacity to redefine the inhibited instinctive adjustment in the light of imaginally experienced trial and error, and (3) the volitional capacity to realize the modified instinctive adjustment into overt behavior to the advantage of the individual as a social animal. These are respectively the inhibiting, analytical, and persevering aspects of intelligence.

Among other views expressed in the symposium are two which limit intelligence strictly to conscious thinking. Thus Henmon accepts the definition that "intelligence is intellect *plus knowledge*," and Terman defends the view that "An individual is intelligent in proportion as he is able to carry on abstract thinking." Terman's view is, in fact, rather far removed from the broad concept of intelligence discussed above — that is, the conception that intelligence includes social traits and motor ability. To quote from his argument: "It cannot be disputed, however, that in the long run it is the races which excel in abstract thinking that eat while others starve, survive epidemics, conquer time and space, and substitute religion for magic, science for taboos and justice for revenge. The races which excel in conceptual thinking could, if they wished, quickly exterminate or enslave all the races notably their inferiors in this respect. Any given society is ruled, led, or at least moulded by the five or ten per cent of its members whose behavior is governed by ideas." Terman is interested in excluding from intelligence all forms of adjustment that do not involve abstract analysis. He does not regard the skill required of street car motormen as a form of intelligence. However, his argument clearly points to successful adjustment and even dominance over others as the final criteria of intelligence.

It will be noticed that despite the variety of standpoints

which they represent, these definitions of intelligence do not differ on questions of fact. For instance, considered as descriptions of actual psychological phenomena, the respective statements of Colvin and Terman are in no respect contradictory. As our previous chapter disclosed, practically all organisms learn through experience. Moreover, men and animals in general employ the same learning methods. If the student were given 50 curves of animal learning and 50 of human, both obtained from a maze or a problem box experiment, he would experience considerable difficulty, in the absence of labels, in distinguishing between the two. On the other hand, no psychologists question the superiority of human over animal mental development and thinking capacity. The psychological gap between human and animal mental achievement is indeed large. Our sole question is whether intelligence should be applied to all cases of effective learning or restricted to those cases which clearly involve the higher mental processes.

So far as scientific psychology is concerned, the two opposed concepts of intelligence can be made equally serviceable. It should be repeated that they are based upon the same body of facts. To be more explicit, the student will find both concepts entirely in harmony with the facts and principles discussed in both the previous and present chapters of this text. *Intelligence* is primarily a popular term that has crept into psychological literature, and like other psychological terms of similar origin, it suffers from ambiguity. For this reason some psychologists prefer the less popular term, " mental alertness."

Innate versus Acquired Factors in Intelligence. The question of whether human behavior is determined primarily by heredity or environment has been argued countless times. Such arguments are fruitless because they are illogical. Their fallacy lies in their assumption that psychological functions can be classified as either wholly hereditary or completely environmental. As we have seen, all psychological functions are stimulus-response relationships. The pupillary reflex is a function, involving not only a structural mechanism but a stimulus. The reflex mechanism is of course inherited, in the sense that the iris and its nerve connections are inherited, but it can function only with reference to environmental stimuli. Not only light but sound stimuli elicit the pupillary response,[17] and for all we know, one is as " natural " as the other. Conditioned pupillary responses very likely begin early in infancy. It is futile, therefore, to argue that pupillary responses are chiefly determined by either heredity or environment, for all of them are determined by both. We might as well argue whether the structure of an automobile or the skill of its driver is responsible for the fact that it can turn a corner. The principles of biological inheritance apply to structures, not to functions determined by those structures when placed in a stimulating environment.

It follows that receptors, effectors, and neural mechanisms rather than traits and abilities are directly heritable. Conversely, traits are heritable only in the sense that they are determined by inherited structures. As a matter of fact, few human traits appear in successive generations according to the Mendelian ratio. If intelligence, for instance, were a unit character, comparable with eye-color, it would either appear or not appear in a particular organism. Consequently, all people could be classified as " intelligent " or " not-intelligent," just as eyes are classified as brown or not-brown. But as L. S. Hollingworth (21) states, " All men can be no more divided into the dull and the bright, than they can be divided into the tall and the short." Human intelligence is found in varying amounts.

[17] See Cason's experiment, described in Chapter III.

The assumption that intelligence is a heritable, Mendelian unit must not be confused with the supposition that the limits and direction of an individual's ability are fixed by his inherited mechanisms. In the opinion of some psychologists, the latter conclusion seems warranted by the available evidence. In Chapters II and III the dependence of activity upon morphological factors was stressed. In the sense of the principle there explained, prize-fighters are born and not made. The question is whether this can be said of poets, using poets, of course, to symbolize intellectual and artistic ability. It has been maintained that the *general level* of an individual's ability is established by innate factors. Assuming this to be true, intelligence could be defined as potential native ability, whether restricted to mental processes or not. Two lines of evidence lend support to this conclusion. In the first place, the mental level of a given individual tends to remain fairly constant during any number of tests. His score in the first test is generally indicative of his scores in subsequent tests. In the second place, siblings (children born of the same parents) and twins (two children developed from the same ovum) respectively tend to show the same degree and quality of intellectual performance. This kind of evidence, however, is inconclusive because the environmental influences are exceedingly difficult to measure.

The Criteria of Intelligence. One source of confusion in discussions of intelligence emerges from the fact that the aspects of behavior to which it refers are measured by two different standards. Even when the term is limited strictly to mental processes it sometimes refers to (1) the *difficulty* and *complexity* of a mental act, and sometimes to (2) the *social value* of the act. Thus, it is usually assumed that intelligence of a high order is required to solve difficult mathematical problems and to translate obscure Greek passages.

The instructor frequently gauges the mental caliber of his students by the facility they disclose in wrestling with intellectual problems. He is flattered on being told that his course is exceedingly difficult, for he assumes that his standards are correspondingly high. Of course, it is not difficulty alone, but difficulty combined with complexity which constitutes this standard. People with prodigious memories are not necessarily regarded as intelligent.

On the other hand, mental acts characterized by both difficulty and complexity are not always regarded as intelligent. Many people admit grudgingly or flatly deny that excellence in playing bridge, solving cross-word puzzles, or anticipating the outcome of mystery stories is an indication of intelligence. When forced to defend their position they fall back on the argument that such accomplishments are less *worthy* than understanding Emerson or studying natural history. The perennial criticism directed against mental tests is that such tests place a premium on " mental gymnastics," and ignore profound thinking. Obviously the individual who belittles Phi Beta Kappa students places little *value* upon their intellectual attainments. He assumes and generally asserts that superior students do not possess the ability required in " practical " success.

At their best, standards for evaluating the products of intelligence and ability are shifting and uncertain. As Thorndike (40) has pointed out, geniuses are characterized by their rarity rather than their relative degree of attainment.[18] The recognition and financial compensation given to the best grand opera singer, as compared with the second best, are frequently disproportionate and unfair. Also, when a product ceases to be rare it is no longer hailed as a work of genius. The aviator who first looped the loop was truly a genius, but the numerous duplications of his feat

[18] *Op. cit.*, p. 181.

have served to detract from his accomplishment. We tend to estimate intelligence from our own individual standpoint, hence we fail properly to evaluate anything beyond our capacities or interests. In such cases we tend toward the extremes of over-estimation or under-estimation. The savage is frequently at a loss to know whether the missionary should be eaten or deified. To give a more pertinent example, a vaudeville act of even mediocre quality demands of the performer an amount of skill and training not always appreciated by the audience. One inevitable result of an inability to appreciate intelligence is, of course, prejudice and dogmatism. As a consequence, we are likely to over-rate the intelligence of an individual who shares with us certain political or religious convictions, and to regard as stupid an individual with opposed views.

When we define intelligence from the standpoint of effective adjustment we are again confronted with the same two standards for its measurement. The problem for which the adjustment is made must present some real difficulty if its solution calls for intelligence. The act of swallowing involves a complicated physiological mechanism; if it had to be learned, it would doubtless be comparable in difficulty with playing a sonata on a piano. But since it is performed at birth with little or no practice it is not an act of intelligence. However, the sheer difficulty of an overt act is a poor indication of the intelligence which it requires. The individual who can hold himself motionless in some posture longer and better than any other individual in the world does not thereby display superior intelligence. At best he can hope only for the recognition accorded by circus or vaudeville patrons. As in the case of mental feats, the added factor of complexity fails to establish the act as intelligent. Many people use the term *skill*, rather than intelligence, with reference to the performances of the professional magician, boxer, typist, or pianist. Some even reluctantly employ " intelligence " to designate brilliant repartee or wit, preferring the term " cleverness."

To summarize, we find that irrespective of the way in which intelligence is defined, it is measured in terms of two standards which logically are distinct but practically are found together; namely, the standards of *difficulty* and of *value*. Furthermore, we have seen that in order to be regarded as intelligent, a difficult act must possess some degree of complexity. Since the standards are poorly defined, they are sources of confusion in both scientific and popular psychologizing.

We must conclude that intelligent behavior is the product of many factors, each requiring careful investigation for its analysis and definition. Thus the psychologist accepts the fact that social values fluctuate and proceeds to devise a technique for their measurement. At present, the values of human intelligence and ability can be studied most advantageously in the realm of commerce and industry, where such traits are at a definite premium. Here the task of the psychologist, connected with a factory or department store, is to ascertain, measure, and evaluate in monetary terms the human traits of its actual or prospective employees. On the other hand, the nature of the factors constituting intelligent behavior, disregarding their social worth, are studied in the psychological laboratory. In the following section of this chapter we show how such studies are made.

Mental Measurements

Perhaps no phase of experimental psychology has attracted as much popular interest as the field of intelligence testing and measuring. But unfortunately, the assumptions underlying the technique of intelligence testing, and consequently the results obtained by this technique, have been generally misunderstood. It is one thing to administer and score tests, but it is another thing altogether to understand the psychological significance of test results.

The Nature of Psychological Tests. First of all should be noted the fundamental assumption underlying intelligence tests. As the name implies, they consist essentially of problems which presumably require intelligence for their solution. Since the purpose of such a test is to ascertain in short time certain facts about the intelligence of the individual tested, it necessarily consists of typical or *representative* problems. In other words, the test *samples* the intelligence of the person who takes it, in much the same way that a blood test made by a physician consists of an examination of a specimen of the blood of the patient. Obviously the intelligence test is valid only to the extent that its problems are truly representative.

Just what constitutes a representative test problem requires some explanation. In the light of our previous discussion it is evident that no test purports to measure directly the factor of sheer intellectual ability divorced from training and experience. This factor, or rather group of factors, is a logical and convenient abstraction, never found in isolation for the simple reason that mental *activity* cannot take place without mental content furnished by experience. Practically all tests of general mental ability include mathematical problems, verbal relationships, logical relationships, extent of vocabulary, various forms of reasoning, and general information.

The following test problems are fairly typical of those found in psychological tests for adults:

(1) Underline the word that does not belong with the other four words: light, candle, lamp, match, torch.

(2) The opposite of *minus* is (underline the correct word) : times, add, substract, plus.

w

(3) The synonym, or word corresponding in meaning, for *haste* is (underline the correct word) : energetic, quiet, rush, hasty.

(4) Write in the appropriate word: England: Europe = China: ——

(5) Correct this sentence: He is larger than any boy in his class.

(6) One of the three lists of words given below contains the words needed to complete the following sentence. Select the words in the correct list and write them in the blanks, one word to each blank: One ought to —— great care to —— the right —— of ——, for one who —— bad habits —— it —— to break them.

(a) Avoid, use, abundance, bad, morals, himself, assortment.

(b) Attach, indulges, awaken, visions, Heaven, learn, hard.

(c) Difficult, sort, contracts, cultivate, finds, habits, exercise.

(7) Write in the blanks two numbers that belong in this series of numbers: 5, 6, 8, 11, 15, 20, ——, ——

(8) Use the margin for figuring and write the answer in the space indicated: what is the average of 12, 29, 60? (Answer ——)

(9) Underline the nearest correct statement: Daniel Webster was a president of the United States — writer of a dictionary — United States Senator — governor of New York.

(10) Write in the parentheses the number of one of the 4 numbered statements that comes nearest expressing the thought of the quotation:

( ) " Do unto others as you would have them do unto you." ——

1. It is easier to tell others what to do than to do it yourself.
2. Industry is its own reward.
3. Treat others as you want them to treat you.
4. Live and let live.

Although the effects of schooling, special training, and everyday experience cannot be eliminated from intelligence tests, they can be fairly well estimated in such a way that the final score made by the subject is a relative measure of his intellectual ability or mental alertness. One method of measuring such effects is to reduce them to a minimum. For instance, in one mental test problem the subject is asked to explain how two railroad trains going towards each other on a single track can be made to pass with the least amount of switching, when the only provision for switching is a single side-track shorter than either train. Since few individuals are familiar technically with railroad switching, this problem is relatively fair for the majority of people. Another method of estimating training effects is to include training elements common to all individuals for whom the test is intended. Since they were selected from tests designed for college freshmen, the test problems quoted above were presumed to meet this requirement.

The Diagnostic Purpose of Tests. The purpose of a psychological test is to predict what the individual tested will do in some field of accomplishment. It measures what he has learned in order to predict what he is capable of learning. A test, therefore, is a psychological device used for mental diagnosis and prognosis. The psychological examinations frequently administered to college freshmen illustrate this purpose, since their aim is to predict scholastic success. Knowing the test score of a freshman, his dean is in a better position to know what sort of work he is *capable* of doing. Clearly the usefulness of tests designed for this purpose depends upon the degree of correspondence between the test scores and the school grades made by the students, and in order to make the scores and grades correspond as closely as possible, tests for college freshmen usually contain many items based upon high school training. Such tests fulfill their purpose with a fair degree of success because they show with what mathematical *probability* a given student will receive a given average grade. Of course factors other than those measured by the tests help determine school grades: no one doubts that the habits of work, adaptation to particular courses and instructors, health, and traits of personality which characterize a student are instrumental in determining his scholastic success. But these facts in no sense militate against the scientific and practical value of the tests; if a student scores high in the test and is graded low in his work, the fact is significant; if the reverse obtains, the fact is equally significant. Far from arguing against the usefulness of the test, such discrepancies often throw considerable light on the intellectual and temperamental make-up of the individuals concerned.

Principles of Test Construction. It is indeed a mistake to suppose that psychological tests are merely thought out and then written. Tests must themselves be tested before they can be accepted as scientific. The most important principle of test construction is known as the *standardization* of a test. In the majority of cases the test scores should show what is called a *normal distribution.* The term distribution refers to the proportion of scores of different values made by the subjects. It can be illustrated by the school grades commonly used, A, B, C, D, and E. A normal distribution of grades is represented by 7% of A's, 24% of B's, 38% of C's, 24% of D's, and 7% of E's. This distribution is expressed graphically by the *curve of normal* *distribution,* shown in Figure 26. This curve is symmetrical or bell-shaped, and its height bears a relatively fixed relationship with its width. The curve of a distribution which radically departs from the normal is non-symmetrical, or *skewed.* Figure 27 shows a marked skew, caused by the fact that the distribution which it represents consists of 15% A's, 45% B's, 25% C's, 10% D's, and 5% E's.

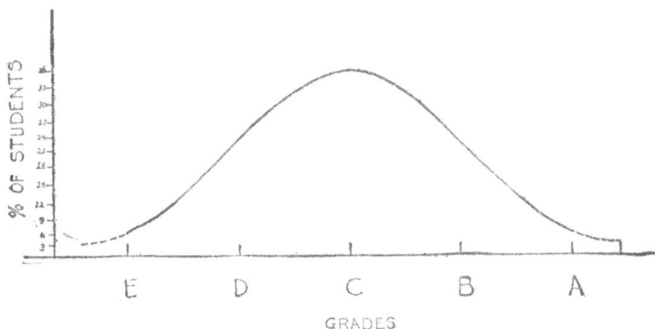

Fig. 26. — Curve of the normal distribution (approximate) of school grades described in the text. In curves of distribution the number of cases are indicated on the ordinate at the left, reading from bottom to top in the order of their increasing magnitude; and the measurements are indicated on the base line, reading from left to right in the order of their increasing value. (Those conversant with statistical methods will note that the extension of the curve represented by the dotted lines includes plus and minus 3 sigma.)

A normal distribution is so-called because it characterizes measurements of many natural phenomena. For example, the heights of adults belonging to a given race tend towards this distribution. In general, measurements of mental and physical human traits are normally distributed. It will be noticed that in the curve of normal distribution the measurements are symmetrically grouped around a *central* tendency or average. Consequently, by means of such a curve it is possible to determine the significance of any given measurement.

Unless a test yields a normal distribution of scores, the chances are that it is either too difficult or too easy. One method employed to insure this result is to try out each test problem on a sufficiently large group of subjects. If 75% of the subjects answer a given test problem correctly, it is assumed to be of the right degree of difficulty. Sometimes a 50% basis is used.

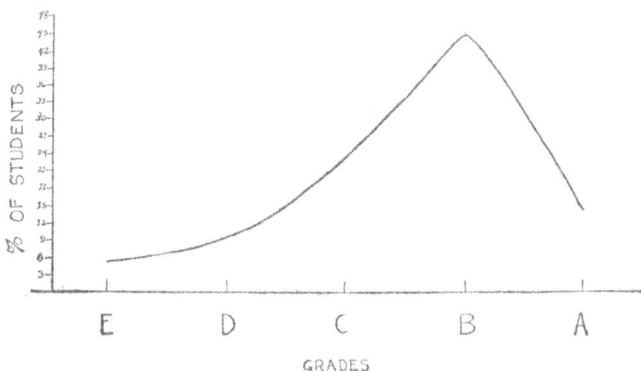

Fɪɢ. 27. — The skewed curve described in the text. This curve is skewed to the right, but skewness may be found in any part of a non-symmetrical curve.

A second principle is concerned with the *validity* of a test. By this is meant correlating or comparing a test with some other test or measure of the same ability. Assuming that grades in a course of instruction, say geometry, are measures of intelligence, a psychological test is valid to the extent that it correlates with these grades.

A third principle is the determination of the *reliability* of a test. Frequently many forms of the same test are devised; and the test is reliable if these forms correlate with each other. It should be emphasized that any test designed for general use must be standardized, validated, and made reliable in order to insure its diagnostic usefulness.

Administering and Scoring Tests. In giving psychological tests the directions for examiners and subjects must be carefully formulated and followed. As a rule, both accuracy and speed are taken into consideration in administering and scoring an intelligence test. Sometimes tests are scored on the basis of the number of problems answered correctly, sometimes on the basis of the number of correct answers minus the number of wrong answers. Frequently one type of problem is considered superior to another, in which case it counts more in the total score than the other. The usual procedure in administering an adult test to a group is to limit the total time. Frequently the time for each individual subject is recorded and counted in the total score, and often a time limit is set for each group of problems in the test. In counting speed in the final score, psychologists are merely following the practice which obtains in vocational life; *e.g.*, the bank teller must be both quick and accurate. Additional justification for this double standard is found in the fact that speed and accuracy vary together in the learning process.

Levels of Mental Ability. The method of constructing, administering, and scoring a test further depends in part upon the age of the individual for whom the test is designed. It is generally stated that intelligence increases from birth to the period from 12 to 20 years, and then remains fairly constant until old age begins. Assuming this to be true, it is generally thought advisable to have different tests for the different age levels up to maturity. For example, tests for 3-year-old children include such items as pointing to parts of the body, naming familiar objects, repeating short sentences, enumerating objects in pictures. In the

Stanford Revision of the Binet scale, made by Terman and his co-workers, problems for higher age levels include tests of vocabulary, the ability to repeat series of digits, understanding the meaning of prose passages, arithmetical reasoning, common information, and other items. Above the age levels of from 15 to 18 all tests are known as adult tests. The final rating on an age level test is usually the Intelligence Quotient, or I. Q., found by dividing the mental age by the chronological age. The mental age is the age level of the test which the subject can pass satisfactorily. According to many psychologists, the classification of individuals in terms of the range of their I. Q.'s is as follows:

Intelligence Quotients	Classification
0–69 [19]	Feeble-minded
70–79	Borderline
80–89	Backward
90–109	Normal
110–119	Bright
120–129	Very Bright
130 and above	Very Superior

Performance Tests. There are classes of people for whom tests involving the use of language are manifestly unfair. Illiterates constitute one of these classes, foreigners another. The intelligence of people thus handicapped can be measured by *performance tests,* which require them to do rather than to write or say something. To illustrate, they are given a *form board,* consisting of blocks of geometrical designs, such as stars, triangles, and squares, cut out from a board, and required to place the blocks in the appropriate holes cut in the board. They are given simple drawings or

[19] It is claimed by some that the feeble-minded group should be determined by the range 0–50.

pictures with missing parts and asked to show what is wrong
with the pictures. The picture may be of a table with one
of the four legs missing. A more difficult kind of performance test consists of a series of related pictures which must
be numbered in the order in which the pictures should be arranged. In still another performance test the subject attempts to draw the true path in the diagram of a maze by
making a continuous line.

Tests of Physical and Motor Capacity.[20] The principles which govern mental measurement apply in general
to physical and motor testing. The latter technique involves
the construction of appropriate pieces of apparatus. An-
thropometric tests should be classified in this group, even
though they include measurements of anatomical structures
as well as physiological and psychological functions. They
comprise measurements of chest capacity, handgrip, strength
of back and legs, standing and sitting height, weight, bodily
proportions, and the size and shape of the skull.

Tests of motor ability measure neuro-muscular functions
of varying complexity. Many of them are designed to measure the elements of coördinated responses enumerated in
Chapter II, namely the direction, force, duration, and timing of muscular activities. Several *tapping* tests have been
devised, to record the number of taps per unit of time an
individual can make with a pencil or stylus held in his
hand. The *tracing* test measures his ability to move a stylus along a straight line. The *steadiness* test requires him
to hold a stylus in holes of different diameters cut into a
metal plate without touching the boundaries of the holes.
In the *aiming* test he tries to strike the points of intersection
of straight lines on a paper held at arm's length, making
one attempt at each beat of a metronome. Muscular

[20] Consult Whipple's *Manual* (47) for a more detailed discussion of
this topic.

strength is recorded by the dynamometer, and muscular *fatigue* by the ergograph. Sometimes different elements of coördination are involved in a single test. For instance, in *card sorting* the subject sorts a shuffled deck of cards into appropriate boxes, labeled and placed before him, as rapidly and accurately as possible.

Tests of Special Aptitudes and Abilities. Very early in the history of intelligence testing psychologists became interested in measuring special talents, capacities, and abilities; and today many tests of this sort are extensively and carefully standardized. Seashore's tests of musical talent and Stenquist's two tests of mechanical ability are excellent examples. We shall describe them in some detail for the purpose of noting the technique involved in their administration. The group of Seashore tests concerned with musical sensitivity is made with phonograph records, and it includes tests of sensitivity to pitch, intensity, time, consonance, tonal memory, and rhythm. The subject is seated before a phonograph with a pencil and a printed form upon which he writes his responses. When taking the sense of pitch test he hears pairs of notes, of varying degrees of pitch difference, sounded in close succession and separated by short intervals of silence, and after hearing the second note of each pair he writes either H or L in the appropriate place on the blank to indicate whether he hears it as higher or lower than the first note. This procedure is modified for the other tests to suit the kind of sensitivity which they measure, differences in rhythmic units, for example, being recorded as S for " same " or D for " different." In each of the records the test becomes more difficult as the record is played.

One form of the Stenquist test, known as the Stenquist Assembling Test, consists of a box containing a number of compartments, in each of which are the parts of some mechanical device. In one compartment is a toy pistol, in another a simple door lock, in another a spring mouse-trap, etc. The subject is given a small screw-driver and instructed to put each device together. The time spent in executing each task is recorded. The Stenquist Mechanical Aptitude Tests are issued in pamphlet form, and consist of pictures. The subject is asked to indicate by a letter system what parts of mechanical devices shown in the pictures belong together. Many other tests of special or vocational aptitude could be described, but the ones referred to illustrate the method of measurement upon which they are based.

It must not be inferred that these and similar tests measure all the abilities involved in the vocations or professions to which they belong. To illustrate, a consistently superior record in all the Seashore tests of musical sensitivity by no means marks the person who makes the record as a potential musical genius. Music is an exceedingly complex phenomenon, and the successful musician must possess a wide range of abilities, social as well as musical. Moreover, some musicians, the pianist for example, use a medium of expression which does not call for all the degrees of musical sensitivity measured in the tests. The pitches made on a piano differ by tones and semitones (a tone being the equivalent of 54 vibrations) whereas those made by the sense of pitch record vary from 1/2 to 30 vibrations. The Seashore tests should be regarded as diagnostic tests of certain specific abilities required in musical performance and appreciation; but these abilities do not constitute musical excellence.

Similar statements can be made regarding all tests of special aptitudes. Their usefulness lies in the fact that they measure the *essential* aptitudes involved in the vocations. Needless to say, their significance is better understood when they are compared with other tests of a more general character.

Measurements of Social Intelligence. A high degree of intelligence is involved in making social adjustments. It assumes various forms, such as tact, a sense of humor, repartee, understanding the motives of people, and a more or less general ability to do and say the appropriate things with respect to others. To say that within certain limits these abilities can be cultivated in no sense differentiates them from other forms of intelligence.

Two sorts of technique are employed in the measurement of social intelligence, namely (1) tests and (2) ratings. Such tests as can be classified under this heading in reality furnish measurements of social attitudes and practices. That is to say, they test social intelligence by measuring ethical standards, aesthetic appreciation, opinions and prejudices, and the forms of emotional response most likely to be shown in social situations. Inasmuch as these are factors in *social adjustment* they are properly regarded as manifestations of intelligence. The tests serve the purpose of establishing norms and of showing how a given individual stands with respect to the norms. Whether conformity or non-conformity to the norm is a sign of intelligence in any one test is, of course, a question of value which cannot be determined by the test itself.

One method of testing the " sense of humor " will illustrate a technique for the study of similar social responses. The subject is given a pamphlet containing 10 samples of good, bad, and indifferent humor as determined, we will say, by a group of " experts." He is then instructed to rank these samples in numbered order from " best " to " poorest." His rankings are then compared with the standard rankings or norms established by the expert judges, or possibly by the group taking the test. In this way it is possible to ascertain his " idiosyncrasy " score, or his deviation from the norm. If the experimenter in charge of the test wishes to compare reactions to humor with intelligence test scores or with scholastic ability he can do so by employing the method of correlation, described below. Many other ways of treating the data could be devised.

The Pressey X-O test for the study of emotional responses follows a different method. In this test the subject is handed a pamphlet containing various groups of words with the instructions to cross out certain words in each group. In one, he is told to cross out all words the meanings of which are unpleasant; in another, he is to indicate by the same method things he has worried about; in a third group he crosses out a number of practices which to him are morally reprehensible; and he indicates words which in his mind are associated with other words. The Pressey X-O test does not purport to measure intelligence, but it is mentioned here for two reasons: it illustrates a psychological testing method, and it does measure certain emotional factors involved in social adjustment. Its results can be treated in the manner described above.

The rating scale provides for the systematic estimation of the traits of an individual by a group of competent judges or raters. The following hypothetical scale will show one way in which this is done (see page 338).

In the type of rating scale illustrated below there is a description of each trait followed by a line representing successive increments of the trait. Just below each line are short descriptions of these increments, or differences in the amount of the trait, so that the line itself is a scale. After studying the individual to be rated with reference to the traits described, each judge places a check mark at some place on the line to indicate his estimate of the amount of the trait possessed by the individual. The ratings are recorded independently and then compared. Usually the median or middle rating is accepted as the final rating of the subject.

The basic assumption underlying the rating scale method-

Instructions

Along the line opposite each quality, place a check at that point which, in your opinion, most accurately represents the student's degree of that quality. The adjectives below the line are merely suggestive; your check may be placed at any point which seems most accurately to represent your judgment. Please place each check directly on the line.

QUALITIES	REPORT				
I. Consider the student's *ability to learn;* the ease with which he grasps new ideas; his thinking ability. Base your estimate on his apparent capacity to learn, rather than on his perseverance and industry.	quick, accurate thinker	alert, learns easily	fairly good under- standing	slow to learn	dull
II. Consider his *willingness to work;* the readiness with which he goes about his work; his alacrity in undertaking new tasks. Is he energetic in his regular activities, or does he tend to "soldier" on the job?	unusually industri- ous	willing, steady worker	only moder- ately indus- trious	somewhat indolent, not active	sluggish, lazy
III. Consider his *ability as a leader;* the extent to which he influences and controls the activity of his associates. Consider especially his ability to induce men to work together effectively, and his success in dominating his group.	forceful, winning, "a born leader"	dominates and in- fluences in most situations	about average in leader- ship	very little leader- ship	sub- missive, always a fol- lower

ology is that personality consists largely of the effects of impression produced by an individual upon others. For example, personal beauty is not an anatomical phenomenon, but rather the responses which the individual who " possesses " it elicits from others. The individual is beautiful in the sense that he arouses certain emotional and aesthetic responses in others. This is shown by the fact that the standards of personal beauty vary from one time to another and from one race to another. That social intelligence likewise consists of effects or responses is apparent. Thus, the leadership of an individual is measured by the behavior responses of those whom he leads; an anecdote is humorous if it is so considered by competent judges.

Everything considered, the rating scale methodology is logically adapted for measuring many socialized phases of intelligence. It is commonly used in factories, and in business and educational institutions where it is desirable to obtain estimates of achievement. It was used in the United States army during the recent war as one method for determining the efficiency of officers.

MENTAL ORGANIZATION

We are now prepared to ask in some detail just *what* an intelligence test measures and samples. To say that it measures intelligence clearly begs the question, for this term is an abstraction which denotes an exceedingly wide range of responses. A vocabulary test measures one kind of response, an arithmetical test another. We may surmise that the abilities which they measure respectively are related, but we can scarcely guess at the extent of the relationship. Still more problematical, in the absence of data, are the relationships which the various mechanical, mathematical, linguistic, literary, artistic, and social abilities bear among themselves and to each other. Whether an analogies test [21] measures general ability to see relationships or merely a specific ability to think of analogies has not yet been discussed. In order to ascertain what a given intelligence test problem measures we must know how the ability which it samples is

[21] No. 4 in the list of test problems on page 326 is an analogies test.

related to other abilities. This is the problem of mental organization.

The Method of Correlation. Relationships among abilities are studied by comparing measurements of these abilities. If algebra and geometry require the same kind of intelligence, people who excel in one should excel in the other, and those who are poor in the one should be correspondingly poor in the other. The nature of mental organization is studied by administering a variety of tests to groups of people and comparing the inter-relationships among the resulting scores. In making these comparisons, the scores from each test are compared with the scores of every other test.

The statistical method employed in comparing two series of scores is called *simple correlation*. It can best be explained by a hypothetical illustration. Let us suppose that 100 students who have completed a course in history have also been given an intelligence test. In order to correlate the two series of measurements it is convenient but not necessary to arrange them in a *scatter-diagram*. The following scatter-diagram contains the results which we will assume to obtain in our illustration:

INTELLIGENCE TEST SCORES

		35-39	40-44	45-49	50-54	55-59	60-64	65-69	70-74	75-79	80-84	85-89	90-94	95-100	Totals
	A							/	/	/	/	/			5
	B				///	///	///	++++	++++	///	/	/	/		25
GRADES IN HISTORY	C		/	/	//	////	++++ /	++++ ///	++++ /	////	++++ //		/		40
	D		/	//	/	///	++++	++++ //	///	///					25
	E	/		/	/	/	/								5
	Totals	1	2	4	7	11	15	20	15	11	7	4	2	1	100

−6 −5 −4 −3 −2 −1 0 1 2 3 4 5 6

In the diagram, each of the 100 students is represented by a mark so placed as to indicate both his history grade and his test score. The grades, ranging from *A* to *E* in descending order, are shown in the rows, while the scores are given in the columns. The scores have been divided into groups, each group including 5 points. The median grades, *C,* are in the row so designated; the median scores, 65–69, are in the column marked " O." As the table shows, one student who scored from 90–94 in the test was graded *B* in the history course; 6 students with scores in the 70–74 group were graded *C* in the course; and 2 students with scores of 45–49 received D's in the course.

The table also shows the *distributions* of the scores and grades respectively. This term has already been defined. We note that both the scores and the grades approximate normal distributions. The mathematical formulae ordinarily used to determine the amount of correlation presuppose normal distributions of measurements.

A scatter-diagram shows to some extent the *amount* of correlation represented by its two series of measurements. In our illustration, there is a fairly definite tendency for those who excelled in history to score high in the test, and for those who fell down in history to score low in the test. This is manifested in the tendency of the marks to follow a diagonal line extending from the lower left-hand corner to the upper right-hand corner of the diagram.

The exact extent or amount of correlation between any two series of measurements is expressed by a number, usually a decimal fraction carried to two places, called a *coefficient of correlation.* This is computed by a formula. The coefficient representing perfect *positive correlation* is the whole number, 1.00. This coefficient would obtain if the individual with the highest score in one measurement would also have the highest score in the second measurement, if

x

the next best person in the first measurement were also the next best in the second measurement, and if the remaining people down to the poorest showed similar parallel relationships in their scores of the two measurements. Below perfect positive correlation, the next highest coefficient is $+ .99$, followed by $+ .98$, $+ .97$, and so on down to about $+ .20$. *Negative correlation* is the inverse of positive. It results when high scores in one series of measurements accompany low scores in the second series. Its coefficients range from $- 1.00$, the coefficient of perfect negative correlation, to $- .99$, $- .98$, $- .97$, and so on to about $- .20$. Between approximately $+ .20$ through zero to $- .20$ coefficients show a minimum, or *absence of correlation*.

In psychological and educational investigations, tests are correlated with school grades, tests are correlated with each other, and school grades are correlated with each other. Perfect correlations, either positive or negative, are never found. As we explain subsequently, practically all coefficients are positive. According to Rugg (35), coefficients of less than .15 to .20 are negligible, indicating absence of correlation; coefficients from .35 or .40 show " present but low " relationship; coefficients from .35 or better to .50 or .60 show " marked " correlation; and coefficients above .60 or .70 indicate " high " correlation.[22] Just what degree of correspondence a given coefficient represents, however, is to some extent a matter of arbitrary judgment and definition.

The coefficient of correlation between the history grades and the test scores of our scatter-diagram is $+ .402$. Ordinarily this would be stated as $+ .40$. In terms of Rugg's interpretation of coefficients, this indicates a marked degree of correlation. As a matter of fact, $+ .40$ is about the average coefficient actually obtained in psychological and educational studies. There are several reasons why coefficients do not run higher, some of which have already been indicated.

The Significance of Coefficients of Correlation. Extreme caution must be exercised in basing conclusions upon coefficients. As several investigators have discovered, students coming from good homes do better school work than those coming from impoverished homes. Since it is reasonable to suppose that the better homes are equipped with telephones, a positive correlation would exist between the two factors, scholarship and possession of telephones. But no one would point to telephones as the *cause* of scholarship, any more than they would to automobiles. Possibly the better homes represent better American stock or superior social and educational advantages. A correlation of this sort indicates an incidental, or concomitant, rather than a casual relationship.

In the majority of instances a positive coefficient indicates the presence of factors common to the two series of measurements correlated. When this is true, the relationship is causal in the sense that both measurements are due to common causes. According to Otis (29), the coefficient of correlation in such cases ". . . may be thought of as the decimal fraction which tells what proportion of the causes affecting the magnitudes of two variables are common to both variables." [23]

This definition may be illustrated hypothetically. A coefficient of + .60, we will suppose, is found between grades in government and grades in economics. This is obtained, of course, by correlating the grades in the two subjects obtained by the same group of students. We will now assume that there are 10 factors of equal strength which determined each of the two sets of grades, but that 6 are common to both, while 4 are common to government alone and 4 others

[23] *Op. cit.*, p. 185.

are common to economics alone. This makes a total of 14 factors. The following factors, we may imagine, are common to both studies: (1) emotional stability, (2) speed of writing, (3) background of training in social sciences, (4) extent of vocabulary, (5) health, (6) retentive memory. As factors which functioned only in determining the government grades we may list, (1) previous training in government, (2) practical experience in politics, (3) personality of the government instructor, (4) special interest in the government course. Although the same students took both courses, the four factors just enumerated were manifested only in the government class. Some of the students, for instance, had previously taken courses in government and some had not; but this factor, in itself, was as potent as any other factor in determining all of the government grades. In the same way, four other factors determined the economics grades, as follows: (1) business experience, (2) difficulty of the text-book, (3) training in a related subject, as history, (4) special interest in economics. Assuming, then, that all of the 14 factors were of equal strength, and that 6 of them were instrumental in determining both grades while 4 others helped determine the government grades and 4 additional ones determined the economics grades, the resulting coefficient would be + .60.

Partial Correlation. At times it is possible to ascertain the cause of a relationship between two abilities by correlating them together and by correlating each with a third ability. The method is known as *partial correlation,* so called because it partials out or eliminates the effect of the third ability upon the other two. Our original illustration will serve to explain the procedure. It will be remembered that the coefficient of correlation between the history grades and the mental test scores was + .40. We will now add a third measurement of ability obtained from the 100 students; namely, their grades in algebra. This gives us three abilities which we will call " history," " algebra," and " mental ability." Using the method of simple correlation, we will now correlate each of the three with the other two, obtaining the following hypothetical results:

(a) history correlated with (b) algebra = + .30
(b) history correlated with (c) mental ability = + .40
(c) algebra correlated with (c) mental ability = + .70

The three coefficients show that relationships exist between history and algebra, history and mental ability, and algebra and mental ability. It is possible, however, that the relationship between history and algebra is due to the third factor, mental ability. The method of partial correlation enables us to eliminate the effect of this third factor; and when it is used, the correlation between history and algebra is reduced to .03, indicating a negligible degree of relationship. Partial correlation, therefore, provides a method for measuring a factor common to three kinds of ability by eliminating the effect of one ability upon the other two.[24]

Theories of Mental Organization. As the result of studying coefficients of correlation among tests, particularly coefficients obtained by simple and partial correlation, psychologists have formulated three different views of the *nature* of intelligence. These are known respectively as the unimodal, the multimodal, and the non-modal theories. It should be explained that the term mode as used in statistics refers to the number or quantity most frequently repeated in a series of numbers. To illustrate, C is the modal grade in the normal distribution of grades represented by 7 A's, 24 B's, 39 C's, 24 D's, and 7 E's, because it is the grade most frequently found. The term is used correctly in the names of

[24] A third kind of correlation, known as *Multiple Correlation*, is omitted because it is relatively of minor importance in solving the psychological problem of mental organization.

the three theories, but in the interests of clarity it can be replaced by the word " kind." Thus the first theory implies that there is only one kind of intelligence, the second that there are several kinds, the third that intelligence cannot be classified into kinds or types.

(1) **The Unimodal Theory.** The first of the three theories assumes that there is only one kind of intelligence; namely, general intelligence or general ability. As the name of the theory suggests, this general ability is supposed to be distributed normally, thus yielding a curve showing only one mode. Since a given individual possesses a certain fixed amount of intelligence, he should do equally well in all forms of achievement. Theoretically, according to this conception, all coefficients of correlation among measurements of intelligence should be perfect and positive, for all individuals of a given mental level should do equally well in all mental performances. In thus stressing the unity of mental life, the unimodal theory conceives the brain to function as a unitary organ and not as a system of distinct organs each having a highly specialized function.

Advocates of this theory are forced to acknowledge the fact that individuals differ in their environment and training. The British psychologist, Spearman, has a modified unimodal theory to provide for such influences. According to his view, the score made by any given individual in any test is determined by two factors operating together; namely (1) a *general factor,* conveniently called general ability, and (2) a *specific factor,* or the specific preparation which the individual has for the test. Thus, his ability in English composition is determined both by his general mental ability and his specific training in English composition. From the physiological standpoint Spearman conceives the general factor as a common fund of neural energy aiding all mental activity, and the specific factor as a particular neural energy.

Assuming the validity of Spearman's view, a hypothetical table of coefficients of correlation would show positive coefficients among *dissimilar* tests. Spearman emphatically states that his principle cannot be established from intercorrelations among similar tests. To cite his own illustrations, correlations between Latin translation and Latin grammar and between French prose and French dictation, although high, do not argue for his theory because they are due in both cases to the operation of the second factor; namely, specific training. But Spearman would expect to find positive correlations between geometry and Latin, history and English grammar, English synonyms and arithmetic, chemistry and English composition. In order to establish his first factor he must *eliminate* the effects of his second.

The coefficients constituting a table of coefficients, so Spearman argues, can be arranged in such a way that they will decrease in size when read from left to right and from top to bottom. Spearman's point can be illustrated by the following hypothetical table of coefficients, obtained by correlating each of five tests with the four remaining tests:

Test	A	B	C	D	E
A	X	.65	.62	.58	.37
B	.65	X	.60	.57	.34
C	.62	.60	X	.53	.32
D	.58	.57	.53	X	.25
E	.37	.34	.32	.25	X

Spearman applies the term *hierarchy of coefficients* to coefficients which can be arranged in the way indicated by the table. Of course he does not predict before the tests are administered what two tests will yield the highest coefficient, what pair will yield the next highest, etc. In our table, the tests showing the highest coefficient are arbitrarily labeled A and B respectively, and the remaining tests are indicated accordingly. The student will recall that the term *hierarchy* was used in Chapter V to designate an organization of habits. In typewriting, the habit of writing the word " through " as a unit and not as a series of seven distinct habitual acts is a habit-hierarchy. Likewise, each word-unit in the repertoire of the typist is a hierarchy. A general factor, namely a more or less general reliance upon word-unit habits, characterizes the achievement of the experienced typist. In the same manner, Spearman holds that a general factor determines in part the test score made in any particular test. Assuming that the tests A, B, C, D, & E are dissimilar and intrinsically unrelated except for the general factor, the coefficient of A correlated with C bears the same relationship to the coefficient of A correlated with D that the coefficient of B and C bears to the coefficient B and D. Using r to designate any coefficient, the relationships just stated are expressed by the formula:

$$\frac{r \quad AC}{r \quad AD} = \frac{r \quad BC}{r \quad BD} = \ldots\ldots\ldots\ldots (1)$$

As is true of the other two theories, Spearman's view finds *apparent* confirmation in some of the facts of daily experience. Some students " naturally " seem to possess superior, all-around intelligence, as is shown by their uniform success in courses of instruction. Moreover, these same students frequently excel in social intelligence. Others by common consent are consistently rated low in the intelligence scale; and the fact that they are inelegantly called " dumbbells " argues for a widespread acceptance of the unimodal theory. To advance more extreme evidence, the nature of feeblemindedness is at least compatible with this theory. Feeble-minded people do, as a matter of fact, show rather uniform levels of low mental ability. Occasionally an *idiot savant* is found, an individual who manifests exceptional aptitude in some circumscribed field of achievement in spite of his feeblemindedness, but such cases are rare and of questionable significance in so far as the present discussion is concerned. It would seem then that general intelligence is a unit factor or closely related group of factors capable of distribution along a single scale. At one end is the lowest possible I. Q., represented by the lowest grade imbecile; at the other is the highest I. Q. discoverable in any quantity.

(2) **The Multimodal Theory.** The second theory assumes that there are *types* or kinds of intelligence. This distribution would obtain if tests of one type of ability should correlate more closely than tests of diversified abilities. Some advocates of this view describe such types as verbal or linguistic, mechanical, and social intelligence; others regard sensory discrimination, memory, imagination, and similar mental processes as kinds of intelligence. The student must not confuse names of tests with the assumptions of the multimodel view; for instance, it is one thing to label the Stenquist tests *Mechanical Aptitude Tests*, but it is another thing altogether to assume that they measure an actual type or kind of intelligence. As the term indicates, a multimodal distribution of intelligence is represented by a curve showing many (or several) modes.

Since many people tacitly accept some form of faculty psychology, we would expect the multimodal view to find frequent expression in popular psychologizing. Thus, the novelist is assumed to possess a highly developed faculty of " imagination," and the individual endowed with " good judgment " is supposed to exercise this faculty, whether he is judging cattle or antique furniture. The majority of people and not a few psychologists seem to regard certain mental processes as general functions. " Concentration " is one of these implied general powers: it is a magic word used to explain why some students make good and others fail in their courses of instruction. Even after due allowance is made for transfer effects and identical elements, in forms of mental achievement, the belief in general powers or faculties is still discernible. Intelligence itself is frequently treated as if it were a unitary mental process or faculty.

(3) The Non-Modal Theory. According to the third view of mental organization, all acts of intelligence are specific, specialized, and independent, except in so far as they involve identical or common factors. If a test composed of arithmetical problems correlates positively with one in the field of history, it is because both of them involve some such factor as ability to read, or perhaps ability to remember figures. Tests of social intelligence and of mechanical aptitude respectively could even correlate, for they might involve in common certain habits of muscular coördination. But aside from an acceptance of the identical factor principle, the non-modal theory stresses the mutual independence of all psychological activities, and criticizes any assumption of formal powers or faculties. It would find graphic expression in a curve showing no fixed modality.

The no-modal concept of intellect is not without its popular champions. Students are prone to emphasize the variability rather than the uniformity of their grades, and to explain any one grade in terms of the specific factors involved in its attainment. Popular views of vocational psychology assume that vocational aptitudes are independent abilities; the problem is to fit square pegs into square holes, round pegs into round holes, and to transfer maladapted pegs to appropriate openings. Only infrequently is it granted that a successful lawyer might have become an equally successful physician, or even business man.

Evidence Bearing upon the Theories. The available evidence concerned with the nature of mental organization discloses two sets of facts. In the first place, there is a marked general tendency towards *positive* correlation among test scores. And in the second place, certain groups of tests show higher intercorrelations than others. Both sets of results must be considered in an attempt to evaluate the three theories under consideration.

The two tendencies are summarized by Thorndike (41) as follows: " If we measure a group of men or children in respect to a random sampling of intellectual tasks, and score each on a scale running from low to high, or bad to good, using those terms in each case as psychologists or sensible persons in general would use them, we find two notable facts. All or nearly all the inter-correlations are positive. The inter-correlations range from low to very high values." To quote another psychologist's statement of the same principle, " All mental abilities are related," and " Negative coefficients of correlation have never been found, except occasionally by chance or selection." [25]

Some examples will help explain the principles. In the article from which the above is taken, Thorndike gives his analysis of the American army mental tests. The intercorrelations among the groups of problems constituting these tests range from + .125 to + .746. Attention is called to the fact that these groups of problems are strikingly dissimilar: the standard form of the test, known as the Army Alpha, includes 8 elements — following directions, arith-

[25] (21), p. 16.

metical problems, practical judgment, synonym-antonym, meaning of disarranged sentences, number series, analogies, and information. The Army Beta test, designed for illiterates, contains 7 elements.

Turning from tests to school courses of instruction, we also find positive intercorrelations. The following table of correlations among university grades, quoted from Hollingworth (20) and based on grades obtained from 50 students, may be taken as fairly typical of results obtained by other investigators:

	Psychol.	Logic.	Hist.	Econ.	Eng.	Germ.	Chem.	Math.	Avge.
Psychology.....		.60	.36	.52	.48	.49	.33	.54	.47
Logic..........	.60		.48	.57	.47	.41	.25	.57	.48
History........	.36	.54		.44	.62	.46	.52	.61	.51
Economics.....	.52	.57	.44		.51	.43	.45	.71	.52
English........	.48	.47	.62	.51		.25	.26	.46	.44
German.......	.49	.41	.46	.43	.25		.39	.38	.4''
Chemistry.....	.33	.25	.52	.45	.26	.39		.57	.40
Mathematics...	.54	.57	.61	.71	.46	.38	.57		.55

The mean coefficient is even higher than in mental tests.

In practically all fields of mental measurement the principle is confirmed: positive coefficients of correlation obtain between intelligence tests and high school grades, intelligence tests and college grades, high school grades and college grades, intelligence tests and the Stenquist tests, intelligence tests and motor tests, intelligence tests and traits such as rapidity in mental accomplishment, tendency towards cheerfulness, desire to excel at performances in which the person is interested, self-confidence, degree of aesthetic feeling, foresight, and between intelligence and money-earning capacity.

The fact that intercorrelations among measurements of

intelligence are positive does not necessarily lend confirmation to Spearman's theory. On the whole, the theory has not received the support of psychologists. On the basis of an experiment in throwing dice, Thomson (38) concluded that the hierarchy of coefficients described by Spearman can be obtained by chance alone, and that consequently it is not an actual psychological phenomenon. As he states his criticism in another paper, hierarchies among coefficients of correlation exist, but they are not necessarily due to the general factor. Summarizing his analysis of Alpha and Beta tests referred to above, Thorndike states that, " We may indeed find factors common to all cognitive performances but not in parallel amounts, factors common to many, factors common to few, factors specific to one." [26] In other words, individuals Jones, Smith, Black, White, and Brown consistently score high (or low) on a group of different tests, not because they possess one factor in common, but because Jones and Smith possess factor a, Smith, Black, and White possess factor b, and Brown possesses factor c. Since factors of this sort have been ascertained by purely quantitative methods, their existence rather than their nature is known. They have been isolated without being described. The results of Haught's investigation are in harmony with Thorndike's conclusions (18). Using four tests of rational learning or thinking, Haught found something in common between each two sets of test scores correlated, but he also found the single factor running throughout all four tests to be practically zero. Many other investigations bear directly or indirectly upon Spearman's view; considered together, they apparently indicate that this view has not been established.

Turning to the multimodal view, our first concern is with the scientific validity of the assumptions upon which it rests.

[26] (41), p. 149.

It will be remembered that the multimodal concept of mind is a modified form of faculty psychology, a doctrine which was criticized in our discussion of phrenology. In brief, faculty psychology holds that the mind consists of separate powers or faculties. One of its earliest forms divided the mind into the three faculties — intellect, feeling, and will, or as they were sometimes described, knowing, feeling, and doing. Subsequent varieties of faculty psychology included such powers of the mind as memory, imagination, reasoning, etc. This view of the mind assumes that imagination, for example, is an entity: a given individual possesses a fixed amount of imaginative ability, irrespective of the field of thought in which this ability is manifested. If he is imaginative in thinking about costume designing, he will be equally imaginative in thinking about machinery. In the extreme form of this doctrine his imaginative power is assumed to be independent of his memorizing or reasoning powers.

Sufficient indication that the belief in mental faculties is popularly accepted today is found in such common expressions as the " power of observation," " power of concentration," " faculty of imagination," etc. It is also customary to speak of a normal man as being in " full possession of his faculties." According to phrenology, the various faculties are located in separate, circumscribed cortical areas. It will be recalled that some of the alleged faculties are amativeness, sublimity, veneration, and secretiveness. We might well add the mental faculties implied in the expressions just quoted. But as Chapter II disclosed, no such cortical areas have been found: the brain does not function in the manner assumed by the phrenologists.

Our present criticism of faculty psychology is voiced from the standpoint of direct, psychological experimentation. Consider, for example, the alleged " power of observation." Even our unchecked, everyday experience points strongly to the conclusion that no such *general* power exists. On the contrary, it suggests that what one observes depends upon his individual interests, habits, and knowledge. The locomotive engineer habitually pays close attention to the different sounds emitted by his engine, but it does not follow that he is equally discerning while listening to a symphony orchestra. In general, an individual attends to what he is trained to notice. Experimental psychology strongly confirms this view. When a subject is permitted to see geometrical designs, words in various languages, and other graphic signs for a fraction of a second only, in an instrument called the *tachistoscope,* his ability to describe what he " sees " is found to be determined largely by his familiarity with it. A familiar English word is perceived in much less time than an unfamiliar foreign word. By a different experimental attack it has been shown that " imagination " is not a faculty or power, but rather a process of associating ideas furnished by experience. The chronic day-dreamer and the mechanical inventor are each imaginative, but in widely divergent ways. Instead of being actual traits of mind, the alleged mental faculties are exceedingly artificial abstractions, the products of a popular disposition to simplify unduly the facts of human nature. Applying the foregoing general conclusions to our present problem, we must conclude that intelligence does not consist of separate faculties. If it did, we could presumably devise tests for these faculties; but such tests do not exist. At best, a psychological test of " imagination " would merely measure the ability of an individual to imagine in terms of geometry, clothes, machinery, finance, automobiles, gardening, and other unrelated fields of experience. Likewise, a psychological test of reasoning would necessarily include specific problems in different fields of reasoning. And there are obviously as many fields of reasoning as there are kinds of problems for human beings to solve. The extent to which an individual who excels in solving one group of problems will also excel in other groups is another question. Our present point is that reasoning, imagination, concentrating, observing, and the remaining so-called faculties are closely related aspects of specific acts of intelligence.

It should be said that a limited confirmation of the faculty theory is found in certain experimental results. The psychologist Woodrow (49) studied the phenomenon of attention under two conditions of complexity. In one of his experiments the subjects reacted to touch, sound, and light stimuli as quickly as possible; in the other, they fixated on a light, reacting with the right hand when it became brighter and with the left when it became dimmer. Woodrow concluded that a general capacity for attention exists, a "certain general ability to *attend* which remains the same, relative to other individuals' abilities, in spite of variations in the type of mental process concerned." Of course Woodrow would make full allowance for the rôle of experience as a determiner of attention, stressed above. His conclusion should not be identified with the original sweeping assumptions of phrenology and of the faculty concept.

Carey's investigation of the mental processes of British school children led to more conservative conclusions (7). This psychologist failed to discover a function of " discrimination "; ascertaining the existence of a small, general memory factor, but concluding that a general process like " painstaking " is much more limited than is usually assumed.

Motor Skill. It is possible that muscular coördinations constitute a group of abilities which are not only closely related but relatively independent of so-called mental abilities. Playing tennis and turning handsprings seem more closely related than either is related to solving algebraic equations.

As we have explained, thinking is largely a muscular process, but it consists, nevertheless, of implicit muscular responses which differ considerably in character from the explicit responses involved in acts of skill. Our question, therefore, is whether motor abilities are more highly correlated among themselves than are motor and mental abilities.

Several investigators have studied motor skill in its relation to intelligence, using the motor tests described elsewhere in this chapter and correlating the results obtained with mental test scores. One of the earlier investigators, Wissler (48), found low correlations between simple motor and mental performances. Wooley and Fischer (51) tested 700 school children of Cincinnati, correlating measurements of memory and association with hand grip, steadiness, tapping, and card sorting. Their coefficients range from .15 to .21. Both Muscio (28) and Perrin (32) found that low positive coefficients obtain among motor tests. Other investigators have reported coefficients between motor and mental tests, and coefficients among motor tests, ranging from zero to .50 or better. These results are somewhat ambiguous, but on the other hand, Garfiel's work points to a distinction between motor and mental abilities (16). She administered a series of motor tests to 50 girls, students in Barnard College, and secured ratings on their general motor ability. Her results include (a) intercorrelations among motor tests ranging from .15 to .25, (b) a high correlation, .77, between a team of motor tests and the combined ratings, and (c) a self-consistency of .92 among the judges. In other words, although her intercorrelations among individual motor test scores were no higher than those reported by other investigators, her composite score, based on several motor tests, agreed with the independent ratings furnished by judges. Garfiel concludes that the terms mental and motor refer to different groups of abilities which tend to show a low positive correlation.

This conclusion, however, in no respect justifies the assumption of a general faculty of motor dexterity. It does not imply that general motor ability can be cultivated by practicing one motor coördination. It should be interpreted as meaning that different motor activities are based on overlapping factors, some of which, in all probability, are common to many of these abilities. Furthermore, many activities, such as playing bridge, obviously involve both mental and motor functions. In general, the nature of motor ability must be ascertained in the light of the entire evidence bearing upon mental organization.

Special Aptitudes and Talents. In all likelihood the so-called faculties are reducible to a few forms of mental ability which are more or less common to all mental activities. Retentive ability is perhaps one such form; ability to make sensory discriminations in a given sense field another. Assuming this to be true, an individual's ability in a given direction is the product of all his so-called faculties, and not merely one of them. It is not so much a unit trait as the resultant of many traits.

This principle applies to the majority of special aptitudes and talents. For example, musical talent is based upon a number of contributing factors which exist in varying amounts and in varying combinations in different musicians. Seashore's inventory of musical talents includes five groups; namely, (1) musical sensitivity, (2) skill in musical execution, both vocal and instrumental, (3) musical memory and imagination, (4) musical thinking, and, (5) musical appreciation. Each of these in turn includes several sub-divisions. Again, literary ability is not a unit trait, but rather a complex group of abilities. Furthermore, a given literary genius represents a group of highly specialized response systems peculiar to himself and collectively designated as his " style." Although Dickens and Thackeray were contemporary novelists, neither could have written the novels of the other. The fact that special aptitudes vary with the individuals who disclose them indicates that they are largely products of individual experience and training.

On the other hand, the most essential ingredient of an aptitude may be at times a unit and perhaps a heritable factor. Book's investigation of ability to typewrite leads him to conclude that the most important element involved, namely, quickness of finger, wrist, and arm movements, is innate (5). In the sense that they possess and possibly inherit the essential factors required in their accomplishments, poets, musicians, typists, mathematicians, prizefighters, landscape gardeners, and various other specialists may be born and not made. But in most instances the possession of the essential factor or factors is in itself no guarantee of successful accomplishment.

The nature and number of unit abilities which coöperate with other factors in determining vocational aptitudes has not been ascertained. Certainly a number of fundamental traits, such as intelligence, pleasing personality, and emotional poise, are important factors in many professions. Indeed, we may surmise that an individual's greatest vocational asset is his level of mental ability rather than some special talent. Scott (36) has pointed out the mistake of regarding vocational guidance as a method of placing square pegs in square holes and round pegs in round holes. As he explains, vocational adjustment is a dynamic process involving an inter-relationship between the factors of the individual and the factors of the vocational situation in which he is found.

The Complexity of Mental Organization. The considerations so far advanced lead to the general conclusion that all the elements of personality are involved in the organization of mental processes. Thus, intelligence cannot be divorced entirely from motor skill, and neither can be separated from its motivating factors. Bridge experts are expected to be interested in the game, whereas poor players may proclaim their lack of interest. But this fact does not explain whether interest is the cause and ability the effect, or vice versa.

Throughout the discussion we have stressed the necessity of studying mental organization by experimental methods. A speculative approach to this problem is futile. Even though motives and abilities function together, it is possible to isolate them by the proper experimental technique. The British psychologist, Webb (46), investigated experimentally certain traits of character and intelligence in schoolboys, and concluded that he had isolated two variable factors, namely " general ability " and " persistence of motive." His fellow-countryman, Garnett (17), discovered two factors which he called " cleverness " and " purpose." Now the existence of such traits as persistence, cleverness, and purpose is verified by everyday observations. Moreover, the technique of both Webb and Garnett is open to technical criticism. The point is that these investigators show the possibility of demonstrating and measuring character traits by purely quantitative methods. All traits of personality, including the traits designated as mental and motor abilities, are thus amenable to controlled investigation. Psychology has indeed progressed far beyond the stage where man's nature was supposed to consist of " knowing, feeling and doing."

PERSONALITY

Our discussion of intelligent behavior has disclosed two significant facts: (1) An individual represents an *organization* of response tendencies. The entire organism and not merely one of its parts, does the responding. It is therefore impossible to study a response without taking into consideration the entire reaction system of the organism concerned. Even a relatively simple human reaction, such as stooping to pick up a pin, involves to some extent all the factors which have been analyzed in the various chapters of this book. It involves a conditioning process, some motivating factor, and the principles of learning; and it may call for the functioning of language mechanisms.

(2) All responses represent attempted adjustments of the organism to the environment. In this sense, all behavior culminates in what we have described as "intelligent behavior." An organism adjusts to the environment, however, by controlling or modifying the environment. As popular writers say, man "conquers" his environment. Intelligent behavior is thus a series of effects, and we measure intelligence by measuring its products. In social behavior, the *responses* of an individual are *stimuli* for other individuals. Such responses consist of gestures, facial expressions, speech, and movements calculated to produce effects upon physical objects. All of these, in turn, elicit responses from others.

Definitions of Personality. The two facts just stated have resulted in the formulation of two concepts of *personality:* (1) the individual considered as a behaving entity, and (2) the series of effects produced by a given individual upon others. Popular usage favors the latter view, as is witnessed by the expressions, "A has a pleasing personality," or "B is entirely lacking in personality." This view is also expressed in psychological literature, notably by Dunlap in the following statement: "The self of one individual, in so far as it is experienced by another individual, or in so far as it is estimated by another, is properly designated as *personality.*" [27]

[27] (13), p. 341.

Views which identify personality with the individual considered as a behaving entity fall into two classes. (a) One of these, to use Gordon Allport's expression, includes all "rag-bag" theories of personality (2). Many writers stress the fact that all responses are organized into systems, but nevertheless define these systems from the standpoint of their constituent elements. Thus, according to Prince (33), "personality is a complex affair in that in its make-up there enter many factors, some acquired and some innate." These factors are "our reactions to the environment, our moral and social conduct, the affective reactions of our sentiments, instincts, feelings, and other conative tendencies, our 'habits,' judgments, points of view, and attitudes of mind." These, in turn, "are determined by the mental experiences of the past by which they are developed, organized, and conserved in the unconscious."[28] To quote another writer, Warren (44) states that personality is "the total outcome of an individual's mental organization, comprising all his permanent mental conditions and organized experiences at any period of life."[29] Watson holds a similiar view, since he regards the individual's total repertoire of responses, active and potential, as his personality.[30]

(b) A number of psychologists find the explanation of personality in some basic principle which determines the behavior of the organism as a whole. Certain theories of motivation, discussed in Chapter IV, are really theories of personality. Psychoanalysts view the individual from the standpoint of the repressions, conflicts, sublimations, and other mental mechanisms which he represents. Psychoanalytical literature contains personality studies of Leonardo da Vinci (14), Darwin (23), Shelley (26), Charlotte Brontë (11), and other celebrities, along with similar studies of neurotic patients and normal men. Berman and some other writers,

[28] *Op. cit.*, p. 306 ff.   [29] *Op. cit.*, p. 409.   [30] *Op. cit.*, Chapter XI.

it will be remembered, explain personality in terms of endocrinal activities. Similarly, Kempf's view of autonomic functions is a theory of personality. Likewise, Cooley finds the origin and development of an individual's personality in the social groups with which he is identified. In views of this sort, personality is practically identified with character and temperament.

Human Traits. Personality studies are chiefly concerned with the analysis of *traits*. Three characteristics of traits should be noted: (1) The term refers to a stimulus-response *tendency* — that is, to some act of behavior which is manifested habitually and characteristically by a particular individual or by human beings in general. When we say that individual A is hypersensitive, witty, or skillful in dancing, we imply that he can be depended upon to show the trait in question more or less consistently. In fact, the aspect of personality known as *character* is usually defined in terms of the stability and dependability of response systems. If responses to stimuli did not tend to become habits we could not trust or distrust people, or select friends and associates. As a matter of fact, all organisms, even the most intelligent, are creatures of habit. We " know " or understand people to the extent that we can *predict* their behavior. Moreover, the fact that we do predict behavior within reasonable limits enables us to transact business, drive automobiles through crowded thoroughfares, and cooperate with others in various social economic undertakings.

(2) A trait is a specific behavior tendency which must be defined in terms of a particular stimulus and a particular response. Any such general term as " strong-willed," " clever," " intellectual," " imaginative," " affectionate," or " narrow-minded," when applied to two people, or even to the same person on different occasions, is likely to designate two different traits. The fundamental error of faculty psy-

chology is found, as we have seen, in its assumption that behavior can be analyzed in such general or abstract terms.
To use a former illustration, an individual may be habitually neat with respect to his person, and characteristically
slovenly in his handwriting or the care of his desk. The
majority of traits are responses conditioned upon specific
stimuli, and they are transferable to other stimuli only to
the extent indicated in our preceding discussions of transfer
and of mental organization.

(3) A trait must possess some social value. In other
words, it must directly or indirectly attract *attention*. The
normal pupillary reflex is not ordinarily regarded as a trait
of human nature, but some peculiar habit of winking, on
the other hand, is usually so designated. Although personal
mannerisms, such as habits of walking, gesticulating, and
eating may not tend to correlate closely with the more fundamental traits of human nature, they are nevertheless important elements in the composition of personality by virtue
of the favorable or unfavorable attention which they attract.
Obviously a trait which is highly desirable in one situation
may be relatively worthless in another. Certain forms of
mathematical ability which are indispensable in playing
chess are quite superfluous in dancing. In stressing the
values of traits in the composition of personality, we are
merely applying one of the criteria of intelligence to all aspects of human nature.

Trait Measurement. Since traits are behavior tendencies, they are objective in character and therefore capable of
measurement. Consider such diversified reaction tendencies
as skill in serving a tennis ball, a tendency to blush, a fond-
ness for ice cream, a habit of flattering people, a proclivity
for day-dreaming, and a knowledge of the French language.
In accordance with the principle stated above, we must regard these as specific responses to specific stimuli: but we

shall assume that they are found in many people. In the first place, if any one of these traits exists at all in a given individual, it exists in some appreciable amount. If 100 such individuals are selected at random, they can be ranged or ranked in the order of increasing or decreasing amounts of any trait chosen from the list. The first trait listed can be scored; the last can be tested; the others can be rated. In all probability, each of the hundred individuals would be found to possess either more or less of the trait than any other one individual; if perchance two or more should be scored, tested, or rated the same, their common rank could be ascertained by the proper statistical procedure. It follows, in the second place, that if a trait exists in some appreciable amount it can be measured. The unit of measurement which perhaps is most serviceable in personality analysis is the one suggested by our illustration; namely, the difference between a given rank and the rank just above or below it. Since this is the smallest difference actually *observed*, it is the smallest unit of difference to which a social value can be assigned. Thus, an instrument that would record exceedingly minute changes in the vaso-motor reflex responsible for blushing would yield finer differences among people than are noted in social relationships. Like this hypothetical instrument, the majority of psychological tests yield finer measurements than are required for statistical or practical purposes. In general, traits are measurable because they are *observable* phenomena; and their quantitative gradations can be made as fine as scientific necessity demands.[31]

Traits are isolated and described by two different methods. The first is analogous to the procedure of the naturalist, who studies animals in their native habitats. The

[31] See Thorndike (39) for a discussion of the principles stated in this paragraph.

psychologist may wish to study human nature where it is normally disclosed — on the street, in the theater, in business institutions, and in the home. In situations of this sort he notices some trait and proceeds to study it systematically. The rating scale or some similar device is admirably suited for this purpose. And just as the naturalist occasionally captures a specimen and brings it into his laboratory, so the psychologist may become interested in an individual and ask him to report to the psychological laboratory. But unlike the animal, the human subject, particularly the adult, is frequently quite willing to be analyzed. Often a trait is first observed in daily life and then subjected to laboratory investigation. For instance, Moore and Gilliland (27) investigated experimentally the tendency of certain people to look others straight in the eye while talking to them. In many instances, the Landis investigation, for example,[32] the psychologist can duplicate in his laboratory the stimulating conditions which are found in social and economic activities.

The second method is similar to that of the experimental biologist. It consists of arranging a stimulus situation in the laboratory and analyzing the response which it elicits. In this case the response may be exclusively a laboratory product, selected because of its promise to reveal some significant trait manifested in normal activity. The Downey Will-Temperament test illustrates this method. This test measures certain volitional capacities of an individual by requiring him, among other things, to write phrases and to trace simple outlines on paper under varying conditions of speed, accuracy, distraction, and hindrance. Of course the significance of such tests must be established in terms of their correlations with other tests and with ratings.

The Doctrine of Mental Types. Popular systems of personality analysis frequently proceed upon the assump-

[32] See Chapter IV.

tion that people either possess or do not possess certain traits. According to this assumption, people can be classified into *types* depending upon whether or not they have the traits in question. Because they are objective and tangible, physical characteristics most commonly form the basis of type differentiations. We are familiar with the alleged blond and brunette types, and the coarse and refined types. A less known classification, based upon the face profile, describes the convex, concave, and plane type of human individuals. Of course such physical characteristics exist; our question concerns the assumption that they are correlated with distinctive mental and temperamental response tendencies. If current beliefs are to be trusted, individuals with red hair have quick tempers, brunettes are highly emotional, and people with convex faces possess an abundance of mental and physical energy. Statements of this sort are to be found in widely advertised systems of " character analysis."

Other theories proceed to describe mental types with no attempt to correlate them with physical signs. Such theories, stated in the most extreme form, are unfortunately found in psychological literature. The traditional sanguine, phlegmatic, choleric, and melancholic temperaments will be recalled. A recent theory, mentioned in our discussion of motivation, describes temperaments in terms of predominating endocrine functions and thus classifies people into the thyroid, adrenal, pituitary, and thymus types, with provisions for mixed glandular types. We have also mentioned the psychoanalytical distinction between introverts and extroverts. Many type classifications are restricted to mental processes. An example is found in the attempt of the earlier psychologists to describe visual, auditory, motile, tactile, and verbal types of mental imagery. People have been classified with respect to their method of making decisions into quick constant, slow constant, quick inconstant, and slow inconstant types. A favorite type of classification distinguishes between rapid learning and rapid forgetting as opposed to slow learning and slow forgetting. In fact, so many assumed psychological types exist that their mere enumeration would occupy several pages of this book.

Criticisms of Type Psychology. One fundamental criticism applies to practically all theories of mental types: they cannot be reconciled with the principles governing the distribution of trait measurements. It will be remembered that measurements of traits tend to show normal distribution; that is, they tend to cluster around a central tendency or average. The majority of men are of average height; fewer men are either tall or short; and an extremely limited number are giants and dwarfs. We have already quoted Mrs. Hollingworth's statement to the effect that men in general cannot be classified as " tall " or " short." Yet this sort of classification is assumed in the majority of type theories. Although such traits as introversion and extroversion, for example, can be found, we have every reason for believing that *typical* introverts and extroverts, like typical tall men and short men, are comparatively rare. On the contrary, the majority of men in all probability are mid-way between the two extremes. The so-called types, therefore, are extremes which are rarely found and consequently not typical. Just as theories which describe two opposed types assume a bimodal distribution of traits, theories of three or more types presuppose multimodal distributions. In his investigation of the socially and the mechanically inclined people, Max Freyd (15) expresses this criticism and states that his trait measurements tend towards normal distributions. Few psychologists, in fact, have ever reported bimodal distributions of human traits. Thorndike summarizes the doctrine of type psychology by saying that variations in measurements of a single trait center around one type only; namely, the average or mediocre type.

Classifications of types based upon physical characteristics are open to additional criticisms. They are theoretically unsound, and they lack experimental confirmation. Most of them are products of reasoning by analogy. Thus, fine texture of hair and skin is supposed to indicate refinement of temperament; and conversely, coarse hair is alleged to show a coarse, brutal nature. At least one theory of this sort has been tried in the psychological laboratory and found wanting. Paterson and Ludgate (30) secured ratings from 94 judges on 26 assumed traits of blonds and brunettes. Each judge was asked to select and rate 2 blonds and 2 brunettes with respect to the traits. Notwithstanding the fact that 187 blonds and 187 brunettes were rated, no correlations were found between their traits and their color: both blonds and brunettes respectively were found to possess an equal number of blond and brunette traits. In general, the claims made by professional phrenologists, physiognomists, and graphologists find little support in facts. Very often, it is true, the health, occupation, and social status of an individual are reflected in his personal appearance and behavior, particularly in his conversation, but this is far from saying that such characteristics represent psychological types.

Types Established by Group Activities. In two essential respects, however, types may be said to exist. People who belong to a given profession, social level, geographical section, nation, or race undoubtedly show certain distinctive characteristics. Business men develop habits of acting, talking, and thinking which differentiate them from artists. Likewise, residents of different parts of the country acquire distinctive accents and mannerisms. In a sense, therefore, we may speak of the typical business man, university professor, actor, politician, Englishman, Frenchman, or perhaps boy or girl. But the differences represented by such types are superficial rather than fundamental. For example, no significant mental differences between the sexes have been established. As Thorndike expresses it, men differ more among themselves than men differ from women; and conversely, women differ more among themselves than women differ from men. In all probability this statement could be paraphrased to include the majority of mental and temperamental differences among races of the same intellectual level. We also have reasons for believing that distributions of human traits are much the same in all localities. Measurements of intelligence obtained from students in different universities are strikingly similar: they show the same range of scores from low to high, and they are distributed normally. According to Brogan's results (6), students from universities located in widely separated parts of the country have practically the same ethical standards. In fact, there are mental types only in the sense that there are levels of intelligence. Undoubtedly, as the Army Alpha mental tests indicate, professional men are more intelligent than day laborers and white men are generally more intelligent than negroes. Aside from differences in mental ability, the so-called mental types chiefly represent variations in custom and tradition.

The following quotation illustrates concretely the conclusions just formulated:

If you were to draw up a list of a thousand human traits, Englishmen and Frenchmen would be bound to have 999 of these traits in common. The 1 per cent. of difference would be found to consist in the fact that the Englishman says "Yes" and the Frenchman says "Oui, oui"; the Englishman prefers beef from the joint and the Frenchman likes his meat en casserole; the Englishman likes to go out into the fields and shoot something and the Frenchman prefers to sit around a table and talk. And yet that 1 per cent. margin is the thing that makes words like "Englishman," "Frenchman" or "American" carry a thrill like very few other words in human speech.[33]

Types Established by Single Traits or Characteristics. Very often the presence of a given trait or characteristic *in any noticeable quantity* suffices for purposes of type classification. In this sense there are " types " of insanity, physical disease, temperament, physical beauty or ugliness, mental ability, goodness, and the like. And in this sense it is possible to describe the type, " red-haired people," provided that no sweeping implications are made regarding other traits in the people so classified. It is likewise possible to describe the " mathematical " type of mind in referring to people who show mathematical aptitudes. But again we should be cautious in assuming a correlation between this trait and any other given trait. The fact that individual *A* is a mathematician in itself tells us nothing concerning his moral character, musical ability, political views, sense of humor, skill as a tennis player, or physical beauty. In the majority of instances type classifications based upon the possession of single traits are relatively useless. The majority of human traits, in fact, are possessed by all people. Only when the relative amount of the trait is known or inferred is the classification of practical or scientific value.

The Elements of Personality. Although any classification of human traits is entirely arbitrary, it is possible to describe three groups of traits which, taken by and large, include the most significant elements in personality. According to our classification the outstanding aspects of a human personality are his (1) physical characteristics, (2)

[33] From an article by Simeon Strunsky in the *New York Times Book Review*, July 20, 1924.

temperament and character, (3) intelligence and ability. The traits included under these headings are primarily effects or impressions produced by a human being upon his fellows. Technically speaking, they are stimuli to which his fellows react. As our brief discussion will show, the last group is the most inclusive of the three.

(1) The physical characteristics of an individual are sources of a large number of the effects produced by that individual upon others.[34] People are attracted by a pretty face and a well-proportioned body, by pleasing manners, by a well-modulated voice, by signs of personal cleanliness; conversely, they are repulsed by ugliness and deformity, by atrocious manners, and by indications of personal uncleanliness. The advertising pages of magazines testify to the popular demand for stylish clothing, personal ornaments, cosmetics, fat reducers, and hair restorers. In daily conversation people give due consideration to the physical characteristics of their associates. Notwithstanding the traditional assurance that "beauty is only skin deep," the majority of people are probably influenced by such factors to a greater extent than they realize.

Physical appeal is frequently responsible for reactions which are highly rationalized. The physical is easily confused with the mental and moral. In myth and fairy story, in the popular novel and in the moving picture, virtue is closely associated with beauty, and vice is identified with ugliness. Cinderella is both good and beautiful; Uriah Heep is morally and physically obnoxious. Of course beauty of person may be a relatively subordinate factor in physical appeal. So far as intelligent adults are concerned, people are attracted or repulsed primarily by personal habits and mannerisms and by such forms of expressive behavior

[34] For a more extensive discussion of physical attractiveness and repulsiveness see Perrin (31) and Dunlap (12).

as facial expressions, gestures, bodily postures, and vocal inflections. It is with reference to forms of expressive behavior that physical attractiveness and repulsiveness become confused with temperament and intelligence.

To a certain extent the physical appeal of an individual is indirectly responsible for his character and temperament. Other factors being equal, physically prepossessing people are more likely to elicit favorable responses from others. Children who are unduly petted tend to become " spoiled." Since physically attractive adults are socially in demand, they presumably tend to be socially active and, as a consequence, they acquire certain traits of character not found in those who lead secluded lives.

The relationships between physical appeal and intelligence have not been fully ascertained. In the investigation mentioned (31), a coefficient of $+ .02$ was obtained between ratings on physical attractiveness and mental test scores, a result which argues against the traditional antithesis between " beauty and brains." On a priori grounds, we could expect to find either a positive or a negative correlation. For the reasons advanced above, physically attractive people might be supposed to excel in social intelligence. Moreover, physical attractiveness, presupposes a certain amount of good health, an asset which is surely not incompatible with mental vigor. On the other hand, attractive people, by virtue of their social qualifications, may be tempted in the direction of intellectual laziness. Probably the coefficient obtained represents a balance among factors operating to a slight extent in both directions.

(2) The traits of temperament and character consist of the *attitudes* which people manifest in response to social situations. The term refers to an immediate, more or less unanalyzed reaction, containing both emotional and ideational elements. The majority of opinions, prejudices, ideals, sym-

z

pathies, antipathies, personal likes and dislikes, aesthetic and ethical responses, and sentiments are attitudes. An illustration of a relatively simple attitude is found in the crouching position of a cat, watching a mouse hole and ready to spring upon its intended victim. In this instance, the attitude is a motor set and its accompanying state of visceral tension; functionally it is a condition of preparation for overt action. A complex human attitude is illustrated by the individual with some pronounced and fixed political bias. Psychologically the two cases have much in common. In both, the attitude is a *reaction tendency* which involves practically the entire physiological equipment of the organism concerned.

Individual differences in character and temperament are represented by differences in attitudes. Professional criminals, for instance, vary greatly among themselves in intelligence and education; they differ from law-abiding citizens chiefly with respect to the attitude which they take towards society. The same can be said of people noted for their strong aesthetic or moral reactions. In both fiction and biography, character analysis takes the form of analyzing personal and social attitudes.

(3) We have already stressed the fact that all human traits are valued ultimately in terms of their effectiveness in adjusting individuals to their environment. For this reason, intelligent behavior has been viewed in this text as the highest form of behavior. To the extent that an individual utilizes successfully all of his response systems for the purpose of achieving social and vocational ends, he is intelligent. From this point of view, such a trait as tact, no less than proficiency, in some mental performance is a manifestation of intelligence. To illustrate further, an " ideal " is essentially a *plan of action,* formulated verbally and valued as " high " or " low " in terms of human welfare. It is indeed significant that the terms used to describe the different

kinds of personality all reflect the standard of adjustment. The personality of an individual is " strong," " compelling," " magnetic," " pleasing," or " forceful " if his social adjustments are successful; otherwise it is " weak," and in extreme cases he is " utterly lacking in personality."

References

1. ALLPORT, FLOYD H. Social Psychology, 1924.
2. ALLPORT, GORDON W. Personality and Character. Psychological Bulletin, 1921, 18, 441–455.
3. ANGELL, J. R. An Introduction to Psychology, Second Edition, 1920.
4. BAIN, ALEXANDER. The Senses and the Intellect, Fourth Edition, 1894.
5. BOOK, W F. Voluntary Motor Ability of the World's Champion Typists. Journal of Applied Psychology, 1924, 8, 283–308.
6. BROGAN, A. P. A Study in Statistical Ethics. International Journal of Ethics, 1923, 33, 119–134.
7. CAREY, N. On the Nature of the Specific Mental Factors. British Journal of Psychology, 1915, 8, 70–92.
8. CLARK, RUTH. An Experimental Study of Silent Thinking. Archives of Psychology, No. 48, 1–101.
9. COLVIN, S. S., and others. Intelligence and its Measurement. Journal of Educational Psychology, 1921, 12, 123–147, 195–216.
10. DEWEY, JOHN. How We Think, 1910.
11. DOOLEY, L. Psychoanalysis of Charlotte Brontë as a Type of the Woman of Genius. American Journal of Psychology, 1920, 31, 221–272.
12. DUNLAP, KNIGHT. Personal Beauty and Racial Betterment, 1920.
13. —— Elements of Scientific Psychology, 1922.
14. FREUD, S. A Childhood Memory of Leonardo da Vinci, 1910.
15. FREYD, MAX. The Personalities of the Socially and Mechanically Inclined. Psychological Monographs, 1924, No. 4, 1–101.
16. GARFIEL, EVELYN. The Measurement of Motor Ability. Archives of Psychology, 1923, No. 62, 1–46.

17. GARNETT, J. C. M. General Ability, Cleverness and Purpose. British Journal of Psychology, 1919, 9, 345–366.
18. HAUGHT, B. F. The Interrelation of Some Higher Learning Processes. Psychological Monographs, 1921, 30, 1–71.
19. HEIDBREDER, EDNA. An Experimental Study of Thinking. Archives of Psychology, 1924, No. 73, 1–175.
20. HOLLINGWORTH, H. L. Vocational Psychology, 1920.
21. HOLLINGWORTH, L. S. Special Talents and Defects, 1923.
22. JAMES, WILLIAM. The Principles of Psychology, 1890.
23. KEMPF, E. J. Charles Darwin — The Affective Sources of his Inspiration and Anxiety Neurosis. Psychoanalytical Review, 1918, 5, 151–192.
24. KÖHLER, W. The Mentality of Apes, 1925.
25. KUO, Z. Y. A Behavioristic Experiment on Inductive Inference. Journal of Experimental Psychology, 1923, 6, 247–293.
26. MOORE, T. V. Percy Bysshe Shelley, An Introduction to the Study of Character. Psychological Monographs, 1922, No. 31, 1–62.
27. MOORE, H. T., AND GILLILAND, A. R. The Measurement of Aggressiveness. Journal of Applied Psychology, 1921, 5, 97–118.
28. MUSCIO, B. Motor Capacity with Special Reference to Vocational Guidance. British Journal of Psychology, 1922, 13, 157–184.
29. OTIS, A. S. Statistical Method in Educational Measurement, 1925.
30. PATERSON, D. G., AND LUDGATE, KATHERINE E. Blond and Brunette Traits, A Quantitative Study. Journal of Personnel Research, 1922, 1, 122–127.
31. PERRIN, F. A. C. Physical Attractiveness and Repulsiveness. Journal of Experimental Psychology, 1921, 4, 203–217.
32. —— An Experimental Study of Motor Ability. Journal of Experimental Psychology, 1921, 4, 24–56.
33. PRINCE, MORTON. The Unconscious, 1914.
34. ROBACK, A. A. Intelligence and Behavior. Psychological Review, 1922, 29, 54–62.
35. RUGG, H. O. Statistical Methods Applied to Education, 1917.
36. SCOTT, W. D. Changes in Some of Our Conceptions and Practices of Personnel. Psychological Review, 1920, 27, 81–94.

37. STERN, WILLIAM. The Psychological Methods of Testing Intelligence, 1914.
38. THOMSON, G. H. A Hierarchy Without a General Factor. British Journal of Psychology, 1916, 8, 271–281.
39. THORNDIKE, E. L. Individuality, 1911.
40. —— Educational Psychology, Vol. II, The Psychology of Learning, 1913.
41. —— On the Organization of Intellect. Psychological Review, 1921, 28, 141–151.
42. THORSON, AGNES M. The Relation of Tongue Movements to Internal Speech. Journal of Experimental Psychology, 1925, 8, 1–32.
43. TITCHENER, E. B. A Beginner's Psychology, 1917.
44. WARREN, H. C. Elements of Human Psychology, 1922.
45. WATSON, J. B. Psychology from the Standpoint of a Behaviorist, Second Edition, 1924.
46. WEBB, E. Character and Intelligence. British Journal of Psychology Monograph Supplements, 1915, No. 3, 1–99.
47. WHIPPLE, G. M. Manual of Mental and Physical Tests, Second Edition, Revised and Enlarged, 1915.
48. WISSLER, CLARK. The Correlation of Mental and Physical Tests. Psychological Review Monograph Supplements, 1901, 3, 1–62.
49. WOODROW, H. The Faculty of Attention. Journal of Experimental Psychology, 1916, 1, 285–318.
50. WOODWORTH, R. S. Psychology: A Study of Mental Life, 1921.
51. WOOLEY, HELEN THOMPSON, AND FISCHER, CHARLOTTE RUST. Mental and Physical Measurements of Working Children. Psychological Monographs, 1914, 18, 1–247.

Additional References on Thinking

DASHIELL, J. F. A Physiological-Behavioristic Description of Thinking. Psychological Review, 1925, 32, 54–73.
—— Is the Cerebrum the Seat of Thinking? Psychological Review, 1926, 33, 13–29.
GIVLER, R. C. The Intellectual Significance of the Grasping Reflex. Journal of Philosophy, 1921, 18, 617–628.
JUDD, C. H. Psychology, Second Edition, 1917. Chapter X, Speech as a Form of Behavior.

LASHLEY, K. S. The Behavioristic Interpretation of Consciousness. Psychological Review, 1923, 30, 237–272 and 329–353.

MARKEY, J. F. The Place of Language Habits in a Behavioristic Explanation of Consciousness. Psychological Review, 1925, 32, 384–401.

WATSON, J. B. Behavior: An Introduction to Comparative Psychology, 1914. Chapters IX and X.

—— The Unverbalized in Human Behavior. Psychological Review, 1924, 31, 273–280.

—— The Place of Kinaesthetic, Visceral and Laryngeal Organization in Thinking. Psychological Review, 1924, 31, 339–347.

WEISS, A. P. A Theoretical Basis of Human Behavior, 1925. Chapter XI, Consciousness. Chapter XIII, The Language Responses. Chapter XIV, Thinking.

INDEX

Ability, definition of, 314.

Accommodation, mechanism of, 26; definition of, 27.

Adjustment, 4, 16–17.

Adler, Alfred, 187–190, 193.

Adrenal glands, 71.

Adrenin, 147–148.

Affection, symptoms of, 163–164.

Agraphia, definition of, 60.

Allport, F. H., 77, 130, 165–167, 169–170, 193, 297–299, 375.

Allport, G. W., 362, 375.

Amplitude, 31.

Anabolism, 192.

Anatomy, 19.

Angell, J. R., 255, 284, 315, 375.

Anger, symptoms of, 161–162.

Animal nature, 19.

Anrep, 95–96, 98–99, 101, 103, 108, 110, 130.

Anthropomorphism, definition of, 91.

Antithesis, Darwin's principle of, 165.

Aphasia, definition of, 60; functional, 61; motor, 61; sensory, 61.

Areas, associational, 49; cerebral cortical, 49; motor, 49; sensory, definition of, 49; sensory, classification of, 51; somesthetic, 51; auditory, gustatory, olfactory, visual, 51.

Association, controlled, 87; criticisms of, 90; definition of, 54;

free, 88; laws of, 82–92; mechanism of, 88.

Attention, definition of, 79, 292; objective conditions of, 79.

Attitudes, 373.

Aufgabe, 86–88.

Autocoids, 69; adrenin, 71; thyroid, 71.

Automatograph, 179.

Autonomic nervous system, 24, 63–72, 147–150; diagram of, 148.

Axon, definition of, 42.

Bain, Alexander, 309, 375.

Behavior, abnormal, 182; and thinking, 307–311; biological foundations of, 19–72; control and prediction of, 16–18; historical explanations of, 73; intelligent, 52, 287–378; learning, 196–286; motivation of, 132–195; original versus substitute, 80–81; psychological foundations of, 73–131; units, integration of, 76.

Behaviorist, 16.

Beritoff, 104, 130.

Berman, Louis, 182, 193, 362.

Bernard, L. L., 127, 130, 160, 193.

Biology, 19.

Bloomfield, Daniel, 128–131.

Bogardus, 213.

Book, W. F., 265, 359, 375.

Brain, diagram showing chief cortical areas of, 49.

For Product Safety Concerns and Information please contact our EU
representative GPSR@taylorandfrancis.com
Taylor & Francis Verlag GmbH, Kaufingerstraße 24, 80331 München, Germany